A Lure of Knowledge

BETWEEN MEN ~ BETWEEN WOMEN
LESBIAN AND GAY STUDIES
General Editor, Richard D. Mohr

BETWEEN MEN ~ BETWEEN WOMEN

LESBIAN AND GAY STUDIES

Richard D. Mohr, General Editor

Gary David Comstock, *Violence Against Lesbians and Gay Men*

Lillian Faderman, *Odd Girls and Twilight Lovers: A History of Lesbian Life in Twentieth-Century America*

Richard D. Mohr, *Gays/Justice: A Study of Ethics, Society, and Law*

Kath Weston, *Families We Choose: Lesbians, Gays, Kinship*

A Lure of Knowledge

∎

LESBIAN SEXUALITY AND THEORY

Judith Roof

Columbia University Press • *New York*

Columbia University Press
New York • Oxford

The author thanks Yale University Press for permission to quote the poem "Artemis" from *Beginning with O* by Olga Broumas, copyright © 1977 by Olga Boumas. All rights reserved.

Library of Congress Cataloguing-in-Publication Data
Roof, Judith, 1951–
  A lure of knowledge : lesbian sexuality and theory / Judith Roof.
    p.   cm.
  Includes bibliographical references and index.
  ISBN 0-231-07486-7
  1. Lesbians' writings—History and criticism—Theory, etc.
2. Lesbianism in literature.   I. Title.
PN56.L45R66   1991
809'.93353—dc20   91-14705
                                                                       CIP
⊗

Casebound editions of Columbia University Press books are Smyth-sewn and printed on permanent and durable acid-free paper.

Printed in the United States of America

c 10 9 8 7 6 5 4 3 2 1

BETWEEN MEN ~ BETWEEN WOMEN
LESBIAN AND GAY STUDIES
Richard D. Mohr, *General Editor*
Eugene F. Rice, *Columbia University Advisor*

John Boswell YALE UNIVERSITY	History
Claudia Card UNIVERSITY OF WISCONSIN	Philosophy
Richard Green UNIVERSITY OF CALIFORNIA, LOS ANGELES	Psychology
Larry Gross UNIVERSITY OF PENNSYLVANIA	Media and Communication
Gilbert Herdt UNIVERSITY OF CHICAGO	Anthropology, Sociology, Political Science
Barbara Johnson HARVARD UNIVERSITY	Literature
Rhonda R. Rivera OHIO STATE UNIVERSITY	Law

Between Men ~ Between Women is a forum for current lesbian and gay scholarship in the humanities and social sciences. The series includes both books that rest within specific traditional disciplines and are substantially about gay men or lesbians and books that are interdisciplinary in ways that reveal new insights into gay and lesbian experience, transform traditional disciplinary methods in consequence of the perspectives that experience provides, or begin to establish lesbian and gay studies as a freestanding inquiry. Established to contribute to an increased understanding of lesbians and gay men, the series also aims to provide through that understanding a wider comprehension of culture in general.

FOR SHARON

Contents

Acknowledgments

I WOULD like to thank the National Endowment for the Humanities and the Center for Twentieth Century Studies, University of Wisconsin–Milwaukee, who supported this project through the 1988 Summer Seminar for College Teachers conducted by Jane Gallop, where work on this book really began. I would also like to thank the editors of *Arizona Quarterly* for their kind permission to reprint portions of "Freud Reads Lesbians: The Male Homosexual Imperative," and the University of Tennessee Press for permission to reprint " 'This Is Not for You': The Sexuality of Mothering" that appears in a different form in the anthology *Narrating Mothers*, edited by Brenda O. Daly and Maureen T. Reddy. Copyright © 1991 by the University of Tennessee Press. I owe a debt to Katherine Burkman, Ann Dubé, Mark Auburn, Stephen Heath, and Charles Williams for providing models, tools, materials, and the stimulus to write something; to Richard Feldstein and Ellie Ragland-Sullivan for their insights on psychoanalysis; to Ann Ardis, Dale Bauer, Barbara Gates, Sandra Harding, Melissa Mowry, Bonnie Scott, Michele Shauf, Ellen Wert, and Lynda Zwinger for their helpful readings of manuscript in process; and finally to Jane Gallop, Sharon Groves, Julie Schmidt, and Robyn Wiegman for their friendship, criticism, support, and inspiration.

A Lure of Knowledge

Introductions

Configurations

 A N ANECDOTE that appears several times in Anaïs Nin's writings is about Nin and her husband, Ian Hugo, going to a brothel on Rue Blondel to see a sexual "show" performed by two women. In a kind of erotic travelogue, the prostitutes demonstrate exotic positions using a false penis. According to Nin, however, nothing stirs until the women abandon the priapus and demonstrate "lesbian poses."[1] At this point they all—the prostitutes, Nin, and her husband—become aroused: "The big woman reveals to me a secret place in the woman's body, a source of new joy . . ." and "Hugo and I lean over them, taken by that moment of loveliness in the little woman, who offers to our eyes her conquered, quivering body. Hugo is in turmoil. I am no longer woman: I am man. I am touching the core of June's being" (72). Configuring a moment of authentic sexual excitement, the thrilling view of the two women turns Nin into a man who desires a woman.

In this scene Nin brings together many of the conventional cultural conceptions of lesbian sexuality. The women's use of a dildo and Nin's masculine transformation establish the sexual activity of the two women as either faked heterosexuality or as masculine. A performance, it belongs to the realm of a licentious underworld. Despite the fact that it begins as an act, its spectacle becomes authentic, exciting both Nin and her husband. Watching it, Nin gains some essential knowledge about female sexuality. But in Nin's scene, the women only momentarily relate to one another sexually as women; the lesbian core of the story is buttressed at beginning and end by masculine transformations (the dildo, Nin's masculinity) compelled by a complementary two-term logic whose obvious superimposition divulges the heterosexual gloss framing the lesbian display. The passage thus exemplifies how attempts to depict lesbian sexuality expose the governing binary logic of heterosexuality. By implicitly challenging the habitual heterosexual paradigm, representing lesbian sexuality conspiciously unmasks the ways gender and sexuality normally coalesce to reassert the complementary duality of sexual difference.

The various figures employed in this depiction of lesbian activity typify its representation. While lesbian sexuality epitomizes the central moment of an authentic and dangerous arousal, the arrangement of these transforming metaphors as they combine both to represent lesbian sexuality and effect a defensive evasion of it produces a configuration—a performance of portrayal and defensive transformation. Its depiction as a nuclear instant of genuine, exciting display can only occur because it is surrounded by a protective, defensive, heterosexualized husk of description. The configuration represents lesbian sexuality, defends against that representation, and exceeds its representation to stand in for something else—in this case secret knowledge of female sexuality or sexual arousal. But configurations also expose what is threatened by the representation of lesbian sexuality in the very terms that constitute the threat—in this story, the primacy of heterosexuality itself.

Nin's alterations of this scene in other texts enact additional, symptomatically visible configurations of lesbian sexuality. Examining Nin's modifications, we see performed a range of configurations that each reveal a similarly complex exposure of the investments of culture and representation in a two-gender, heterosexual model. The version above is from *Henry and June: From the Unexpurgated Diary of Anaïs Nin*, published posthumously in 1986 by Nin's estate trustee. Because this is from a diary that has presumably not been doctored, it is Nin's "authentic" confession or the "true" version. Only this account contains Nin's profession of her arousal as the effect of watching the lesbian acts; the others either replace that admission with something else or omit it entirely. As Nin rearranges and polishes her *Diary* for publication, for example, she not only transposes her husband into Henry Miller, but she also elaborates the posed, theatrical portions of the episode, embroidering her descriptions of the physical ambience of the brothel, the prostitutes, and the element of travelogue. In her *Diary* account, the moment the women shift to their lesbian acts, the arousal they excite is displaced from Nin and her husband exclusively onto the prostitutes, whose response is more colorfully described than in the "unexpurgated" passage. This version ends abruptly: "A moment later they both stood up, joking, and the mood passed" (60).[2]

In this second configuration, excitement evoked by the lesbian moment is experienced only by the participants; even for them, it is a fleeting "mood." Its authenticity is reduced to a joke by Nin, a necessary defense against any possible effect of the moment. Nin's emphasis on the opulent setting of the brothel situates the entire experience as tacky excess, and the women "like mother and daughter" reiterate a grotesque version of what might be simple familial intimacy (59). Within this configuration, however, Nin's allusion to mother and daughter is also a slip—uncanny testimony to a fearsome perception of lesbian sexuality as narcissistic incest. The configuration not only simultaneously represents and defends against lesbian sexuality, but reveals the incestuous terms that instigate the defense.

The episode reappears in Nin's *Delta of Venus*, a collection that bears on its cover the tantalizing inscription: "She did it for a male client for a dollar a page. Now over one million copies in print."[3] Its pornographic context doubled (brothel and erotic fiction), the anecdote of the lesbian show becomes part of the story of the well-endowed Basque, a regular client of the establishment. Enclosed by the story's emphasis on the Basque's superb penile fortitude, the women's activities with the dildo are described at greater length and in greater detail, emphasizing close-up descriptions of the action of the rubber penis. This time "the women" are "beautifully matched, without timorousness or sentimentality. Women of action, who both carried an ironic smile and corrupt expression" (169). Their performance was requested by "foreigners" who "must have asked to see a man and woman together, and this was Maman's compromise" (169). A "foreign" desire and a "compromise," the women's performance is witnessed by the Basque from a prearranged voyeuristic vantage point. Though the foreigners are "fascinated," the women never begin any sexual activity without the dildo or drop their pretense of heterosexuality. At the moment where in other versions they do, the Basque enters: "Viviane looked at him gratefully. The Basque realized she was in heat. Two virilities would satisfy her more than that teasing, elusive one" (170). They are saved by the phallus at the point where their behavior might have become overtly lesbian.

The candid lesbian moment of other versions replaced by a scene with two phalli, the anecdote is completely heterosexually recuperated in a way that suggests almost a male homosexual performance in the active presence of two penes. What threatened to be lesbian is completely recovered by the Basque's hyper-heterosexual entrance. The suggestion of lesbian activity, heterosexual simulation as it is, becomes only foreplay to the greater climax introduced by the Basque. This passage configures lesbian sexuality as the spectacle that instigates heterosexual intervention and relief. A "compromise," it can only lead to something better and more fulfilling. In this narrative, which drives toward completion rather than arousal, as Nin's first version did, lesbian sexuality becomes the inauthentic rather than the authentic, a "foreign" imitation that prepares for the real thing.

Appearing through the range of Nin's work, textual transformations of this anecdote enact multiple symptomatic configurations of lesbian sexuality related both to common cultural perceptions and their specific literary contexts. Even in her correspondence with Henry Miller, Nin comments. "Certain gestures (I felt that in the Rue Blondel) destroy the magic."[4] Here the editor asserts in a note attached to the name Rue Blondel that Nin went to the brothel on the "recommendation" of Miller, with whom Nin was having an affair. At the time, as Nin recounts in her *Diary*, she was also attracted to Miller's wife, June. The episode thus not only centers around an authentic, biographical "core," but this core appears only in the "authentic," but albeit still fictional version and increasingly becomes more and more defended as it is more and more fictionalized.[5]

In configurations analogous to those employed by Nin, lesbian sexuality occupies certain specific locations or positions in the arguments, subject matter, and rhetoric of cinema, psychoanalysis, Western European and American literature, and literary criticism. Across these discourses, lesbian sexuality tends to be represented in the same range of configurations in similar rhetorical or argumentative positions. As titillating foreplay, simulated heterosexuality, exotic excess, knowing center, joking inauthenticity, artful compromise, and masculine mask, configurations of lesbian sexuality embody the conflicting impetuses of representational insufficiency and recuperation. Operating as points of systemic failure, configurations of lesbian sexuality often reflect the complex incongruities that occur when the logic or philosophy of a system becomes self-contradictory, visibly fails to account for something, or cannot complete itself. Simultaneously, lesbian sexuality instigates the overly compensatory and highly visible return of the terms of the ruptured system that mend and mask its gaps. As a point of failure, lesbian sexuality is the phenomenon that evades the rules; as a point of return, it is the example that proves the rule and reveals the premises upon which the rules depend. Attempts to depict or explain lesbian sexuality spur anxieties about knowledge and identity—two terms that inevitably and often unaccountably appear linked in discourses as diverse as Freud's psychoanalytic writings, soft-core pornography, and feminist reader-response theory. Revealing or forcing logical inconsistencies, configurations of lesbian sexuality undo discursive claims to mastery and wholeness and occupy positions of penultimateness, immaturity, and incompleteness that exist alongside of, but not in opposition to, neat systemic closure.

I chose these four discourses—psychoanalysis, cinema, literature, and literary criticism—because they are all, though not exclusively, both discourses and metadiscourses about sexuality and the way sexuality is perceived in and through Western culture. And while none of these discourses may contain the "truth" about any sexuality, all enact the terms by which sexuality is culturally understood. Configurations of lesbian sexuality in these discourses are complex representations whose particular location in a text and strategic combination of elements reveal not lesbian sexuality per se, but the anxieties it produces. Because the collision of gender and sexuality becomes so visible in configurations of lesbian sexuality, they also illustrate how irreconcilable conflicts between the two are representationally resolved. Thus by reading these discourses for the lesbian sexuality in them and analyzing its textual enactments, we see how lesbian sexuality is configured and how that configuration functions in the text, in the discourse, and, by extension, in the culture.

This is different from an analysis of lesbian images, a study of lesbian portrayal, or making any claims for lesbian women or lesbian

sexuality per se.[6] While the discovery and analysis of images is important, I am more concerned in this book with the political context of
those representations: how lesbian sexuality is used as a figure signifying something else and why it appears when and where it does.
Configurations, like representations, have very little to do with any
facts about the wide range of lesbian women, either as authentic
descriptions of their lived experience or as accurate accounts of development or cause. Insofar, however, as configurations affect self-rep-
resentations or the cultural positioning of groups of individuals, the
rhetorical presence of configurations of lesbian sexuality is a symptom
of the kinds of perceptions that underlie cultural treatment and placement of lesbian women, since these same discourses reflect and shape
cultural myths. Politically and critically, understanding these configurations may help us identify the oppressive sources of ideology that
tend to delimit the cultural possibilities of individuals. It can also help
us understand the ideology and rhetoric of sexual difference itself and
how gender interacts with other paradigms of difference, helping us
pierce through what seem otherwise to be gender-neutral formulations.

The quandary of how to define the lesbian sexuality that demar-
cates these configurations is already a product of the complex intersection of political, historical, and identificatory issues. Because the arguments of this book do not depend on biographical verifiability, but
rather on a broad cultural category operating in textual representations, I define lesbian sexuality as women's real or imagined sexual
desire for or sexual activity with a woman. This definition is clearly a
product of a heterosexual ideology that privileges sexual categories,
but it is also the concept most typically identified as "lesbian" in
Western culture. The political and critical issues about definition I
take up in chapter 3 in the context of feminist reader-response criticism. Studying configurations of lesbian sexuality does not stake a
claim exclusivity for the functions they perform. Other figures or
moments—male homosexuality, colonized non-Westerners, the figure of the witch, the female body, Woman—serve as analogous but
slightly different configurations in Western thought and culture.[7] Alice
Jardine's *Gynesis: Configurations of Woman and Modernity,* for example,
takes up one aspect of the figure of Woman in modernist discourse
and culture.[8] Finally, though these configurations are historically determined, this book focuses on their striking repetition through differ-

ent discourses and times rather than on any concentrated attempt to define a cause/effect relation between particular historical circumstances and the appearance and shape of the configurations.

Two More Examples

PROPHYLACTIC INTRODUCTIONS

The two examples of multiple configurations of lesbian sexuality that follow are introductions written by editors or translators to books containing lesbian subject matter: Francis Birrell's introduction to Diderot's *Memoirs of a Nun* and Joseph Collins's introduction to Colette's *The Pure and the Impure*.[9] In the specific context of literary value, these introductions reflect the cultural conflict and anxiety around questions of moral decency, cultural significance, and the underlying economic interests of the publisher, who often benefits from the artfully indirect implication of a book's impropriety. The introductions' investment in explaining, defending, and evaluating the texts they precede makes them particularly prone to contradictions and evasion, especially when the text that follows is famous for containing what some might consider scurrilous content. The introductions try to neutralize the books' material, making them consumable without guilt while ensuring their marketability. Given their contradictory tasks, these introductions contain a plethora of lesbian configurations, more concentrated, perhaps, because of the immediacy of the problem.

Sometime before 1928, Francis Birrell undertook the translation of Denis Diderot's *La Religieuse* for the Broadway Library series of eighteenth-century French literature. In his brief introduction to the volume, Birrell defends what he sees as the "artistry" of Diderot's novel while disavowing its admittedly "perverse" content. To deflect imputations of voyeurism and pornography, Birrell concentrates on the literary history and historical context of the novel. "*La Religieuse* is in great part a practical joke," he affirms, "a fact which should be borne in mind by readers over-inclined to be serious" (vii–viii). It is "little more than a *pièce justificative* intended to make "more convincing" Diderot's faked letters from a "Madame Madin," protector of the escaped nun Suzanne Simonin, to the Marquis de Croismare, who was interested in her case and whom Diderot and his friend Grimm hoped to lure back to Paris (viii). The novel's spectacular and shocking lesbian content was a lure, according to Birrell, employed by Diderot to enhance the reliability of the letters that accompany the account. But while "Diderot certainly got carried away by artistic enthusiasm, . . . it is well to remember that the author's tongue was probably never for a very long time together completely out of his cheek" (viii).

Otherwise, for Birrell the graphic lesbian activity in the novel primarily reflects both the range of Diderot's worldly knowledge and his realist abilities. "As a study of female perversion in three different forms, *La Religieuse* is extremely subtle and staggeringly modern in treatment" (ix), a fact that reveals Diderot's "enormous knowledge of life in all its forms." And despite Birrell's recommendation that "the proper way in which to approach *La Religieuse* . . . is after all the simplest one, the artistic approach" (viii), the novel's artistry resides in its authentic portrayal of Diderot's extraordinary human and sexual knowledge. "*La Religieuse* is interesting because it is a splendid novel, full of character, variety and human feeling. . . . For this reason the commentary and erudition have been reduced to the minimum necessary to show the realistic detail which Diderot employed, presumably the better to mystify M. de Croismare" (x). Finally, Diderot's knowledge and realist adeptness exceed his translator's abilities. As Birrell confesses at the end of his brief introduction, "I have on occasion been much embarrassed by the undiluted femininity of the society described, and have found my vocabulary sadly at fault. . . . It has been found necessary to omit a few words and phrases which, however, do not in any way interfere with the meaning of the paragraphs in which these omissions occur" (xi).

The specter of an educated reading audience infected with a twentieth-century squeamishness (as Birrell seems to imagine) might invite this mercurially apologetic, defensive, laudatory, and ultimately diverting introduction to a novel that overtly depicts sexual activity among cloistered nuns. But in addition to rescuing Diderot from his readers' prudish misunderstandings and eliminating any idea that the author might have applauded or enjoyed the nuns' behavior, Birrell's contradictory, evasive, and euphemistic rhetoric also reflects his own reaction to the sexual subject matter of Diderot's novel. The parts Birrell "found necessary to omit" are the portions of Diderot's descriptions of lesbian activity that take place below the waist.[10] Somehow, words fail him here, and the loss of these parts (omissions signified not with asterisks, as Birrell advises, but, symptomatically, with ellipses, making invisible even the locations of these omissions) does not "interfere with the meaning of the paragraphs," since without the phallus, there is no meaning.

Within the four and one-half pages of Birrell's prefatory frame, we find that the cloister culture and its sexual activity constitute an "undiluted femininity" for which the translator has no words. Sexual acts that approach the genital both lack signifiers and have no meaning anyway. We find that the realistic depiction of such activity is evidence of Diderot's extraordinary knowledge and constitutes a lure and mystery for M. de Croismare, designed to pique his desire to return to Paris. We also are told that the novel depicting such activity is a joke and—whether or not this is a suggestive slip of Birrell's tongue—in writing about it, Diderot's tongue is rarely out of his cheek. In this introduction, lesbian sexuality, rather than simply serving as a representation of two women who are sexually engaged or even as part of the subject matter of a novel, functions as the place of mystery, as a lure, as evidence of Diderot's knowledge, as an untranslatable, "undiluted" femininity, and as the elliptical gap, the place where the translator's abilities break down.

As the simultaneous point of systemic return and reinvigoration, the depiction of the lesbian galvanizes controlling strategies that reintroduce, with a vengeance, defensive and often conservative mechanisms prototypical of literary/critical discourse. For Birrell, the lesbian sexuality of the novel is contained not only by the circumstantial unnaturalness of the cloister, but also by its literary/critical function as both lure and joke. It is, finally, practically eliminated: as a lure, it is misleading—not what it seems to be. As a joke, it no longer exists at all. Historical context eliminates literary content; author and culture are saved from the veritable existence of such "unnatural" practices. And in so doing, the author is celebrated for his insight and an artistry that relies upon the simultaneous depiction and erasure of lesbian sexuality.

The introduction to Collette's *The Pure and the Impure,* another book with lesbian content, adds to the configurations of lesbian sexuality present in Birrell's introduction and makes even more apparent the kind of defensive overcompensation necessary to neutralize lesbian subject matter. Translated into English by Edith Dally in 1933,

Colette's collection of portraits *Ces Plaisirs* . . . (1932) was published in the United States under the title *The Pure and the Impure*. Subtitled *A Case-book of Love* for the purposes of its American publication, Colette's essays are preceded in the American edition by a verbose table of contents, replete with pithy descriptive quotations from the chapters, and an introduction by Joseph Collins. Like Birrell, Collins finds it necessary to "save" the author by simultaneously appealing to the depths and circumstances of her unusual knowledge and distancing her from the culture about which she writes. Beginning with a connection between sexual exploits and gossip, Collins performs the perverse gymnastics necessary to license and recover Colette:

> Many years ago, the author of *The Pure and the Impure* gained a certain reputation, deservedly or undeservedly, of not being like other girls. She has liked to talk about it, and in this book she likes to tell about it. The net result of her narrative insofar as it concerns herself is that her amatory feeling and her genesic instinct were directed mainly to the normal—though they sometimes peeped, they never strayed. She had, and has, a lively sympathy with those who are otherwise gaited and she understands them—at times she applauds them. She tells why when young, she aped man in dress and manners, and she gives lengthy and brilliant description of her contacts and intimacies with the strange sisterhood. (ix–x)

Like Diderot, Colette has a superior knowledge, a knowledge Collins reaffirms again and again in introductory overkill. But equally important to Collins is Colette's self-salvation from the "strange sisterhood" whose stories she writes in fits of excess, in an inability to keep "sin" silent. Fortunately, according to Collins, Colette has the appropriate sympathetic heterosexual perspective on the lesbian phenomenon, one he does not hesitate to repeat: "She is firmly of the belief that love-making amongst women is far less common than between men and that it constitutes an entirely different sociological and ethical problem. In her own sex it derives largely from idleness, ennui, and alcohol, and from the activities of vicious and depraved proselyters" (x).

That these women are worth writing about is also argued by a perplexed Collins who undertakes to explain the mysteries of God to prospective readers: "I think it was Job who said that God does things past finding out, unsearchable things. One of these unsearchable things is that out of every one hundred human beings created in His image, there at least are two who can be incited to the emotion of love only by persons of their own sex" (xi). Having justified their pedigree and their worthiness as Colette's subject matter as well as Colette's own "platonic intimacy" with them, he states again their intrinsic interest, not as lesbians, but as "anomalous" talent who are also interesting characters:

> It is of the [gifted], their conversations and conduct, their antics and antimonies that Mme. Colette writes. When women got off the leash, they began to wander—they found that the street called 'Straight' was difficult to stay on. There seemed to be an increasing inclination to get off it in couples, and Mme. Colette met and played around with a lot of them and a considerable part of this book is taken up with telling their daring and their doing. (xii)

Giving Colette authority without implicating her, Collins performs the symptomatic list of cultural perceptions about lesbian sexuality. Animal-like ("off the leash"), often "aping" men, they are bored alcoholics, anomalous anomalies (less prevalent than male homosexuals), but sometimes gifted. Their emergence seems to be a result of a liberation—something like feminism—that left them uncontrolled, taking the wrong path (away from that street called "Straight"). But they are nonetheless interesting, worthy of a view. The redemption process undertaken by Collins on behalf of culture, Colette, and God is continued in those features added to the American edition. The change of title from *Ces Plaisirs . . .*, a simple, pleasant reference to the phrase "ces plaisirs qu'on nomme, à la légère, physiques . . ."[11] from *Le Blé en herbe* is translated into the melodramatic and binary *The Pure and the Impure*. The shift from pleasure to categories of purity is a shift from an unmoralized license to moral judgment and issues of sexual virtue, lending the book a righteous fervor not present in the essays. The interpolation of the "case-book" subtitle not only makes Colette's descriptive portraits scientific, distancing them from her tone of familiar friendliness, but also overtly imitates psychoanalysis in situating Colette's portraits as the study of anomalies, of unusual cases. Science explains and authorizes Colette's knowledge as well as its transmission. Protecting both the public and Colette by transferring her sympathetic descriptions into the proper realm of psychological study, the case-book approach insulates readers from the poten-

tially deleterious example of such figures as Pauline Tarn and makes
the lesbian subject matter safe for consumption. Though originally
concerned with interesting lesbian characters, the rest of the book is
transmuted into a lesson in what to avoid.

What Follows

THIS BOOK is organized loosely around the broad categories of seeing, writing, and reading. In the context of each of these
processes, configurations of lesbian sexuality tend to bring into question central assumptions or axioms within discourses. In practices of
viewing or perceiving, configurations of lesbian sexuality challenge
the stability of a visible, rigidly defined sexual difference. The first
section of chapter 1, "A View to a Thrill," takes up questions raised
by the cinematic imaging of lesbian sexuality. The regular use of
lesbian scenes in soft-core pornographic films such as *Emmanuelle* and
Melody in Love reveals not only how lesbian sexuality functions in
narratives devoted to heterosexuality, but also how the semiotics of
lesbian scenes brings into question theoretical issues about the relation between gender and viewing and the dependence of film theory
on clearly delineated categories of sexual difference. The second
section examines the overly defensive portrayal of lesbian sexuality in
the mainstream women's films *Desert Hearts* and *Lianna*, observing
that the cinematic portrayal of lesbian sexuality in these instances is
highly fetishized. In the third section an analysis of feminist depictions of lesbian sexuality in *Entre Nous* and *I've Heard the Mermaids
Singing* suggests that they both create "a different measure of desire"
in a visual and narrative aesthetic based on sustaining and frustrating
both narrative and visual pleasure.

In the context of questions about creativity and writing, lesbian
sexuality configures both the desire to desire and an authorizing originary moment that is subsequently emphatically denied. At the center
of the two chapters on writing, " 'This Is Not for You': The Sexuality
of Mothering" and "Beginning with L," is the projection of a preoedipal, utopian lesbian origin that is both asserted and denied by
feminist theorists. The paradox of this sexualized mothering as it
appears in the writings of Julia Kristeva and Nancy Chodorow is the
subject of chapter 2, which compares their mainly heterosexual utopian vision of mother/daughter relations with the denial of the mother

in such lesbian novels as Jane Rule's *This Is Not for You* and Rita Mae Brown's *Rubyfruit Jungle*. Comparing the position of the mother and particularly the mother's connection to an accessible, preoedipal origin leads to an understanding of a differing structure of narrative desire that exists between Kristeva's and Chodorow's accounts and the novels.

Chapter 3 treats feminist theories of writing and reading. The first section, "The Lure of Origins," explores the relation between questions of origin and theories of women's writing and community as formulated by Hélène Cixous and Luce Irigaray. Like Kristeva and Chodorow, both Cixous and Irigaray want to premise a lesbian originary moment that they evade and deny. While their descriptions of feminine experience look suspiciously like descriptions of lesbian sexuality, they propose a somewhat different feminine aesthetic from that practiced by the lesbian poet Olga Broumas. The section on reading, "The Lure of Identity," examines how the figure of Emily Dickinson incites questions about the relation of reading, gender, and identity. Reading through the work of such critics as Adrienne Rich, Judith Fetterley, Patrocinio Schweickart, Jean Kennard, Bonnie Zimmerman, Dale Bauer, and approaches such as encodement theory, this section traces how the threatening multiplicity of lesbian sexuality becomes the assurance of a more centered feminist identity.

Chapter 4, "Freud Reads Lesbians," focuses on the relationship among identity, desire, and knowledge configured in the body of Freud's work by lesbian sexuality. A reading of his treatment and theories about lesbian patients yields the configurations of lesbian as a decoy for knowledge, as a mask for both male homosexuality and heterosexuality, and as a fleeting, transitory stage that functions metonymically.

The final two chapters of the book treat critical questions that arise as the contexts of seeing, writing, and reading coalesce in more pragmatic circumstances. Chapter 5, "All Analogies Are Faulty: The Fear of Intimacy in Feminist Criticism," examines how black and lesbian become symptomatic parts of an oppressor/oppressed analogy prevalent in feminist criticism. The unacknowledged reliance upon this analogy actually keeps differences separate and prevents the development of critical diversity. In chapter 6, "Polymorphous Diversity," the differences among lesbians are explored through a reading of homophobia instigated by Margaret Court's criticism of Martina

Navratilova, an analysis of Butch/Femme, a mention of s/m and a brief prolegomenon to a lesbian critical practice.

This survey and analysis reveals a kind of haunting regularity to the positions occupied by lesbian sexuality. Despite cultural perceptions of its marginality—as Colette observes, it is "less common" than male homosexuality—its configurations are surprisingly central. As Freud observes: "Homosexuality in women . . . is certainly not less common than in men, although much less glaring . . ."[12] And even if lesbian sexuality is less visible, its very evasiveness promises a thrill that is finally only a lure of knowledge and a desire for desire.

View to a Thrill

Just a "Foretaste": Lesbians in Pornography

I've NOTICED as I've watched (probably 100 times) the clips for the films I discuss that I'm still both stimulated and embarrassed by them. I suspect the titillation comes from two divergent places: my acquiescence to the voyeuristic structures of the apparatus and my identification with the activity and characters on the screen. It's hard to determine which comes first, my seduction by the apparatus or my identification with something on the screen, or if either does: they seem to coexist in a kind of circular interdependency that creates both tension and pleasure as I view. My identification with whatever—the characters, the activity, the idea of the activity —is the sign of my undoing, because that engrossment means that I've also been lured into an alignment with a camera, an identification with a third party who looks from a distance. This voyeuristic scope both enables my identifications (it is the condition that fosters them) and alienates me from the image, embarrasses me, and obstructs my pleasure, making me want in turn to distance myself, to dissociate myself from the screen image, which I do by analyzing, theorizing, writing a book to erase my discomfiture, trying to master the apparatus as it has mastered me.

As a viewer I find myself in two double-binds. I am subject to the contradictory tensions of cinematic identification—identification with on-screen characters and identification with the camera view—experienced by most film spectators. But I am also caught in the peculiar impasse of the female spectator, a chronic dilemma exacerbated by pornographic films' overt appeal to metacinematic structures of voyeurism and the erotic as they operate conspicuously in the field of sexual difference. On the one hand, by consenting to watch these films, I submit myself to their masculinist ideological and political constructions of viewer identification that posit the female image as the object of a voyeuristic consumption in a narrative that controls and degrades her. Accepting the film's conventions and its point of view, I can "enjoy" the film. On the other hand and at the same time, unless I forget I am female, I am continually alienated from images produced by an apparatus that is antinomic to my position as viewer, which poses me simultaneously as voyeur and as chastised recipient—witness—of a patriarchal lesson in sexual regulation. Watching these films, like discussing them, seems to require a tension of pleasure, denial, and masochism.

The only moment in porn films where this dilemma seems to dissolve itself is the conventional lesbian interlude. Remarkable for its superficial erasure of on-screen sexual difference (two women, no man), the cinematic depiction of lesbian sexuality seems momentarily to enfranchise the female as a sexually aggressive participant, erasing some of the objectification of the woman, and appearing to provide a simple screen identification and place for the female viewer, at least as a lesbian. But even if there is a site on the screen for a female viewer's sympathetic identification, the apparatus itself tends to reproduce its scopophilic posture; the two women are still objects of the viewer's voyeuristic look. And narratively, while enhancing the heroine's libertinism and desirability, soft-core porn's inclusion of lesbianism as merely one of a number of sexual permutations provides another version of erotic domination for the male viewer.

Even if the lesbian scene is included expressly for voyeuristic purposes, the portrayal of lesbian sexuality renders uncomfortably visible the narrative operations and semiotic strategies by which women and sexuality are represented. That two women occupy traditionally heterosexual positions makes visible the gender stereotypes that inhere in representations of sexuality. While the project of imaging a phallusless sexuality results in a scene that is in some ways more conventionally portrayed than heterosexual scenes, that lesbian sexuality is forced into a traditionally heterosexual model causes the images to slip away from and break down these conventions. With the absence of two "complementary" genders, something on the level of the operation of the apparatus breaks apart, disturbing the alliance between camera and viewer, between viewing subject and screen object, freeing up the lines of cinematic identification and the conventional objectification of erotic images. Why the portrayal of lesbian sexuality would incite this temporary cinematic breakdown is part of the subject of this chapter.

Because there is a tendency to explain lesbian sexuality in terms premised upon a heterosexual norm, I want to question the gendermen and heterosexism of film theory itself by looking at these cinematic depictions of lesbian sexuality, points where sexual difference, sexuality, and the visual are asymmetrically misaligned. I will focus my examination on soft-core pornography because it is widespread, aired on television, easily available in video stores, artily narrative, and cornily stylized to make it seem worthy of consumption by the self-proclaimed "art" film viewer. The pretense of soft-core porn toward art, discretion, and a mixed audience makes its exploitation of sexuality more insidious than that of hard-core porn. Its distinguishing difference from "hard-core"—sexual scenes are faked rather than authentic—gives soft-core porn an artistic leeway that enables representational latitude. Not tied to the cinematic exigencies of portraying real sexual activity, soft-core porn can instead concentrate on playing symptomatically with the tensions of voyeurism and sexual excitement. I realize that in looking at pornography at all, I risk valorizing a genre that is generally oppressive to women, but I think it is crucial to understand how such oppressive forms are constructed, how they oppress, how they titillate, and why they regularly include the lesbian.

EMMANUELLE AND MELODY

Emmanuelle, a prototypical soft-core porn film, and *Melody in Love* both contain lesbian scenes.[1] Narratively, these are not central or climactic moments in the films, whose plots generally consist of a series of episodic sexual encounters. Both films appear to be aimed at a mixed audience and contain the formula typical to soft-core porn films: a series of sexual encounters arranged in an episodic narrative about the sexual initiation of a woman or a young man. Combining initiation rite, sexual education, and erotic travelogue, *Emmanuelle* and *Melody* are structured around the acquisition of sexual knowledge; these narratives follow their heroines through a series of sexual lessons, in which they are tutored by a more experienced, liberated teacher whose role it is to help the young women lose their hampering inhibitions. Loosely set in a trajectory toward perfect sexual satisfaction, the lesbian scenes occur only in the first half of the film following episodes of autoeroticism, but preceding the resolution offered by the films' "satisfying," climactic heterosexual encounters. In this way the parallel between narrative and sexuality becomes overtly apparent in a trajectory that links completion to heterosexual intercourse and often to violence.[2]

Emmanuelle is about the young wife of a French embassy official, who travels to Bangkok to join her suave and presumably liberated husband, a man interested only in promoting his wife's complete sexual education. He disavows jealousy and possessiveness and urges her to experiment in the bored French colony of diplomats, recommending particularly the erotic sexagenarian Mario as guide.[3] Emmanuelle ventures into this community and attracts both the precociously promiscuous Marie-Ange (her "sex professor") and Ariane, a jaded, jealous, middle-aged, controlling diplomatic wife. But Emmanuelle is interested in the colony's outcast, Bea, an archaeologist with a mysterious reputation. Though Marie-Ange attempts to educate Emmanuelle with a masturbation exhibition and Ariane tries to introduce her to the joys of sex in a grope on the squash court, Emmanuelle pursues Bea at a party while (and not coincidentally) Mario makes overtures to Emmanuelle, setting a date that Emmanuelle breaks to follow a hesitating Bea into the wilderness. Though still professing love for her husband, Emmanuelle is completely taken with Bea, but Bea rejects her, admitting, after a brief sexual affair at an archaeological site, that she doesn't love Emmanuelle. The heartbroken Emmanuelle returns to her husband, who has been angry and jealous at Emmanuelle's defection with a woman. Still sexually inhibited (relatively speaking), Emmanuelle allows herself to be tutored by the hedonistic Mario, who, through a series of lessons in passivity (including gang rape), teaches Emmanuelle to be a "real" woman.

An imitation of *Emmanuelle*, *Melody in Love* follows the sexual initiation of Melody, who has come to visit her suave and liberated cousin Rachel on a volcanic island. Naive and virgin, Melody wants only Rachel as lover until Rachel convinces her that men are better, setting her up with a cute hotel manager whom the married Rachel tries out first. Melody's attachment to Rachel, who is depicted as a nursing mother, is clearly the attraction of a child to a parent. At Rachel's insistence, Melody timidly tries out heterosexuality, but never quite satisfactorily until she and the manager are caught on the volcanic slope during an eruption, when, in rhythm with the spurting lava, Melody learns to shed her inhibitions. The Melody plot is paralleled by the sexual initiation of a native girl, who, in love with her homosexual teacher, tries to follow him on vacation only to end up in the arms of Rachel's husband, Octavio, and ultimately in a three-way sexual encounter with him and Rachel.[4]

The lesbian episode is carefully situated as part of a natural development in the films' lessons about the inherent qualities of female sexuality, part of the education offered both to the heroines and to the viewers. The knowledge they seek is natural rather than cultural; the process involves a return to nature—to bestial natives in the case of *Emmanuelle*, to primordial volcanos in *Melody*. The plots of the films as well as the characters' sexual educations are unified under the aegis of nature, which orders the homosexual and heterosexual, making a place for both. But "nature" consists of a contrived path of female sexual development only posed as natural. For Emmanuelle, the process is artfully arranged by her husband; her deviation from the heterosexual as well as her return to it are seen as normal, necessary, and predictable stages in a female sexual exploration. In fact, the naturalness of her experimentation is emphasized precisely at the point when the question of lesbian behavior arises between Emmanuelle and her husband. When he asks Rachel if she wants to make love to Marie-Ange, Emmanuelle rejects the possibility, but adds that what is attractive about Marie-Ange is that her sexuality is "natural" and, further, that sexuality itself is "all natural."

Melody's progress is even more tritely "natural," following the timing of a volcanic eruption on the island. Clearly a stage of "normal" development set within a familial, even oedipal model, Melody shifts from her desire for the mother figure, Rachel, to desire for the father, to an interest in men outside of the family. In this trajectory (quite like the one Freud posits for female development), Melody's lesbian interest is located as the penultimate point on a line to maturity/ fulfillment that leads to the heterosexual finales of Melody's encounters with the hotel manager and the three-way scene among Rachel, her husband, and the native girl. The very naturalness of it is transparently revealed in one of Melody and Rachel's initial conversations:

M: I honestly don't think I want a man.

R: Everything works the way nature intended it to.

M: I don't need to find anyone, I've got you.

R: Darling, all I can give you is a foretaste of what you can have with the right man.

M: I don't believe that.

R: Oh, I think you'll change your tune when the right man comes along.

While both films are replete with a variety of sexual episodes — sex with prostitutes, voyeurism, "spin-off" sex of natives and servants, pickups, and other variations appended onto the narrative — the key elements of these stories: sexual knowledge, sexual questing, and sexual satisfaction, coalesce first in the films' lesbian scenes. In both films, the protagonists undergo a kind of transitory but transforming lesbian experience located crucially between stages of innocent fidelity marked by masturbation and rampant heterosexual promiscuity (the desired end of a sexual education). For example, Melody's sensual training with her polymorphously perverse sex-guide cousin Rachel primes her for the volcanic heterosexual climax she fears and craves, quieting her anxieties and easing her into the ultimate sexual experience. In a lesbian episode with Rachel that occurs simultaneously with Rachel's arrangements with the hotel manager, Rachel reassures a reluctant Melody as she begins to make love to her with the line: "Don't worry, darling; I'll see that you get the best of all possible worlds."

While insistently naturalized and perhaps the reason for this persistent naturalization, these lesbian affairs are also depicted as potentially threatening to the heterosexual order. While casual sex between women is seen as desirable, emotional and sexual engagement between women threatens the fabric of the liberated marriage. For example, Emmanuelle's initial discussion of adultery occurs at the same time she is pursued by Ariane (casual sex) and first sees Bea, with whom she falls in love. The predatory Ariane asks if Emmanuelle has ever betrayed her husband. Emmanuelle, denying that she has, immediately asks Ariane about Bea, who is sitting on the other side of the pool. Ariane responds that Bea has "never quite made the group" and goes on to ask Emmanuelle if she has ever "betrayed him [her husband] with a girl." Emmanuelle asks if it "counts" with a girl, to which Ariane responds, "One day try it with me and you'll see if it counts." Emmanuelle tries it with Ariane, and it doesn't count—doesn't affect her—but Bea, her first extramarital love, the first one for whom she will defy her husband, does count. Her attraction to and rejection by Bea is pivotal; the failure of this courtship induces Emmanuelle's surrender to the self-destructive tutelage of the aged Sadian Mario.

As both natural and threatening, lesbian sexuality emerges at the point where multiple and contradictory sexual postures begin to co-exist. Preceded by the first tentative gropings toward sexual knowledge and pleasure in overt masturbation scenes, lesbian encounters function as a second or mediate stage—a transitional step—between autoeroticism and heterosexuality. Though the lesbian affair in both films is seen as a stage characterized by sexual timidity, adolescent childishness, and fear of the "real" thing, it steps outside of the bounds of "normalcy." It seems a deviation from the desired trajectory, particularly in *Emmanuelle*, where the sexual education of Emmanuelle is attached to her desire to please her husband. The contradictory natural/transgressive nature of lesbian sexuality implies a kind of excess attached to the lesbian episode, especially when it takes place, as it does in *Emmanuelle*, in the wilderness with a social outcast away from the sexual "program." It is also excessive because it is a false path that generates very unliberal behavior in others. Despite his interest in her sexual development, Emmanuelle's husband becomes uncontrollably drunken, jealous, and angry when Emmanuelle runs away with Bea, and in *Melody* the libertine Rachel always tightly controls Melody's desire for her, never allowing it to get out of hand.

This lesbian excess is, however, narratively crucial in these films not only to reaffirm ultimate heterosexuality, but also to provide part of the complication, the twisting, that a heterosexual conclusion resolves. Lesbian sexuality becomes the way the problem of sexual inhibition manifests itself in the narrative, creating the narrative complication that delays completion and introducing the problem of multiple possibilities. Lesbian episodes provide a doubling (a couple) that anticipates and mimics heterosexuality, but a doubling (too many women) that typifies the perverse excess of the exploratory period it represents. This perverse excess is reflected in and perhaps also produces a narrative doubling and splitting that characterizes the narratives of these films. Both *Emmanuelle* and *Melody* have parallel plots and doubled characters that converge as the lesbian moment is recaptured for heterosexuality and patriarchy. In *Emmanuelle*, the Emmanuelle character is doubled by the ingenue Marie-Ange as well as by the servant girls who take her place in her husband's bed. Marie-Ange and Mario are also doubles; had Emmanuelle followed the advice of Marie-Ange, who tried to introduce her to Mario, Emmanuelle would have found the correct sexual path sooner. As it is, Emmanuelle's lesbian interest takes her away from her husband; its failure and her tryst with Mario bring her back. Melody's experiences are paralleled by the initiation process of a native girl that weaves around and through Melody's discoveries. Near the end of the film, Melody's volcanic sexual fulfillment parallels the native girl's satisfying engagement with Rachel and her husband.

The doubling of plots and characters also parallels other kinds of filmic duplicity and splitting. Both films are dubbed, a circumstantial splitting that creates a disjunction between image and voice. There is a split between native (dark) and foreign (white), reflected both in the narrative and in the exotic settings of these films: *Emmanuelle* is set in Bangkok and *Melody* in Sri Lanka. Aligned with racial and national differences are splits in wealth and privilege, emphasized in "politically aware" local color scenes at the beginning of both films. The sexual activities of the wealthy foreign protagonists are leisured pastimes, during which the male Europeans can only profit from— colonize—female natives' "closer-to-nature" sexual knowledge. For the poor male natives, sex is a stolen commodity attached to violence, as Melody is attacked in a marketplace and Emmanuelle is raped by the customers in an opium den. The differences between European and native, male and female, young and old are mended in bed, as are almost all differences in these films, and usually at the expense of the woman and for the pleasure of the male sexual "imperialist," whether white or native. *Melody*, for example, ends with Melody seducing a teenage native boy who has been spying on her naked swims. The cultural splits existing at the beginning of these films are realigned by the end into the classic ideology of sexual difference where the male has power and the female serves him. Lesbian episodes tend to instigate this "democratic" realignment as they draw attention to sexual difference through the exclusion of the male.

Mediate and excessive, the lesbian scenes also constitute foreplay, for the film's characters and viewers. Parts of unhappy love affairs, the lesbian affairs are never quite successful, often ending before any climax. Staging, thus, an uncompleted or perpetuated desire that they arouse but do not assuage, they constitute a kind of crisis, a roving unfixity. The crisis is one of the woman's choice—of a fear that it might work out between women—a crisis of desire that must be fixed or completed by a heterosexual conclusion. Heterosexuality becomes the aim, the goal, the only way anything can be concluded. As an element in a larger narrative, lesbian sexuality is quickly made a part of a heterosexual system where its seemingly liberalized variety ultimately assures a heterosexual trajectory for female sexual development.

As one of the crisis points in the narrative, it is fairly clear that the lesbian scenes operate as disturbances to be corrected and recuperated even as they provide their own titillation and variety. But while the narrative ascendancy of heterosexuality may explain some pleasure for some viewers (such as those who enjoy narrative completion or who are more comfortable with heterosexuality), the narrative shape of the films does not entirely explain why lesbian scenes are a regular feature of soft-core pornography. Curiosity about the nature of lesbian sexuality may constitute another motive; so might pleasure in the very lack of fixity and the generation of desire stimulated by the scenes. As second stages in the protagonist's sexual quest and education, lesbian episodes are represented as excursions into the mysterious realm of female sexuality, extensions of the autoeroticism that precedes them. Including a lesbian scene enables the film to present what is presumably a privileged view of the forbidden secrets of female sexuality especially for the spectator's eye (and pleasure). As Annette Kuhn suggests, seeing what two women do together is going to the heart of pure femininity, of what women do alone without the man.[5] This imaging of what the male viewer would normally not see both supplies a voyeuristic opportunity and provides knowledge, subordinating the activities of females to the exigencies of viewer delight, giving the viewer an illusion of mastery and even ownership over their activities and creating the delight inherent to peeping. Finally, lesbian sexuality is fascinating because it is lesbian sexuality: that which the male can never see except in porn or as a voyeur. In this sense, lesbian scenes are the quintessential porn scenes; they don't have to be incursions into pure female sexuality to function as the forbidden.

While pleasure in transgression—in "unlawful viewing"—is a feature of pornography in general, like Kuhn, both of the films equate lesbian sexuality with female sexuality. I am suggesting that lesbian sexuality can function as a search for female sexuality only within a matrix of binary assumptions about gender and sexuality. Equating lesbian with female sexuality assumes that there is such as thing as a "pure" and separate female sexuality, different from the kind of sexuality a woman would have in the company of a male. It also implicitly suggests that all women are the same and presumes that this "pure" sexuality would simply duplicate itself with another woman. The theoretical equation of lesbian sexuality and "pure" female sexuality in the films would seem to be supported by their situating of lesbian sexuality just after the films' masturbation scenes as part of a continuing process of self-discovery. This also supposes that there is little difference between female sexuality, autoeroticism, and female homosexuality: what differences might exist within female sexuality only occur in the realm of heterosexuality. If perceived or imaged as a search for self, lesbian sexuality becomes primarily a narcissistic process: the female looks in a mirror or at someone who functions as a mirror to find the secrets of feminine sexuality. At the same time, something of the lesbian in these films escapes the self-enclosed homogeneity of the identity of lesbian and female. Lesbian sexuality turns out narratively *not* to be the film's version of "real" female sexuality, a sexuality that can only be comprehended in these films as heterosexual. Lesbian sexuality thereby becomes a deviance, a difference, that which is not homogeneous, a bad substitute for heterosexuality.

In her analysis, Kuhn remarks that lesbian scenes "neatly sidestep a cultural embargo on representing male genitalia" (32). They provide viewing pleasure because they have all the attributes of sexual scenes minus the image of the (threatening? disappointing?) embargoed penis. I suspect this is only half of the story, because most sexual scenes in soft-core porn do not image male genitalia, but we know (or assume) that it is there. What is different and crucial in lesbian scenes is that the phallus is not *supposed* to be there at all, either in image or in "person," an absence that creates a gap, a place for an on-screen yearning that invites phallic fulfillment. Kuhn's choice of the word "sidestep" offers a useful clue to how this implied invitation works. If lesbian activity "sidesteps" the need to represent the penis, it does so by representing it in absentia by imaging the sexual excitation that is the imagined effect of the penis. It is there in spirit. In the oppositional and complementary phallocentric, heterosexual system by which sexuality is most often comprehended, the phallus should be there, it's not there, it needs to be there. The phallus we know to be absent reserves a place for a phallus: the women's lack of penis creates an open-ended craving that awaits the satisfying penetration of a phallus even though the women are sometimes represented as satisfying one another (or one satisfying the other, since there usually remains one open end). This actually constructs a place in a screen-audience threesome for any viewer who can enjoy the women's pleasure, because, finally, such pleasure is open, requiring completion that in these narratives has already been introduced as specifically heterosexual. This subordinates the lesbian episode to a greater narrative phallic exigency and thus augments rather than threatens the importance of the penis and the primacy of heterosexuality. The three-way scene in *Melody* between Rachel, the native girl, and Octavio literalizes the place reserved for the phallus by lesbian sex, providing an on-screen model for the place of the male viewer. The scene brings together lesbian and heterosexuality, native and European, under the gentle guiding hand of Octavio, the third party for whose benefit the desire generated by the two women accrues; the three-way incorporates voyeurism and male participation within the realm of heterosexual pleasure.

The homogenous notion of female homosexuality and its function as a kind of innocent quest for sexual self-knowledge plays against other, very contradictory conceptions of lesbian sexuality implicit in these films. Sex between two women tends to be depicted through the gloss of sexual difference: one woman must be masculinized, aggressive, insensitive. In *Emmanuelle*, Bea, though stereotypically attractive, is businesslike and cold. We suspect, though we are never told, that her exclusion from the community is because she is primarily homosexual and independent and she works, rather than being like the playgirl swingers who constitute the "group." Emmanuelle's other lesbian admirer, Ariane, is also aggressive, acquisitive, and

unemotional. Melody's desire for Rachel, though cast within clear
signifiers of a mother-child relationship, is a desire for an authoritarian
figure, for one who knows. In fact, it is an oedipal desire for both
Rachel and her husband (the only man Melody is initially interested
in), for the heterosexual unit barely hidden behind Rachel's nurturing
tenderness. In both films, the protagonist's search for self-knowledge
ends up not with another woman, but with a male pastiche with whom
the heroine is unhappy and dissatisfied. While posed as narcissistic,
lesbian sexuality also ends up as a version of heterosexuality, not
because women are different from one another, but because within
the context of these films, lesbian episodes become a heterosexual
imposture. When these two conceptions of lesbian sexuality—"pure"
female sexuality and heterosexual copy—come together, the narrative result is that the protagonist's search for self-knowledge is thwarted
by her lesbian experimentation and she discovers that the best place
to find her own sexuality is with a man. The notion of lesbian sexuality as simulated heterosexuality dominates, and female sexuality, the
prize of all of this, is properly a heterosexuality where its nature is
revealed as purely complementary to the male libido. In this way the
lesbian neatly "sidesteps" the phallus, but it does so by making
female sexuality step to the side of man in a narrative and ideological
lesson about the neat complementarity of nature.

  The differing cultural assumptions and sexual politics that govern
the representation of lesbian sexuality are important because, though
not explicit, they are part of the films' systems of representation,
creating a tension both with the apparent liberality of the narrative
and with the actual imaging of the lesbian scenes. Reliant upon binary
oppositions based on a polar notion of sexual difference, lesbian
scenes augment the narrative logic by which the films' protagonists
are driven to heterosexual conclusions. Positioned culturally and narratively as unfixed, mediate, and roving, lesbian sexuality is impossible to sustain. Not only do oedipal leanings drive toward conclusions
and climax, apparently antithetical to the films' representations of
lesbian sexuality, but cultural assumptions force a reduction of that
lesbian unfixity to a position within a paradigm of sexual difference:
either as a mock heterosexual couple or as lost in the endless narcissistic maze of a pure femininity whose essence is to require masculine
complement. Unfortunately, it is equally difficult to account for or
describe lesbian sexuality except in these same terms of sexual differ-

ence that invade our logic of sexuality and underlie film theory itself. But if we look closely at the semiotics of lesbian scenes, we see the binary oppositions of sexual difference unravel as they come up against a different, nonbinary, representational economy that brings into question gender oppositions, the genderment of theory, and any assumed primacy of mastery and completion.

DISTURBING SCENES

The imaging of the lesbian sexual scenes in *Emmanuelle* reiterates the narrative positioning, crises, and tensions surrounding lesbian sexuality in the narratives. In these scenes the representational tensions configured by the lesbian become visible, escaping narrative containment briefly and revealing a cinematic uncertainty that brings gendered systems of identification into question. *Emmanuelle* has two lesbian scenes, Ariane's rather desperate preliminary introduction to lesbian sexuality and Emmanuelle and Bea's scene in the wilderness hut. The first scene between Ariane and Emmanuelle is not only brief, it is imaged almost entirely within the film's heterosexual convention, already established in the first scene between Emmanuelle and her husband. Defining masculine as active and feminine as reactive, these scenes of heterosexual sexual activity usually begin with an establishment shot of the two people, followed by a series of cause and effect close-up shots that alternate between the actions of the male and certain effects or responses in the female, which are represented by close-up shots of her face. While not clearly the point of view of the male who participates in the scenes, the close-up shots of the woman's body suggest the close perspective of a lover rather than the distance of a voyeur. The scenes are elliptical, appearing to focus on sexual technique, while cutting the response time in favor of a rapid trajectory toward satisfaction, toward the effects of the technique. In this way, the power of the male is registered through the response of the female, clearly connecting male action to female reaction, which again is often imaged from a point approximating the closer, often high angle view of the male participant. The series is augmented by the sounds of gasping breathing, the universal signifier for sexual arousal in pornography.

Taking place on a squash court, the brief scene between Ariane and Emmanuelle fits this pattern. Emmanuelle plays the part of the female object pursued by the aggressive Ariane. Ariane's manipulations are registered on Emmanuelle's face, and the cause and effect is clearly demonstrated, even though Ariane's rough gropings seem insufficient to evoke Emmanuelle's response. Her approach is like that of the men in many of the heterosexual encounters already imaged in the film: she zeroes in on erogenous zones, like pushing buttons, a technique necessary both for rapidity and for the clear establishment of cause and effect. Ariane's own reactions, like those of male lovers, are barely imaged at all, while the activities of her hands are carefully recorded.

While quite heterosexually conventional, this scene deviates in two ways that introduce the manner in which Emmanuelle and Bea's later scene will be imaged. The scene is dominated by whiteness, the color of both the squash court and the women's clothing. While this monochromic indistinguishability may reflect a notion of the sameness of the participants in this lesbian interlude, it also creates some disorientation. The scene is cut in medias res, and the cutting of the scene after Ariane's initial advances thwarts the voyeuristic desire to see the process through, leaving the women with an aroused desire that is not fulfilled in the viewer's vision. Cutting this first lesbian scene in the middle makes it a kind of foreplay to be completed in a later scene, situating lesbian sexuality as suspended desire.

The second lesbian scene, between Emmanuelle and Bea, is graphically isolated in a green wilderness, as the interlude is introduced and ended by long shots of a lone hut in a forest. This isolation sets this scene off from Emmanuelle's normal life, sequestering the lesbian interlude away from the patriarchal culture of the diplomats within a kind of wild and untamed "nature." Within this wilderness frame, a brief but completed lesbian interlude is imaged in four shots.

The first is a close-up tracking shot, taken through bars that separate the camera from the action. This shot, interrupted by the bars that pass as the camera moves, follows Emmanuelle's lips kissing the surface of a body; both the parts of the body being kissed and the identity of the lover are initially undiscernable because of the limiting closeness of the camera. After Emmanuelle has kissed up to the point of what turns out to be a shoulder, Bea's face is revealed and the scene culminates in a series of kisses.[6] The second shot shifts to an oblique, slightly high angle medium two-shot of Emmanuelle and Bea kissing and caressing. The angle from which we watch is skewed, disorienting their faces and making the activity difficult to see. As Emmanuelle slides down Bea's body, the film cuts to the third shot, a very high angle medium two-shot taken through the bars of shot one. As in all of the shots, the framing of the shot is disorienting; the character's heads point toward the lower left part of the frame and their bodies are angled toward the upper right. The final shot of the sequence is a high, oblique angle close-up of Bea that pans down and stays on Bea's face tilted almost upside-down as she reacts to Emmanuelle.

Unlike conventional heterosexual scenes, this scene is shot entirely from the perspective of the voyeur, a third party, rather than from the perspective of one of the participants. The voyeur of this scene is not provided the maximal view, as the apparatus appears to alternate or layer a screen ambiguity and camera control, oscillating between an image made uncertain by the action of the apparatus and an uncertain image. The scene begins with the ambiguity incident to the close framing of the shot of Emmanuelle kissing a body. The closeness of the shot disenables anything but a pleasurable gaze at Emmanuelle kissing. Because what she is kissing is missing, there is an uncertainty, which turns out retrospectively to be a confusion about Bea's anatomical orientation that lasts until the camera tracks Emmanuelle to Bea's shoulder and Bea turns over. Her turning over resolves the disorientation of her position and signals another turn from the confusing closeness of the opening shot to the more domineering distance introduced by the first cut. The high angle medium two shot of the women's caressing that follows gives the illusion of a superior view, aligning camera and viewer in the position of someone who could only be voyeur. But the illusion of mastery created by the shot's distance plays against the shot's oblique angle, which thwarts the view, constructing a kind of tantalizing visual bondage of seeing but not quite seeing what the women are doing. The next high angle medium shot appears to establish the viewer in a truly superior position, standing above the two women who continue to caress, but the final close-up shot of Bea's face repeats the upside-down angle of the second shot, frustrating the view again. While we are asked to witness her pleasure as it registers on her face and while we are offered the conventional tormented gasping sound of sexual activity, our view of Bea is upside down and at an angle. Her pleasure is there, but written in such a way that we can't completely read it.

This oscillation of disorientation and clarity replicates the bondage of Bea's initial position, displacing the inconvenience of her back presentation onto the viewer, who sees most of the scene upside down, as if watching on her or his back. The intervening bars also repeat a scenario of entrapment and interruption, again for the viewer rather than for the screen characters, for whom the bars work as a signifier of privacy ad separation. By alternating high angle medium shots and close-ups and by skewing the high angle shots to an angle from which it is difficult to see, the apparatus frustrates, enfranchises, and teases by alternately and even simultaneously offering and withholding a good view, a view that promises mastery. Every disorienting scene appears to be cured by the next shot, which anticipates a trajectory toward orgasm, clearing up one confusion while creating another. In this sense, the montage of the shots in the lesbian scene is a series of questions and answers that ends with a shot—that of Bea's face—that functions as both question and answer. She appears to be in the throes of jouissance, and we see it, but upside down; even if the act ends conventionally in Bea's pleasure, Emmanuelle apparently remains unsatisfied, leaving the scene open-ended. In the context of the scene's return to the wilderness (the shot that follows the fourth shot) and in light of Bea's refusal to love Emmanuelle revealed in this next, very conventional postsex scene, even the slight bondage of confusion and disorientation of the sexual interlude is a trick, providing a thrill because it is temporary, because it is precisely the illusion of a lack of control rather than a real lack, as the prodigal Emmanuelle and the wandering camera return to "normal." The real thrill of mastery exists when mastery is only momentarily lost.

Melody in Love presents this interplay of confusion and mastery in more straightforward, conveniently self-reflective terms. More artfully (or artlessly) disorienting, its self-conscious staginess with a mirror produces a metacinematic split consciousness. The scene consists of only two shots, the first creating a confusion that the second clears up.

The first shot is a medium long shot of a bedroom with a bed parallel to a large mirror. The two women enter from the right and get on the bed, Rachel to the right and Melody to the left. The camera slowly zooms in to a medium two-shot of the women that images Rachel affectionately caressing Melody. The camera then pans right to include both the bed and the women's image reflected in the mirror. This doubles the scene for a moment as the camera continues to pan right from the bed to the mirror. The camera then lingers on the mirrored scene, which has not only reversed the positions of the characters relative to one another—Rachel is now on the left and Melody on the right—but also as the camera moves, Melody shifts position to become the active party in place of Rachel. The telephone rings, the camera pans rapidly back to the medium two shot, and the mirror image disappears. After the phone call, which is from the hotel manager Rachel wants to lure as a lover for Melody, there is a cut to a reverse angle two shot, which zooms gradually back to a high angle two shot from above the women, where it stays for the remainder of the scene.

The first part of the scene is produced through a series of divisions in the visual field. The mirror that dominates the scene is connected to the metaphorical self-seeking reflectivity narratively connected to the sexuality, but used by the camera partially to confound the view of lesbian sexuality it presents. As soon as the naked Rachel instigates the lovemaking, the camera pans to the mirror in a shot that multiplies the women's images, mixes up active and passive, and rearranges the women's positions on the screen, which disorients, at least momentarily, the spectator. As the camera zooms finally to the mirror reflection of the women, it eliminates one image of them, but confusion about the characters' relative positions continues, drawing attention to a sort of cinematic difficulty in finding what to focus on as the camera work tends to break up—even at the moment it clearly directs our vision—the illusion of any visual mastery. The second half of the scene restores order over the uncertainties of the first half, superimposing a second model of viewing onto the first. Narratively, the phone call introduces a third party into the confusing mirroring dualities of the first part of the scene and initiates the shift of camera position, enabling a more superior two shot, which appears to untangle the confusion of the mirror. From the point of the phone call on, when we know that heterosexual help will be on the way, the camera takes a clear, distanced position; the mirror disappears; the disorientation and shifting of the first part of the scene are now organized within the field of a camera in control, fortified, as if it were necessary, by Rachel's totalizing reassurance: "Don't worry, darling; I'll see that you get the best of all possible worlds." No other sexual scene in the film is constructed on either such arty alienation or such a conscious restoration of a camera-eye mastery.

Compared with the heterosexual convention already established in *Melody* in scenes between Octavio and a prostitute, this scene deviates by being unfinished and much less explicit and by lacking the cause/effect cutting characteristic of those scenes. Though unlike *Emmanuelle*, the heterosexual scenes of *Melody* do not always complete themselves, they usually are quite graphic and entertain no confusion about what kind of sexual activity is taking place. The camera in the lesbian scenes provides a mixed message. Searching through the room, it takes a consistent voyeuristic position, while it has trouble finding the place from which to view, though the artiness of the scene signifies a camera well in control. The paradox of a controlled confusion, as in *Emmanuelle*, creates a layering or oscillation of confusion and mastery that creates a thrill when the apparatus repeatedly works itself out. The oscillations of confusion and mastery manufacture a series of small visual triumphs as confusion is created and controlled. The thrill of this oscillation, however, is dependent upon an alignment of viewer with camera in an acquiescence to the apparatus where the viewer is subject to the apparatus. The viewer thus has no real mastery or ability to perceive the working of the apparatus beyond the apparatus itself.

The production of this uncertainty in the imaging of lesbian sexual scenes replicates the prototypical configuration of lesbian sexuality already narratively and ideologically established in the films. The camera work metaphorically matches the narrative treatment of lesbian sexuality. In *Emmanuelle*, the camera's typical focus on erogenous zones and responses and its clear cause and effect cutting are undone—almost parodied—as the camera doesn't quite know what to focus on or from what angle. This unravels, or makes visible the conventions of the heterosexual scenes. In *Melody*, the insertion of the third party and the reestablishment of control that happens in the film's narrative (the hiring of the hotel manager) as well as in several of the film's heterosexual scenes (the three-way) are played out in the structure of the scene as the phone call reestablishes an unconfused, superior camera view.

The lesbian scenes in both films promise a view to a thrill, backed essentially by the power of the camera to reveal what the viewer could not otherwise witness. But this clear view is also obviously not quite what it is supposed to be. The thrill it views—women making love—only mimics sexual behavior. While this mimicry is one element that distinguishes soft-core from hard-core pornography, soft-core film is usually adept at artfully hiding what is not taking place. Thus ellipses and obscuring camera movements and angles in scenes depicting heterosexual sex tend to work toward the maintenance of illusions of sexual continuity, covering over moments of overt mimicry rather than revealing the artificial nature of the actions. Because the mimicry is less than artful in the lesbian scenes, it creates an impression of a sexuality that is both manqué and magical: parts that are supposed to touch are visibly not even close. This failure of illusion creates a gap between cause and effect and presents a hypothetical lovemaking—what they would do if they were really doing it—rather than soft-core porn's conventional attempts to create the convincing illusion of sexual activity. Emmanuelle concentrates on Bea's inner thigh, while Rachel approaches Melody's nipple from a sharply oblique side angle. Just as lesbian sexuality "sidesteps" the representation of the phallus, so it also visibly sidesteps all but the idea of lesbian sexuality.

Piercing the illusion of verisimilitude that other scenes try to preserve also points to the essential artificiality of the other scenes. In this sense the apparatus is finally too masterful, revealing lesbian sexuality as empty; but in so doing, it implicates the emptiness of all of the sex scenes in the film. The obviousness of the lack of real sexual activity in the lesbian scenes also removes any threat of lesbian sexuality, since these actresses aren't really "doing it" after all. What is imaged is imaginary, but this pretend quality combined with an oscillation of confusion and mastery is what provides the thrill—an incursion into the forbidden with the security of a safety net. No knowledge of real-life lesbian sexuality is present; as education it is a failure for both heroine and viewer, but as that which reveals the economy of anxiety and mastery that generates the thrill, the lesbian scenes are quite informative.

Another way to read the camera work of the lesbian scenes is to read it against the literal heterosexual narrative trajectories of the films, as in service of a larger "natural" heterosexual whole, but not extinguished or eliminated by it. As part of a layering that simultaneously attests to camera control and presents the specter of a loss of control, the coexistence of anxiety and mastery is equally dependent on the presence of both. The pleasure of control exists as a coefficient of a visible challenge to that control. While narratively the heterosexual resoundingly and, in *Emmanuelle,* painfully wins out, the coexistence of control and confusion eroticizes anxiety. If we reject the primacy of the urge toward mastery, part of the allure of the lesbian scenes may be this confusion itself, as embodied by a desiring camera eye that roves rather than masters or roves and masters at the same time, creating two coexistent models of viewing that are in fact interdependent, the second relying on the first. It is a matter, finally, not of what the film does, because the film offers multiple alternatives, but of what we privilege in our viewing or analysis of the film. If, for example, we privilege narrative completion—if our reading itself desires mastery—the end would take precedence over the middle and this scene would appear to head toward a reconstruction of the viewer's camera identification, allaying anxiety with both fetishes and a masterful view. But narrative mastery—privileging the end—is connected in these films to a narrative resolution linked to the happy discovery of heterosexuality, which is itself premised in the joinder of two clearly defined genders. If we challenge the connection between heterosexuality and narratives of mastery or question the desirability of completion and instead see beginning and end as equal or layered, the two modes—unfixity and mastery—coexist, neither privileged except narratively or chronologically.

The filming of the lesbian scenes suggests this coexistence; in fact, they are the point where multiple perspectives can coexist precisely because no culmination in expected. The roving plays against notions that all should be completed, posing an alternative of ending or not. The coexistence of multiple alternatives at the point of the lesbian suggests that privileging the kind of Hegelian synthesis of opposites comprising the heterosexual culminations of porn narratives is a kind of heterosexism enacted not only in narrative, but also in the analysis of narrative. Seeing mastery and wholeness as a desirable goal may be just as much heterosexist ideology as it is any psychologically based human tendency. Privileging, even unwittingly, trajectories of mastery and completion requires a monolithic perspective that accepts sexual binaries and their complementary joinder as inevitable aesthetic truth. The lesbian episodes raise questions about the interrelation of sexuality and mastery as well as about the relation among gender, sexuality, and viewing as the scenes play for multiple positions at once, bringing any theoretical genderment of viewing and its premises into question and raising questions about the validity of reading solely on the level of narrative.

VIEWER, VOYEUR: THE FIXED SPLIT

While most porn films don't challenge strategies by which the viewer is constructed as all-perceiving—in fact, most rely on it—porn films do define this screen mastery in a way that more consciously splits the fictional position of the viewer between illusions of mastery and chaos. This fictional split position is a reflection of the cultural splits that attend pornography in general, represented on one side by Andrea Dworkin's position, which attributes an affective narrative mastery to pornography's representations of women and on the other by those who argue that the effect of porn is largely dispersed and illusory—a reflection rather than a cause.[7] In either case, pornography, shown in special places at special times, with an age requirement, both is what we aren't supposed to watch and is created to be watched—made for the viewer's delectation. It is transgressive and authorized—sneaky and part of the master discourse—in ways that replicate the tensions between the unfixity of the camera and its mastery. Porn films situate the spectator as a voyeur quite overtly but have an equal stake in maintaining the ideological naturalness of the events, something that requires that the film pretend that the voyeur is not there, that things occur as if they are not witnessed or created for the special purpose of titillating the viewer.

This contradiction in viewer position in these films is mediated by the lesbian scene in ways that reiterate the conflicting coexistence of mastery and unfixity. In a metapornographic moment at the beginning of *Melody in Love*, the voyeur is narratively a transgressor; Melody is upset by an adolescent boy who masturbates as he witnesses her swim nude. While a substantial portion of the sex scenes in the film are witnessed by other characters, both male and female, which creates a model position for viewers of either gender, those positions are authorized only after the lesbian scene. The cure of the split identifications that exist in the first part of the scene serves as a narrative initiation, but also ensconces the viewer in a position of camera mastery as the place from which he/she should watch, a positioning that authorizes the transgression. While various servant-class voyeurs are still chased from the scene (by one another), the hotel manager's voyeurism is implicitly accepted as the third party is given a place in the sexual activity. The voyeur becomes a participant. The film ends with Melody inviting the masturbating adolescent Peeping Tom to a sex lesson, rewarding the voyeur with a one-on-one favor.

Thus an identificatory circle is constructed: transgressors are authorized viewers; uncertainty becomes mastery. The terms are interreliant and interdependent: one cannot master unless one has first been uncertain. Gendered constructions of viewing follow the same circuit; viewer positioning creates gender roles, and gender roles create positions. As E. Ann Kaplan observes, the objectification of the woman's body tends to repeat a cultural pattern by which men find pleasure in looking and women in being looked at, a tendency that relies on and returns to gender bifurcations.[8] Perhaps the breaking point in this gendered stasis is the lesbian scene, and by breaking point I mean the place where we might move away from circular repetitions of gender and culture, though the lesbian scene itself is obviously a part of the circle. While the pleasure for a male viewer might come from a controlling view of an objectified and fetishized female body, something psychoanalytic film theory can account for, psychoanalytic film theory has not accounted for lesbian sexuality except in the essentialized gender oppositional terms that tend to define active as masculine —in fact repeat Freud's claim that libido is masculine. But if we read psychoanalytic depictions of lesbian sexuality positively as transitory, penultimate, roving, in effect as truly heterogeneous rather than as a homosexual version of the dynamics of sexual difference, might that not suggest that the lesbian scene enables oscillating identifications that provide other places for the viewer as not fixed as either subject or object, but as lesbian or as all three (or more) at once? If we take cultural portrayals of the lesbian at their word, why can't unfixity be positive as a contrast to an accompanying mastery and heterosexuality? This is not to glorify an essentialized, gendered negative or the hidden mastery of a kind of postmodern fragmentation, but to suggest that among other things, lesbian sexuality is a configuration that stands for unfixity in relation to mastery, that both shares in and undoes gender oppositions that align women with a long string of passivity, objectification, etc. The lesbian position as configured in soft-core pornography is not an essential quality of lesbians, but rather a pattern that reappears in attempts to represent lesbian sexuality.

Though we might claim that the illusion of mastery and the explicit invitation to scopophilia seduce the viewer, I would argue that this seduction is only possible by playing out a drama of suspended or lapsed mastery, a kind of scenario of unrequited desire that is relieved by the suturing, controlling operations of the medium itself. What titillates in pornography, as the lesbian scenario suggests, are the cinematic operations themselves—the layering of anxiety and mastery.

In drawing this all out of a cheap and truncated lesbian scene in a grade-B foreign soft-core porn film, do I thus unwittingly valorize pornography as an industry? Do I ignore what I think are actually the ideological investments of a film like this, which are to show women "the way" and titillate male viewers as the possessors of a developing image of a healthy heterosexual female object?[9] I think in their heavy investment in sex porn films like this one reveal the engagement of cinema in general in sexually motivated scenarios of mastery that coexist in relation with rather than in answer to confusing lapses in mastery. This suggests that the monolithic theories of single and somewhat simplistic viewer identification that found political arguments about the efficacy of porn are based on an appeal to the very operation that is the most oppressive and the most enjoyable—the construction of mastery itself. The violence occurs when we leave no space for play, for the kind of deferral of mastery that represents exploration, multiplicity, desire that we cut off with monolithic demands for censorship or with the evocations of a gender binarism that is in the end primarily heterosexist.

WOMEN WATCHING WOMEN: REVIEWING THE FEMALE SPECTATOR

In the same way that an analogy can be drawn between lesbian sexuality's position as narrative excess and the interplay of confusion and mastery in its cinematic imaging, so can the lesbian bring into question film theory's reliance on sexual difference in its formulation of theories of cinematic identification and viewership. In its play of cinematic uncertainty and its temporary narrative opening of multiple possibilities, the lesbian configuration momentarily detaches the sexual narrative and voyeuristic politics of viewing from their heterosexual premise, disturbing any easy alignment among gender, viewer, and screen image and creating other viewing and identificatory possibilities that may enrich our understanding of how film identification works. If desire is the engine of both narrative and the spectator's pleasure and if porn films equate narrative pleasure and sexual desire, then the presence of lesbian scenes in otherwise heterosexual scenarios of desire raises the question of what the relationship is between desire, sexual difference, and sexual orientation. The lesbian adds what may be disturbing elements to the otherwise neatly gendered oppositions relied upon and argued for in various theories of cinema spectatorship.

Following Laura Mulvey's essay "Visual Pleasure and Narrative Cinema," feminist film theory, as Judith Mayne observes, has been "a response, implicit or explicit, to the issues raised in Laura Mulvey's article: the centrality of the look, cinema as spectacle and narrative, psychoanalysis as critical tool." [10] The feminist analyses of all of these issues have emphasized, in one way or another, the importance of sexual difference whose mechanisms, imported from psychoanalysis, tend to conflate vision and desire within a binary gendered model that aligns mastery, activity, and masculinity on one side and objecthood, passivity, and femininity on the other. As Mayne points out, this begins in Laura Mulvey's crucial essay, whose purpose is to discover "where and how the fascination of film is reinforced by pre-existing patterns of fascination *already at work* within the individual subject and the social formations that have moulded him" (my emphasis, Mulvey 6). For Mulvey, the mechanisms described by psychoanalysis already function in culture. Cinema constructs its pleasure by replicating or reiterating these paradigms that are characteristic of representation in general; the gendered models of the fetish, the castrated woman, and the ego-reinforcing model of Lacan's mirror stage. But in Mulvey's adoption of psychoanalytic mechanisms all becomes even more oppositionally aligned. Her accounts of the gendered constructions of cinema ("Woman as Image, Man as Bearer of the Look") are astute readings of the operation of mainstream cinema restated so as to emphasize cinema's reliance upon sexual difference. But while her reliance upon what is essentially also a heterosexual model may accurately describe one possible operation of cinema that creates one position for a woman viewer, it does so by establishing quite a rigid binary and complementary system, reliant upon the premise of heterosexual desire.

How does Mulvey get to this point? Where and how does sexual difference become imbricated in psychoanalytic readings of cinema? And how does sexual difference become bound to assumptions of heterosexual desire linked to both gender and the idealization of mastery? While sexual difference always plays in representations, it is not necessarily true that representation is either defined or limited by the heterosexually oppositional politics appended to sexual difference as it is represented by film theories. Mulvey's notion that the psychoanalytic precepts upon which she relies are already operative in the human psyche simply relocates the source of a gender-aligned system of operations to an intrapsychic domain best described by psychoanalytic theory. Assuming that cinema is a symptom of culture that repeats unconscious mechanisms, Mulvey's analysis is an attempt both to see how cinema reflects the more widespread cultural practices of patriarchy and to pinpoint a source and/or explanation for the cultural paradigm of sexual difference Mulvey sees at work in narrative cinema. While this is partly a restatement of the issue Mayne identifies as the use of psychoanalysis as a tool, I think it is actually more than that, extending to the kinds of biases and presuppositions that inform readings of psychoanalysis as well as psychoanalytic readings and the way they are applied in film theories. Not, of course, that psychoanalysis is an innocent or unbiased set of constructs, but that in importing psychoanalysis to cinema, certain concepts become more skewed in ways that offer clues to how film theory becomes heterosexually bound—that is, to how accounts for the operation of identification and narrative in film are welded to assumptions of heterosexual desire affixed to clearly and essentially gendered positions. This happens through mechanisms that echo the interplay of mastery and confusion, monolithic and multiple, signaled by the lesbian configuration in porn films.

One of the cornerstones of narrative pleasure is the concatenation of pleasure and mastery, seen as a masculine, active positioning created by an urge toward mastery enabled by a mechanism of visual disavowal. The suggestion of pleasure in a lack of mastery, in the possible coexistence of multiple positions configured by the lesbian, plays against the insistent dialogue of mastery produced by Freudian-Lacanian psychoanalytic film theorists of the 1970s, when Mulvey was

formulating "Visual Pleasure." The establishment of founding constructions of sexual difference in cinema relies upon cinema theories'
adaptation and combination of three psychoanalytic mechanisms: Lacan's mirror stage, Freud's fetish, and the function of woman as
"other." Insisting upon the primacy of mastery in a presence/lack
scenario, such psychoanalytic readings as those devised by Christian
Metz and Jean-Louis Baudry easily (and rather insidiously) become
gendered when the mirror is conflated with the fetish.

The theoretical fix on sexual oppositions begins with an adaptation
of Lacan's mirror stage. The mirror stage is an analogy for the point
when a developing infant first perceives itself as a whole, separable
being in relation to what it perceives as the image of a separable being
in a mirror. This perception of wholeness is premature, anticipating
the infant's motor abilities to act as a separate being, an anticipation
that creates what Lacan calls "jubilation."[11] But perceiving that
potential power also enables the infant to recognize the fragmentation and chaos in which it has lived in the past. Thus the mirror stage represents both mastery and chaos, creates a perception
of history, and casts the infant into a dialectic of before/after and
chaos/mastery.

Lacan's mirror stage is also a model of power disparity created by
the distinction between seeing and being. What the infant sees is
what the infant is not; seeing endows greater power than being. The
infant sees only an illusion; it misrecognizes as its own the condition
of wholeness in the mirror image. Though the infant may have organized the image of a whole being, it mistakes the source of that
being's wholeness as a product of the image already there rather than
as a product of its own maturing perceptive processes. There is no
self-reflexive reciprocity in the mirror, no natural or optical equation
between viewer and reflection. Instead there is an inherent visual
asymmetry in the mirror image, which is both temporal and perceptual. The infant sees its mastery before it can accomplish it, and the
mirror cannot reflect the entire field of the looker's vision, capturing
and framing only a part, which is thus privileged and separated from
its environment. The difference between the mirror image and the
field always leaves a remainder of the field that is not reflected due to
the limitations of the mirror's frame and the reflective angles of light.
The point is that the mirror stage analogy is no model for visual
mastery, but is rather a model for a visual misrecognition of mastery.
This misrecognition founds notions of identification and also inaugu-

rates together perceptions of mastery and chaos, separation and fragmentation.

Relying on a mirror stage analogy, Jean-Louis Baudry and Christian Metz describe the ways that film spectators come to believe in the integrity of the world depicted on the screen and in their all-perceiving position in relation to that world. Their interpretation of the mirror stage privileges visual mastery seen as the result of the mirror stage at the expense of the mirror stage's inherent duplicity and its attendant asymmetries. Speculating that the cinema screen works like the analogical mirror, both Baudry and Metz appeal to a notion of viewer omniscience created by the apparatus that invites an identification not with the inherently multiple images of the mirrored field, but with the unified one who looks at him/herself looking—with the camera itself.

The cinema viewer is not like the mirror stage infant caught between anticipation and fear, but has become identified with the camera, with that which organizes by virtue of a captivation with the illusion of wholeness and mastery that results from the operation of the apparatus. This shifts the asymmetry and power disparities of the mirror stage to a cause/effect symmetry that situates the screen image as a product of viewer/camera perception where view equals camera inscription, where what is on the screen is made to seem equal to the total perceptual world of the projecting, perceiving camera perspective. In order to devise this balance, identifications with screen images primary to the mirror stage become secondary in the mirror's cinematic analogy, a reversal that reveals cinema theory's fixation on mastery and its trend toward singularizing perspective and making perception equal literal cinematic projection. While this still entails a misrecognition of the screen world as a whole, that mistake does not alternate with introspective or historical perceptions of any complementary or accompanying chaos. Rather, the mechanism is made to lean toward and rely upon visual mastery in a denial of adherent chaos or lack of mastery.

Desiring transcendence, film theory reorders and hierarchizes identifications. In "The Ideological Effects of the Basic Cinematic Apparatus," Baudry explains:

> But, because the reflected image is not that of the body itself but that of the world already given as meaning, one can distinguish two levels of identification. The first, attached to the image itself, derives from

the character portrayed as a center of secondary identifications, carry-
ing an identity which constantly must be seized and reestablished.
The second level permits the appearance of the first and places it "in
action"—this is the transcendental subject whose place is taken by
the camera which constitutes and rules the objects in this "world."[12]

The primary mirror stage identification with the figure in the mirror
in psychoanalysis becomes secondary to cinema as Baudry attempts to
overcome two problems with the application of the mirror stage model
to cinema. One is that cinema is not the mirror stage; and because the
viewers have presumably passed through the mirror stage, cinema
cannot reenact it. The repetition of the analogy therefore requires a
reordering. The other is that Baudry's argument is precisely about an
ideology of mastery connected to the invisible creation of a monolithic
perspective characteristic of Western cinema and operating within the
apparatus itself. This ideology is an ideology of mastery that Baudry
accounts for in part in Lacanian terms, but only through skewing the
Lacanian model toward mastery by making the more controlling secondary identification primary. In accounting for the masterful ideological operations of cinema, Baudry makes them reflect the mastery he
already sees. He is, in other words, unaware of his own ideological
bias toward mastery, a bias that motivates him to ignore any idea of
the coexistence of multiple identifications, which would undermine
any monolithic notion of apparatus control.

Following Baudry, Christian Metz in *The Imaginary Signifier* privileges this position of spectatorial wholeness by describing the cinematic inscription of the spectator as "an all-powerful position which is
that of God himself, or more broadly of some ultimate signified."[13]
This is at the expense of what Metz perceives as a coexistent and
structuring absence. Because the spectator is literally absent from the
screen "as perceived" (54) as s/he would be in the mirror stage, but is
" 'all-present' as perceiver" (54), any viewer wholeness is founded on
a mechanism of mastery, which works to deny absence as it constitutes the viewer's presence in a more powerful position. Metz, like
Baudry, must establish a reversal of identifications counter to the
mirror stage in order to account for the cinema as a device that endows
visual mastery:

> The mirror is the site of primary identification. Identification with
> one's own look is secondary with respect to the mirror, i.e., for a

general theory of adult activities, but it is the foundation of the cinema and hence primary when the latter is under discussion; it is *primary cinematic identification* proper ('primary identification' would be inaccurate from the psychoanalytic point of view; 'secondary identification', more accurate in this respect, would be ambiguous for a cinematic psychoanalysis). (56)

The ambiguity Metz wants to avoid by reordering identifications from the psychoanalytic to the cinematic model premises cinema on a preconceived model of mastery. While this may be theoretically necessary, since cinema is not the mirror stage and since viewers already can organize the visual world, it unnecessarily devalues or makes disappear in theory the confusion and chaos that may still attend viewing, particularly when one is viewing constructed scenes that shift the expected rules of the everyday world. As an examination of the behavior of the apparatus in the depiction of lesbian scenes reveals, this camera mastery exists in a symbiotic, oscillating relationship with chaos, both preexistent and created by the apparatus. While we can only see cinema because the camera eye looks for us and though we may often desire visual mastery, we may still shift our identifications even with the camera, sometimes seeing from outside it (the position of film theorist, for example), sometimes looking against what it seems to privilege in its framing and editing, often in collision rather than collusion with it in one way or another. The lesbian scenes point to this alternative reading of the mirror stage in cinema by revealing the oscillations between chaos and mastery, bringing the primacy and mastery of camera identifications into question.

But Metz takes his investment in cinematic mastery a step further, conflating the mirror image coherently organized by the "all-perceiving camera" with the fetish, gendering cinema's investment in mastery and cohesion. While Metz sees three distinct "unconscious" roots of cinema—the mirror identification, voyeurism and exhibitionism, and fetishism—he actually aligns all three as manifestations of a drive to deny lack, the real absence figured by screen images whose presence as image covers over the fact of their actual absence. He ends up connecting visual mastery to the fetish, combining the operations of the mirror stage with the mechanisms of the fetish in a way that both reiterates and erases chaos and difference. While fetish operations here are metaphorical, they slip rapidly into a theoretical appeal to a reliance upon literal gender premised upon fairly rigid notions of sexual difference. Metz's use of the fetish drives toward a very singular view of the spectator and masculinizes viewing and the somewhat contradictory fetishization/feminization of screen image in a replication of traditional active/passive gender stereotypes.

Metz extends the Freudian connection between vision, fetish, and woman one step further. For Freud the fetish is a visual object, like the glint on a nose, that stands in for the mother's missing phallus. The male child, seeing his mother's lack of penis, cannot accept its absence; he therefore manufactures an imaginary phallus that he appends to the mother's body.[14] The fetish is thus an ambivalent phenomenon that simultaneously signifies both presence and lack: the lack of phallus that necessitates the fetish and the presence of phallus figured by the fetish. That the fetish is a visual phenomenon appended to the female situates the woman's body as a kind of screen where absence must be disavowed and presence written by the psychological and organizing action of the viewer, who is, by definition, a male. The screen, the fetish, and the image of the woman thus coalesce. Metz situates the fetish as "the lasting matrix, the affective prototype of all of the splittings of belief" (70), effectively superimposing the ambivalent visual dynamics of the fetish over the dialectic of the mirror stage, in part supplanting the mirror model, in part conflating fetish with mirror as commensurate visual phenomena in the operation of the cinematic apparatus.

While questions of identification and belief are affected by the fetish, according to Metz, the real fetish in the cinema is its technical equipment, "the cinema as technical performance, as prowess, as an *exploit,* an exploit that underlines and denounces lack on which the whole arrangement is based (the absence of the object, replaced by its reflection), an exploit which consists in the same time of making the absence forgotten" (74). The fetish here is not a disavowed absence but the "performance" of a power, the action of something unseen but present, manifested in its "prowess"—a phallic thing (or something culturally associated with phalli) that masculinizes the apparatus itself. Since Metz has already connected the viewer's primary identification with the camera as an organizing and "all-perceiving perspective," he implicitly relates the viewer to the fetish, to wanting to see the fetish in order to disavow the lack represented by the absence of presence on the cinema screen. In this way, viewers almost erotically seek to see the fetish evidences of the technical apparatus at work, which reflect, in their own camera identifications, themselves, inscribing potency in the place of absence, certifying the power of viewing, and gendering the process of viewing film, even if we are to take Metz's analogies metaphorically. And if the apparatus is gendered as male, the places left for women are the place of absence and lack, of the imaged and looked at, or the place of the "masculine" view.

This psycho-cinematic transformation, which appears to have been intended to explain systems of cinematic belief, parallels feminist attempts to delineate the gendered operation of the apparatus and questions about how a female spectator can find pleasure in a cinema that objectifies women unless she identifies against her gender—that is, identifies with what has become defined as a masculine position. Mulvey's first response to these questions in "Visual Pleasure" is that the image of woman in cinema creates visual pleasure by disavowing castration and lack. This literally gendered positioning of the image relies entirely upon a gendered reception of the film text, which cannot account for the pleasure (if any) of the female viewer, since she is trapped on the side of the fetish. In a 1981 follow-up essay, "Afterthoughts on 'Visual Pleasure and Narrative Cinema' Inspired by *Duel in the Sun* (King Vidor, 1946)," Mulvey tries to account for how women can find pleasure in cinema, which "seems[s] to impose masculinity as 'point of view.' "[15] Connecting the experience of the female spectator with the example of the "resistant heroine" of melodrama, her answer is that female spectators oscillate, much as resistant heroines do, between an acceptance of "masculinisation" in a kind of culturally necessitated "trans-sexual identification" and "being out of key" with the pleasure offered. This oscillation, which seems like a step away from a gender-bound account, is modeled on the resistant heroines' inability to achieve a "stable sexual identity." So while appearing to lead away from gender boundaries, Mulvey reinscribes the process back within a dualistic, very heterosexual system that sees "stable sexual identity" in only two heterosexual terms—masculine and feminine. The woman viewer's ability to identify with a "masculine" perspective is culturally acquired, "a *habit* that very easily becomes *second Nature*" (13). "Stable sexual identity" assumes the essentialized gendered sides of a binary opposition of sexual difference that unfortunately reproduces the terms of the same devotedly gendered system. Because Mulvey is trying to account for a problem within the confines of a system—vision and sexual difference—that she still sees as preexistent, she has no choice but to reproduce the terms of that system, but those terms may be partially creating the dilemma in the first place. The question is not only how to describe obvious patriarchal operations in representation, but also to what extent we have selected gendered scenarios from psychoanalysis to account for the sexual politics of viewing we see.

One problem with some theoretical accounts for female cinema spectatorship is that the position of Woman in the representation of sexual difference becomes confused with the psychical activities of real women so that the representational function of Woman limits and defines the positional possibilities for women. The binary gender system, which both relies upon and reproduces sexual difference, sees gender as an oppositional and complementary structure, describing representations of sexual difference as they play in culture, including psychoanalysis. But an insistence on sexual difference independent from desire or sexual orientation necessarily limits identificatory possibilities to those working within a binary system that tends to conflate biological gender with the activity/passivity stereotypes it finds operant in cultural expressions of sexual difference. Stephen Heath's 1978 essay, "Difference," is an example of this tendency, following through the dynamics of a psychoanalytically based, binary-bound representational system as it creates the problem for any theoretical description of how gender, filmic enunciation, and reception actually do interrelate:

> The representation of sexuality—'masculine', 'feminine'—is one of the most dangerous operations of equivalence (in which psychoanalysis has played and plays its part), and it is no surprise that such representation should be the great problem, the great affair, of dominant cinema today (with its 'new sexuality'). A crucial question for any alternative practice is thus how *not* to contribute to this representation, how not to valorise its terms of identity and identification.[16]

Heath's essay really poses a second question about gender and viewing: how do we avoid reproducing in theory or film practice the gender alignments that seem to structure representation?

E. Ann Kaplan takes up this question in her thorough review of the question of the masculine viewing position in her chapter "Is the Gaze Male?," from her 1983 book, *Women and Film*. Kaplan attempts to find a way out of the binary fixation of gender by observing that masculine and feminine positions may also be seen as versions of a dominance/submission dialectic, an opposition she tries to detach momentarily from its gendered association. Using experiential data collected by Nancy Friday, Kaplan points out that lesbians can fantasize themselves in both dominant and submissive positions so that a dominance/submission dialectic is not necessarily gendered and does permit female identification with the dominant perspective.[17] Generalizing from lesbian to all women, Kaplan resituates the dominance/submission pattern itself back into the unconscious of patriarchy via the shift from a literal male viewer (who is now unnecessary) to a metaphorical masculine position that is subsumed within what Kaplan sees as a "male unconscious" (30).[18] While the example of the lesbian allows escape from the gender fix momentarily in her analysis, the escape is rather quickly reappropriated under a patriarchal supersystem where dominance is part of a metaphorically masculine positioning that returns viewership and the gaze to the realm of the male.

Continuing to rely on the gender bifurcations that define the unconscious, other feminist film theorists attempt to find ways that the female viewer may be situated as a viewer without necessarily having to be masculinized. Teresa de Lauretis in "Oedipus Interruptus" restates the question in this way:

> If we leave the point of view of Oedipus, and instead ask the question from the place of the historical woman spectator, we may prefer to put it like this: in which ways does narrative (in or through cinema) solicit the female subject's identification in the narrative movement? Does it offer any pleasure beside that of a purely passive, narcissistic or masochistic, position (which is, I think, an impossible place for identification, a non-subject effect)? What manner of seduction operates in cinema to procure the complicity of women in a desire whose terms are those of Oedipus?[19]

Recombining psychoanalytic questions of narrative and desire with a psychoanalytic tradition of film theory represented by Metz, Mulvey, and Heath, de Lauretis also arrives at a theory of dual identification that enables the female spectator to escape from the impossible bind of "two incommensurate entities, the gaze and the image" (39), which either make the female identify against her gender or reduce her to the status of passive "non-subject." This double identification, different from Mulvey's, "consists of the double identification with the figure of narrative movement, the mythical subject, and with the figure of narrative closure, the narrative image" by which "a surplus of pleasure [is] produced by the spectators themselves for cinema and for society's profit" (39). By suggesting that a female viewer can make more than one identification at once, de Lauretis frees her from the necessity of any one gendered positioning, while maintaining gendered positions. De Lauretis also suggests that the way out of the dilemma is by assuming both positions with a vengeance and, at the same time, enacting the contradiction inherent to the combination of positions in relation to the female spectator *as contradiction,* making visible the tensions that exist between representational paradigms of sexual difference—Woman—and the impasse of women consumers of representation.

Another way of simultaneously assuming multiple positions both with and against gender positions is masquerade, suggested as a tactic by Mary Ann Doane in her 1982 essay, "Film and Masquerade: Theorising the Female Spectator."[20] Doane recasts the female spectator's "problem" in terms of a lack of the distance necessary to create the voyeuristic gap between "desire and its object": "Both the theory of the image and its apparatus, the cinema, produce a position for the female spectator—a position which is ultimately untenable because it lacks the attribute of distance so necessary for an adequate reading of the image" (87). Asserting that "sexual mobility would seem to be a distinguishing feature of femininity in cultural construction" (81), Doane puts forward Joan Rivière's model of masquerade as that which constructs gender as a mask and therefore holds gender "at a distance." This assumed distance, created by interposing a consciousness of gender as gender, defamiliarizes gendered images and gives the female spectator the necessary distance to view cinema in ways that resist the "masochism of over-identification or the narcissism entailed in becoming one's own object of desire" forced on female spectators in the fetishistic and voyeuristic operation of the apparatus.

Doane's idea of sexual mobility, however, is a mobility between clearly defined genders, resulting from a consciousness of gender itself as a construct. This necessarily locates masquerade's mobility within the binary opposition of sexual difference in a heterosexual oscillation between masculine and feminine poles that are still attached to active/passive, viewer/object positions. While masquerade could destabilize the essential genderment of viewing alignments if it also shook up the certain heterosexual premises of desire—if, for example, it were admitted that no one's desire is strictly for the opposite sex—Doane's version of masquerade repeats the gender essentialism it tries to avoid. And it is around this question of lesbian desire that her model reveals its foundations in a rather rigid notion of sexual difference. In an analogy to lesbian sexuality similar to the one Kaplan employs, in *The Desire to Desire* Doane brings up a lesbian moment as that which confuses gendered positions and reveals "the convolutions of female spectatorship."[21] But Doane delimits the operations of the moment when a female spectator is asked to gaze at the image of a female to a "narcissistic framework which collapses the opposition between the subject and the object of the gaze" (157). Not only does this assume that the woman's gaze at woman is a function of narcissism (like Kuhn), but it also presumes that gender identity dominates. At the moment she introduces the possibility of a different, lesbian model, Doane encapsulates this model in a preexistent narcissistic frame and returns it to the binary terms of essentialized gender oppositions. When a woman spectator looks at a woman:

> The woman's sexuality, as spectator, must undergo a constant process of transformation. She must look, as if she were a man with the phallic power of the gaze, at a woman who would attract that gaze, in order to be that woman. . . . The convolutions involved here are analogous to those described by Julia Kristeva as 'the double or triple twists of what we commonly call female homosexuality': " 'I am looking, as a man would, for a woman": or else, "I submit myself, as if I were a man who thought he was a woman, to a woman who thinks she is a man.' "
> (*Desire* 157)

Using Kristeva's model, which describes female homosexuality as the operation of a cross-gendered masquerade, Doane reduces the excessiveness of the "convolutions" introduced by the possibility of lesbian desire to versions of a very stable sexual difference. In this heterosexual logic, woman's desire for woman is masculine. Rather than questioning the heterosexual logic of this, Doane relies on it to fix the female spectator in a narcissistic dilemma from which she can only be freed by assuming masquerade—by consciously assuming the same fixed terms that fix her in the first place.

Doane imagines finally that the operations of cinema require the female spectator to be both narcissistic and "transvestite," to be "ultimately, a hermaphrodite" (*Desire* 19). Like Mulvey and de Lauretis, Doane proposes an oscillation, a multiple positioning with object and subject that necessarily renders female spectators multiple and finds a way to empower women as viewers. This multiplicity and oscillation may be the only way to account for the dilemma of the female spectator both in relation to gender and in relation to the desire connected to narrative and visual pleasure. But as the lesbian configuration in soft-core porn films hints, this oscillation and multiplicity is even more complicated once the confines of a heterosexually premised desire are removed. It only makes sense, if we accept the terms of Freudian psychoanalysis at all, that no viewer is securely stable within either gender or sexual orientation. Instead of fixing female spectators as hermaphrodites, transvestites, or in mixed gender positions that actually secure the stability of sexual difference, it is worthwhile to look again at the "convolutions" Doane sees surrounding female homosexuality—at precisely the connection between what Doane calls the "hysterical" camera, which is "frantically searching for, retracing the path of, the lost object, attempting to articulate what is, precisely, not there" (*Desire* 155) and the possibility that desire itself is not heterosexually monolithic.

This is what the lesbian configuration reveals. There is more to sexuality and sexual difference than the mere fact of gender; desire and sexual orientation already destabilize any binary system and with it any necessary hegemony of the heterosexually premised machine, as Teresa de Lauretis points out in *Alice Doesn't* and reiterates in *Technologies of Gender*.[22] Walking "out of the male-centered frame of reference," as de Lauretis suggests, recasts gender as only one of a number of differences, all of which have an effect on viewer identification. While *gender* is one term, *desire* is another. No gender owns the look; no gender owns desire for woman or for man. And while the combination of narrative, gender, and desire may lead in one direction, the very fact of essentially unstable sexual and gender identities may already mitigate against that narrative trajectory, a tension that may account for narrative surplus or defensive mechanisms that try to pin the viewer even more tightly into narratives. In this context, then, the alliance among narrative, female image, and fetish observed by Mulvey is an attempt to combat this lack of fixity and potential slippage, rather than necessarily the governing trend in the operation of cinema. If we pose the question of cinematic pleasure from "outside the heterosexual social contract," a tactic recommended by de Lauretis for looking at constructions of gender, the combination of gender and sexual orientation constitutes a spectrum of differences that destabilize the very terms by which gender is reproduced.[23] Seeing gender and sexual identifications as unstable multiplies again identificatory oscillations, suggesting instead that a single viewer could conceivable identify with the male as male (or in line with the politics of the narrative), with the male as a female or lesbian desiring the women (both in and out of line with the narrative), with the female object as desiring subject, as a viewer in the cinema who desires the woman (or the desire of the woman) or the man (or the desire of the man), or more. These multiple identifications might be layered, occurring simultaneously, or they may be like the camera roving among positions that might also include a consciousness of the camera itself. The surplus of possibilities may provide as much visual pleasure as the oedipal shape of the narrative; viewers may acquire visual pleasure not only from a heterosexual trajectory of completion perceiving from a masculine perspective, but from a surfeit of desiring possibilities constructed by the narrative, the apparatus, and the viewer. The viewer either may not be quite so pinned into the hegemony of narrative and apparatus as some theories suggest or may be watching an apparatus that in its very structure allows for this multiplicity.

If the configuration surrounding the lesbian suggests a tremendously complex structure of viewer identifications, the very complexity of these viewing identifications explains how women can, in fact, gain pleasure from viewing an apparatus that seems narratively to exclude and objectify them. If mastery and disavowal of lack are not necessarily the prime movers of cinema, if we unmoor theories of the cinematic apparatus from their fixation on sexual difference, their privileging of mastery, and their investment in castration, we might see how the apparatus is both more problematically and more intricately self-contradictory, containing tensions between an oedipal narrative impetus dependent upon clear gender alignments and the uncontrollably multiple identifications created by the interference of unstable sexual identities. Not only does this suggest that there is no such thing as *the* female or male spectator, it also suggest that screen identifications may be even more complicated if we take into account the alterations that race, class, age, and other differences might make in the politics of identification.

This is not to say that cinema is a free-for-all or to suggest a pluralistic leveling. What the lesbian configuration exemplifies is the possibility of multiple coexisting alternatives that work because they are situated within a structure that does pit chaos against mastery, that does reiterate mirror stage structures of visual identification. But rather than substituting this mastery/chaos pair for other sets of oppositions, I think the lesbian configuration illustrates not one or the other, but three (or more) interdependent modes: the illusion of mastery, chaos, and neither one. And all can coexist.

Lesbians in the Mainstream

FETISH WITH A VENGEANCE

In the early 1980s, I was excited when I heard rumors that a film about a lesbian woman was being distributed for mainstream audiences. When the film, *Lianna*, finally played in Columbus, Ohio, I went, anticipating a vindication of sorts, but fearing that the film would misrepresent lesbian experience.[24] My desire to see a sympathetic portrayal of lesbian sexuality arose from my own narcissism, from wanting to see something other than heterosexual romance on the screen, and from a sense of recent political disenfranchisement coming from the 1980 election of conservative government officials touting a fundamentalist line. If the film was mainstream, that meant that despite growing conservatism, the power of the media might continue to represent a liberal perspective on the world by providing "positive" images of alternative choices. My premature doubt about the film sprang from the way mainstream films seemed always to adulterate the world they depicted. While I didn't particularly care if screen fantasy romances weren't true to life, it was somehow important that the portrayal of a lesbian relation be authentic, not only to combat the habitual cultural distortion of lesbians as fake men, social misfits, alcoholics, and nymphomaniacs, but also because if it weren't recognizably familiar to me as a lesbian viewer, I would be unable to enjoy the film. *Lianna* met both expectations: it was a sympathetic portrayal, but wrongheaded in perverse ways that made certain parts uncomfortable and embarrassing to watch. I was alienated from the one film I thought was made for me.

After I left the theater with mixed feelings, it took me years to analyze what had discomfited me. I now think that my disaffection was generated by *Lianna*'s subtle political, ideological, and representational defensiveness that actually works against the lesbian narrative it offers, while the film's veneer of liberalness disarms any suspicion. The product of a skillful independent filmmaker, its sometimes metacinematic and/or clumsy moments (Lianna's husband's lecture on documentary editing, the actresses' awkwardness in the opening scenes) actually contribute to an artsy counterculture liberalness that camouflages the film's controlling impetus. Paradoxically, however, while the sexual explicitness of overtly sexist, low-budget soft-core porn films tends to expose the potentially complex layers of multiple viewing positions during the lesbian episodes, progressive 1980s lesbian films such as Donna Deitch's *Desert Hearts* and John Sayles' *Lianna* defensively avoid any suggestion of multiplicity and gender uncertainty in favor of consciously polished imitations of libertinism.[25]

A Hollywoodish antiestablishment pose and appeals to a contrived familiarity are part of the allure of *Desert Hearts* and *Lianna*, which employ such conventional tropes as gay bar scenes, anecdotes of familial rejection, and, most crucially, coming out stories, the quintessential form of lesbian lore and erotica. Centered on issues of sexual knowledge and identity, the coming out story is about the relevation of a woman's potential to desire another woman. As versions of the coming out story, *Desert Hearts* and *Lianna* transform questions of sexual identity into a spectacular seduction, where looking at the woman is not a quest to discern the direction of her desire, but is instead a drive to see her desire staged for the viewer. This shift from the coming out story's desire to know to the film's desire to see the sexual behavior of women translates questions of sexual knowledge and identity into a "reheterosexualized," visually gratified quest for the lesbian as the paradoxically accessible and forbidden sexualized object.

As presumed cultural vindications of lesbian/feminism, the narratives of *Desert Hearts* and *Lianna* appear to authorize lesbian sexuality. Replete with the slick production values typical of first-run fare, both are love stories in the traditional Hollywood sense, a stylistic equation that situates lesbian and heterosexual desire as alternative forms of commercial romance. The films' illusion of social affirmation relies both on this narrative normalization and on undisturbed viewer identifications with film characters—not with idealized male heroes, but with female protagonists apparently in control of their own sexuality. By means of this rudimentary gender reversal, these "women's" films "liberate" simply by making the main characters women in an otherwise "normal" romantic scenario.[26] But the illusion of this lesbian enfranchisement is undone by the heavily conventionalized apparatus of mainstream film techniques that tend to contain and objectify the characters at the moment they appear to gain a subjective status.

Much more carefully made than porn, the political investments of these films in the "normalization" of sexuality extend the overcompensatory impetus already incited by the lesbian figure, resulting in tightly controlled and overinvested love scenes. The metaphor of this control—sexual knowledge—remains the diegetic and extradiegetic pretext for seeing sexual behavior on the screen. Echoing the pedagogical erotics of *Emmanuelle* and *Melody*, the spectacularly sexual moments of these films occur in conjunction with moments when sexual preference is revealed, a coincidence that links knowledge, sexuality, and its spectacular rendering. In this sense, at least superficially, the sexual act that confirms sexual preference for the film characters also provides an illusory sexual knowledge for the film's spectators, producing a superficial pretense for a curious scopophilia —"what do they do in bed?" What appears to be the protagonists' quest for sexual identity is really the film spectator's quest for a knowledge about sexuality, a knowing that helps neutralize the more threatening discoveries the protagonists act upon. While the protagonists are subject to the controlling operations of cinematic imaging, the spectators are aligned with the illusion of camera mastery, a position that reinforces a sense of scopophilic omniscience that tends to objectify and eroticize the protagonists' activities.

Desert Hearts, directed by Donna Deitch and based on *The Desert of the Heart* by Jane Rule, and *Lianna*, directed and written by John Sayles, present similar narratives. In *Desert Hearts*, a college English professor (Vivian) goes to Reno to divorce her husband and meets Kay, the orphaned daughter of Vivian's landlady's ex-lover. Kay, who has a reputation for being "that way," is pursued by her boss, Darryl, but seeing the fragile divorcée, falls in love with the older Vivian, pursues her, and eventually succeeds in convincing her that she also has lesbian feelings. After an engagement party for Kay's best (and most tolerant) friend, Kay and the drunken Vivian drive to a lake where Kay confesses her preference to Vivian and kisses her. The preliminary kiss forces the eviction of Vivian from the boardinghouse to a hotel, where the two continue their affair quite explicitly. The film ends with Vivian's departure and Kay's ambiguous consent to board the train "only until the next stop."

Lianna tells nearly the same story with two reversals: the younger woman is seduced by the older professor, and the love affair ends rather than continuing ambiguously. While the unhappy ending to the affair might suggest a simple negative reading of the film's attitude toward lesbian sexuality, *Lianna* is far more complex and the ending a little more positive than it might seem. The wife of a college English professor, Lianna falls in love with her child psychology teacher, Ruth, who seduces her, though not until she has made certain through a kind of anecdotal investigation that Lianna might have lesbian propensities. When Lianna announces the affair to her husband, he uses it as an excuse to divorce her and force her from the house. Lianna then expects to have a relationship with Ruth, which plays out briefly in scenes of sexual activity and tortured moments of jealousy, since Ruth is also in love with another woman, whom she ultimately chooses over Lianna. Lianna, apparently happily accepting her new sexual orientation, ends the film tentatively reestablishing more platonic female bonds with her best (and married) friend.

Because, presumably, the lesbian behavior presented in these films is "atypical" at best, the films' narratives build in reassuring defenses against potential escapes from heterosexual normalcy. The fear of no sexual difference triggered by the same-sex couple is alleviated by the compensatory marking of this difference through sets of physical oppositions that overinscribe contrasts. In both films the two lesbians who form the couple are depicted as being of unequal power and experience, a legacy from the pedagogical trope employed, but an imbalance that resituates lesbian relationships within a version of a dominance/submission paradigm associated with the inequities of sexual difference in heterosexual relationships. The elements of the films echo one another: as in the soft-core porn films, both couples include a combination of teacher/student, elder/younger, experienced/inexperienced. Kay is brunette, Vivian blond; Kay wears light clothing, Vivian dark; the lake and sky are light, the land dark; their first kiss occurs during a rare rainstorm in "dry" Nevada. Lianna is brunette and Ruth blond, Ruth a self-proclaimed "jock" and Lianna a traditionally "feminine" housewife.

To complete a narrative defense against the films' subject matter, the stories feature arguments against lesbian relationships: lesbian sexuality is not represented without its heterosexual opposition represented by the men and families the women "abandon." This could perhaps be a bow to authenticity, but it also acts as an immediate antidote to potential feminine excess. The insistently present male characters—Kay's tenacious boyfriend, Darryl, and Lianna's philandering husband—stand in as sources of a constantly oppressive disapproval, which provides a heterosexually sympathetic counterpoint to the protagonists' lesbian behavior. The male characters function as part of the voice of "normal" culture, which also includes Kay's stepmother, Lianna's best friend, and educational institutions that have expelled Kay and threaten to punish Ruth. Thus the narratives are not just coming out stories or same-sex romances but also exemplify the social dilemma of making a lesbian choice, not in a way that clearly endorses the women's preference, but in a way that subtly and insistently features the damage such a choice can wreak on nuclear families, rejected boyfriends, careers, communities, etc. Unlike similar scenarios of heterosexual coupling, where such opposition is generally depicted as unproblematically self-interested or wrong and where the weight of the culture is in favor of romantic love between women and men, in these two films this disapproval has the curious effect of being unresolved or of being not altogether unjustified, something that always brings the women's choice into question.

Though appearing to inhibit the frank portrayal of lesbian sexuality, this defensive narrative armor is actually what enables lesbian sexuality to become a spectacle. The defensiveness itself is induced by the fact that the lesbian identities sought in the film are already known to be there from the beginning. Deciding that the film is about lesbian sexuality contributes to the decision about how to make and market the film. The desire for a knowledge of an already-known drives the narratives of these films, which leads to on-screen confessions used as foreplay and pretext for the sexual spectacle that follows. And the contradictory stance of knowing and pretending not to know has additional protective functions. For example, sexual preference must be already apparent so that it is clear that lesbian sexuality is an ingrained propensity, an aberration characteristic of certain women whose marriages have already failed (Vivian, Lianna). Not only do these women independently create their own difficulties (patriarchy is certainly not to blame), but if lesbian sexuality is a given, then there is an assurance that no male loses a woman through his own incompetence. Masculine failure with lesbians is not a sour reflection on anyone's masculinity but only evidence of a man's charitable but stubbornly wrongheaded choice of girl. And there is no real lesbian "seduction" of innocent heterosexual women, since the characters' lesbian preferences are already apparent; the probing dates that serve as pretext for the confessions are founded on the existence of an already visible attraction between the protagonists. The "comforting" sense that these women were already lost exonerates the heterosexual unit from any responsibility for creating such deviations. Nothing is on the line here: we can watch these lesbian aliens with ease; the armor of knowledge that creates a first line of defense disinfects the potential threat of sexual activity.

The second line of defense in these films is to locate lesbian sexuality in the spot heterosexual union occupies in narrative. While lesbian sexuality constitutes the foreplay stage in soft-core porn films, in these mainstream films images of lesbian sexuality become the climax—the completing joinder—even though in *Lianna* this joinder occurs only halfway through the film. Shifting lesbian activity from an immature, penultimate point in the narrative to the climax is accomplished by delaying the visual revelation of a knowledge of sexual orientation that is known from the beginning of the film. Soft-core porn films' tendency to image lesbian sexuality early in the narrative translates into anecdotes about romantic love in these mainstream films, while "real" recognition of sexuality is reserved for the delayed spectacle of sexual activity on the screen. The denouement of *Lianna* is shifted to yet another kind of knowledge—the revelation of Ruth's disaffection and her rejection of Lianna. That Lianna still reaffirms her sexual identity after that rejection seems to be a more human, positive, and less exploitive rendition of lesbian sexuality than that produced by *Desert Hearts*. Despite her rejection, however, the film still images more lovemaking between Ruth and Lianna at the end of the film, lovemaking made poignant by its impossibility but providing visual reaffirmation as a kind of climactic anticlimax.

Despite their differing narrative trajectories, both *Desert Hearts* and *Lianna* situate narrated confessions about sexual preference and stories about the characters' first recognitions as foreplay. The substitution of narratives about lesbian activity for images of lesbian sexuality shifts the source of titillation from the eye to the ear, which constitutes a practice of "now you have it but you don't"—an extended suppression of the visual that feeds the oedipal desire for culmination. In narratives specifically about sexuality, this misalignment of narrative knowledge and visual affirmation has the effect of displacing and delaying knowledge altogether, whetting curiosity, providing narrative foreplay, but postponing its spectacular proof, considered the "real" place of recognition in these films. Vivian, for example, holds out until the very last moment, after she is in bed with Kay, never affirmatively admitting her attraction. Even the kissing scenes—the first visual proof offered—frustrate and delay a certainty that is elided into scopophilia, providing a pretext for more and yet delaying the gratification of the desire to see more.

In *Desert Hearts*, Kay's confession of her lesbianism to Vivian precipitates and/or motivates her literal pursuit of Vivian and their first kiss, but simultaneously delays any more intimate sexual activity. At the beginning of the kiss scene, which occurs about halfway through the film, after the engagement party of Kay's best friend, Vivian is drunk and lets it slip that she feels she is doing "something," a vague hint that Vivian understands the nature of Kay's attraction. They drive to a lake where Vivian inquires about Kay's relation to Darryl, a relation Kay defines as narcissistic ("I let myself become attracted to his attraction for me"), confessing further that "it didn't exactly get the brass ring." Vivian pushes for more: "How do you get it?," to which Kay responds, "With a woman." Vivian's quest for sexual knowledge results in Kay's confession, but Vivian responds to the information with a strange displacement: "Are you trying to shock me?" That Kay's admission might be shocking (since part of the ideology of lesbianism is that it is shocking) to a stranger is understandable; however, for Vivian, who has heard several intimations and accusations about Kay's preferences, Kay's sexual preference can hardly be news. Her imputation that Kay is *trying* to shock her is a displaced admission that she is not shocked, that in fact she "knows" already, but the entire process of shocking and knowing is displaced onto Kay as the actor, a position of responsibility Kay assumes at the beginning of the scene ("if any rules get broken, I'll take the blame"). Kay's reiteration that her confession is "only the truth" causes Vivian to reveal her real fear, that she might have "misled" or actually revealed to Kay the same "truth." She asks, "Have I misled you in any way?" The questions of truth and knowledge constitute a kind of titillating foreplay reminiscent of familiar habits in lesbian communities: "Is she or isn't she?" as a kind of typical curiosity or voyeurism about sexual identity that is linked to the first steps of sexual interest.

In *Lianna* the confession scene is also centered around a question of knowledge, as Ruth investigates Lianna's past for evidence of previous lesbian inclinations. Her questions about first crushes elicit Lianna's narrative about her camp counselor, a painfully stereotypical but prosaically comforting episode of a teenage infatuation. Lianna tells Ruth that she was in love with her camp counselor, a woman she and her bunkmate used to follow to her nightly rendezvous with a boy from the next camp. Describing the scene of the counselor and her boyfriend, Lianna details even the glint of the boy's "white buttocks gleaming in the moonlight." Fixed on the boy's fetishized butt, the two go back to their cabin and reenact the heterosexual scene, her bunkmate calling out the boy's name and Lianna pretending that her bunkmate "had breasts." Overtly cast as an imitation of heterosexual activity the two campers had just witnessed, the lesbian activity between them is safe, only undone by Lianna's curious desire that her partner have breasts. While the storytelling provides knowledge and evidence of Lianna's potential lesbianism, the scenario Lianna recounts parallels her situation on Ruth's couch. Just as the adolescent girls of Lianna's story use an identification with their camp counselor as pretext for their own sexual explorations, so does Ruth (and the film) use Lianna's confession as vicarious (and voyeuristic) impetus for her own sexual engagement with Lianna. As Lianna recounts the story and admits her crush on the counselor, Ruth increasingly conveys desire in her tender look, stroking Lianna's face with her hand as Lianna tells the story and finally, climactically, kissing her. The process of coming to "know" Lianna's sexuality is also the process by which Ruth comes to "know" Lianna carnally.

However, the combination of confession and kissing provides the matrix for the films' revelations of lesbian sexuality; as such they are both full of defensive imaging strategies and still threatening in themselves. The cinematic renditions of the kissing scenes wherein issues of sexual identity, confession, and spectacle first come together embody an ambiguous mixture of confession and delay and figure the defensive posture evident in the films' narratives. Like the soft-core porn films, the sex scenes are high points, subject to and created by visual and temporal ellipses, a practice that moves the scenes more quickly to their osculatory revelations. But this cutting is both defensive and for the viewer: it creates a temporal control and pacing and makes seeing sexuality the structural focus of the films, a structure that inherently privileges the consumer of the images. Kay and Vivian's ride to the lake ends in a series of wipes that cut time and space and force a focus on the confessional moment as well as on the kiss, which occurs elliptically almost immediately after the confession in a manner reminiscent of soft-core porn films' "cause-effect" imaging of heterosexual sex scenes. Lianna and Ruth's after-dinner conversation that provides the backdrop for the revelation of sexual attraction is also elliptied, moving it more rapidly to its conclusion and focusing it exclusively on the parts of their conversation directly related to sexual desire. The middle section of *Lianna,* after the initial sexual contact, consists of Lianna quite literally marking time until Ruth returns from a trip. Her newfound lesbian identity is sustained during this period by her "knowing" looks at other women, a scene comically imaged by Sayles as almost a metacommentary on both the centrality of looking and how changing orientation changes the view.

That the images of the women's kiss are actually reassuring is accomplished by the scenes' implied inclusion of the spectator in the circuit of looks between the women, which prevents the lesbian activity from escaping scopophilic exigency. In *Desert Hearts* the spectacular problem for the confirmation of a lesbian propensity is depicted by means of searching looks at Vivian's face, which is situated as the repository for that knowledge. In the imaging of the kiss scene in *Desert Hearts* the symbolic car window, which Vivian voluntarily rolls down, figures the moment, the almost literal (sexual) flow as Kay, standing in the rain, kisses (and wets) Vivian seated in the dry car. The kiss, reluctant at first, increases in intensity, until Vivian withdraws and rolls up the window. In the car Kay asks, "Where did you learn to kiss like that?," to which Vivian responds, "I don't know where that came from" and "it's back where it belongs." Kay's suspicions confirmed, the kiss is depicted as a moment of recognition for both of them. The question of sexual orientation in this cinematic rendition is translated into the question of the camera's look, answered by Vivian's face, then reaffirmed by the imaging of the kiss, shot from behind Vivian's head. The actual kiss is occluded first by Vivian's head, then by the appearance of Kay's controlling hand on the back of Vivian's head. Knowledge of sexual preference is gained, but affirmation of it is also delayed, first by the hand, then by Vivian's denial.

The kissing episode in *Lianna* inscribes the scene of the spectacle of confession in a slightly different and perhaps more insidious paradigm. As Lianna and Ruth talk on the couch, the camera moves gradually closer through a series of shot reverse shots and two shots that focus on the look of Ruth at Lianna and at Lianna's more distanced, nonspecific look into the past she is narrating. Lianna's mixed lesbian confession and story of heterosexual imitation becomes the knowledge Ruth needs to initiate the kiss. Prepared for and defended against by a voyeuristic story that clearly situates lesbian sexuality as a version of heterosexuality, the kiss between Ruth and Lianna is far more clearly imaged than in *Desert Hearts*.

At the beginning of both kissing scenes, the camera gazes straight-on at the faces of the women—Kay and Ruth—who know and who seek the reassurance of contact. Their looks of desire at the other women—Vivian and Lianna—literally reiterate and parallel the camera's looks at them. A triangle of looks is created: the viewer via the camera looks at the woman looking at the woman, to find through this looking a certainty about the looked-at woman's sexuality—more specifically, about her potential desire for the looker, who is both the other woman and the camera/viewer. Because these scenes are imaged in shot-reverse-shot, the camera/viewer is both included in the exchange and positioned as a third party voyeur to an exchange between the women. Instead of disrupting or confusing the camera's mastery as soft-core porn films do at this moment, mainstream films' metacinematic system of interlocking looks expressly includes the viewer/camera, which works against any question of escape from camera mastery, seducing viewers, male or female, into the economy of looks that promises knowledge—into what has become the foreplay of the scene by virtue of the concatenation of knowledge and spectacle.

Finally, the system of interlocking looks erects a scenario of control through viewing that locates the women's behavior and looks at one another as commodities for screen consumption from the position of an unquestionably masterful apparatus. The spectator, who is situated in identification with the looking woman, "owns" what is defined as a "female" look (or the look of a female) but is structured in the same sexualized subject/object, passive/active paradigm noted by Mulvey in "Visual Pleasure and Narrative Cinema." The viewer for whose eyes the scene is constructed becomes the active party for whose benefit the women's looks are generated. Even though their looks may actively exchange with one another, in relation to the film spectator, those looks become objects to be looked at. This recreation of the viewer/subject versus image/object alignment undermines any illusion of lesbian sexuality or a lesbian viewing position as an independent, nonpatriarchal choice as it is constructed in these films. While lesbian sexuality appears to provide a space for an active female viewer, that viewer is also defined as both masterful and lesbian (nonsynonymous terms) and as a lesbian who accepts a stereotypically masculine, active, subject position in relation to women, whose sexual secrets may be gleaned by looking at them. In this way, by a kind of retroaction, the lesbian on the screen who looks stands for a lesbian look and is masculinized by the operation of the apparatus as it subsumes the lesbian's look within a larger system of scopophilic looks that depend upon the maintenance of mastery in the sustained effacement of camera operations. The lesbian look in these films configures mastery and knowledge instead of confusion and multiplicity and parallels the camera/viewer look.

When the looks disappear, the illusion of viewer inclusion is maintained by the appearance of an obvious fetish object to allay anxiety and to construct what is finally a controlling image of containment over that sexuality that might seem not to need the penis. Unlike soft-core porn films, which either slip away from and then reestablish camera control or oscillate between identificatory confusion and mastery, both films solve the problem of imaging lesbian sexuality by providing a fetishistic hand that stands in for—is a metaphor of— what exactly cannot be seen in the scene. The hand literally orchestrates the kiss, substituting a synechdochal image of control for the confusion or frustration of the partially invisible kiss. The hand itself also functions as a fetish, providing something to see, disavowing the lack in the camera's mastery of the scene as its scopophilic gaze is partially blocked, standing in for the phallus literally absent between the women. The lesbian recognition and kiss is cinematically rendered both narratively and visually in a way that reinscribes it almost as a parody of the disavowal/fetish mechanism identified by Laura Mulvey and Mary Ann Doane.

The two defense mechanisms—viewer inclusion and fetish—are actually connected. The practice of viewer inclusion requires the play of a fetish to occupy the shadow position of the viewer in the scenario. The entrance of this fetish is occasioned by a temporary occlusion of the view of the kiss, not like the confusion created in soft-core porn films, but as a momentary transition from the image of the women to the foregrounding of the fetish itself. The camera, previously positioned in identification with the woman looker's look, is positioned generally behind the head of the woman object but not from her point of view. Reminiscent of porn films' frustration of the view, the kiss, the contact and proximity, is hidden by the woman object's head and by the camera's distance from the action. The sexualness of the kiss in both films is conveyed instead by the increased proximity of the two characters, by decreased camera distance, by the increasing tempo of their actions, and by the appearance of the pursuing woman's controlling hand as a kind of separate signifier of intensity.

It may be obvious why the fetish would appear, especially if we see the fetish, as both Mulvey and Doane have seen it, as screen images of women that provide an illusion of plenitude in the face of cinema's lack. In fact, the fetish in these mainstream lesbian films operates far more literally than the fetish usually discussed in film theory, which is seen as generally metaphorical in one way or another. While Christian Metz sees the operation of cinema technology itself as the fetish, Laura Mulvey sees the figure of the woman as fetish, as film turns "the represented figure itself into a fetish so that it becomes reassuring rather than dangerous." [27] Mary Ann Doane emphasizes the distancing effect of the fetish: that the fetish "is a phallic defense which allows the subject to distance himself from the object of desire (or, more accurately, from its implications in relation to castration) through the overvaluation of a mediating substitute object." [28] Kaja Silverman sees lack itself as a kind of structuring fetish of film theory. [29] Annette Kuhn does point to the fetish function of parts of female bodies in pornography, but as a rationale for pornography's attention to them as well as for why women's bodies are fragmented more than men's.[30]

The fetish that appears in these lesbian scenes is closer to Freud's notion of the penis stand-in, the visual sign of both the presence and absence of the penis on the women. In fact, in these lesbian scenes the fetish is often quite literally a penis substitute. The appearance of this literal fetish in images of sexual scenes between women exemplifies the relation of the fetish to crises of sexual difference—in this case a crisis of no difference at all.[31] Though literal fetishes do appear in images of women in cinema, often in the form of jewelry or other clothing or, as Kuhn points out, in fragmented body parts, these lesbian films' reliance on the fetish *as* the primary signifier of sexual activity reveals the castration anxiety (or maybe here more an anxiety about exclusion or superfluity) that underlies the imaging of these scenes and, at the same time, allays that anxiety. The literalness of the fetish in its rendition as hand (a potential instrument of vaginal penetration) or nipple (phalluslike in images of its erection) or veiling strands of hair that fall between the women points up the rather literal nature of the anxiety in these images: while lesbians may never avoid patriarchy or phallocentrism, they may well avoid the literal penis. Its insistent presence as part of the women's body, as intimate participant in their sexual activity, defends against its obvious exclusion.

But the fetish in these scenes tends also to reveal the basis of a more metaphorical function in the presumed absence of sexual difference. Since these films are bound up in questions of knowledge, precisely questions of sexual knowledge involving the absence of the phallus in sexualized scenarios, the fetish functions to mediate the difference between knowledge and vision where vision, especially a vision of the fetish, protects against the knowledge of no phallus at all. When what is seen cannot be known, the fetish hand intercedes to provide the illusion of knowledge, a second rephallicized, reheterosexualized knowledge that stands in the place of the first knowledge and defends against it. At the point we begin to see images of lesbian sexuality—the point that has been delayed—we can no longer see and the fetish appears to give the eye what the mind cannot comprehend, not because lesbian sexuality is incomprehensible, but because it does not necessarily fit into the narcissistic confines of a heterosexually defined system of representation. Lesbian sexuality in this mainstream system is a point of the failure of and a return to a heterosexual system that is defined not as male/female, but as male and not male, a system of no difference at all signaled by the insistent appearance of the fetish as the signifier of no difference. In this sense the function of the fetish is made transparent: it not only provides something to see, it also imports the heterosexual and phallic terms within which sexuality must be seen.

This reading of the fetish returns to a cinema whose representational politics are overtly dependent upon a reiteration of the terms of sexual difference. But this makes sense, given the fact that these films are precisely about an already culturally stereotyped instance of no sexual difference—lesbian sexuality—that can be and is defined that way only because of a rigid governing notion of sexual difference in the definition of sexualities. What I am suggesting here is that because lesbian sexuality is the subject of the films, it imports a more conscious set of assumptions and is already seen in the context of heterosexuality. This very consciousness of lesbian sexuality as a social issue begets defensiveness, even if the modes of that defense are unconscious. Seeing lesbian sexuality already in terms of sexual difference galvanizes the stereotypical gendered operations of the cinematic apparatus. Though multiple identifications are still possible —the cinematic system is still neither monolithic nor totalitarian— the binary gendered terms of viewer/object, masculine/feminine return with an almost parodic vengeance, revealing gendered investments in the context of an excessive and presumably independent femininity. Chaos or lack of control is the one mode not permitted in this otherwise licensed exhibition; lesbian sexuality can only be deliberately represented in rampantly heterosexual terms where sexual difference is stamped on every operation. Since it is the focus of these mainstream films, it cannot escape this marking, as its more minor role in soft-core porn permits.

This system is familiar because it works the same way as do kissing scenes in regular "straight" films. In *Desert Hearts* and *Lianna*, the pursuer woman takes the cinematic place of the man, but is a woman. Her look is "camerized" if not masculinized, in association with a preceding camera look at the woman object and in relation to "normal" paradigms of societal (and cinematic) heterosexual behavior. One difference, however, is that the camera looks at the woman who pursues more than it usually fixes on the romantic look of a male lead, because both women in a lesbian scene are really sources for a scopophilic look at female desire. But the fact that the characters are women also instigates excessive images of female desire creating a disturbance that must be alleviated by returning her to the masculine and/or by providing an extra fetish in the form of the controlling (and arousing) hand. In this excessive triangle of desiring, overtly female looks, the operations of cinema become more starkly evident, since they must scramble to translate this from and into the habitual heterosexual system. And what becomes evident are the ways the viewer is inserted into the duo as recipient of the erotic look of the woman. This is enacted not only because sexual activity is imaged from the perspective of a participant, but also because sexual activity is translated precisely into a system of eroticized looks that take the place of less erotic and spectacular sexual contact. To preserve the erotics of the look, the films must retain the distance between the women, which also preserves what Doane identifies as the distance necessary for scopophilia.[32] But this distance also quite literally conserves the place of the viewer in the activity, creating, as it does in soft-core porn films' imaging of heterosexual sex, the illusion of participation from the perspective of a participant. When the distanced view disappears, the fetishized hand appears.

SEALED WITH A KISS

If a mere kiss can arouse the fetishistic defenses of the apparatus, what protective mechanisms might more overtly sexual behavior bring to light? Providing the pattern for the exposition of sexuality that follows, the kissing scenes in *Desert Hearts* and *Lianna*, posed as they are as narrative foreplay, are actually more threatening than the full-blown sex scenes, since the kiss is the only sexual activity actually completely imaged in the film and is the most specific information the viewer will ever receive about the nature of lesbian sexuality. The answer to the sexual question posed by the films and presumably provided by the films' climactic sex scenes is, as in the kissing scenes, an undiscernible, nonthreatening, nonspecific titillation that never exceeds the bounds of familiar heterosexual activity. Whether the style and limits of these depictions are made for the sake of decency, art, or filmic mimesis of jouissance or because lesbian sexuality is in fact unimageable, the effect is erotic and defamiliariz-ing, sexual and nonmenacing. This cinematic ambiguity removes any potential threat to phallocracy lesbian activity may have and reduces it to the familiar category of benign diversion. But even this ambiguity is marked by the proliferation of fetish objects that phallicize and control the sexual activity of the scenes.

In *Desert Hearts*, the ellipses and anxieties about knowledge that plague the confession/kiss scenes reappear with more extensive sexual activity. At the initiation of the scene Kay, who has jumped naked into bed when Vivian's back is turned, "knows" better than Vivian what Vivian wants. At Vivian's claim that she wants Kay to "put on her clothes and leave," Kay responds, "No, you don't." As Vivian acquiesces, her remaining problem is that she "wouldn't know what to do." They both seem, however, to rush into bed, to focus on a narrative and visual point that overtly fulfills sexual expectations. It has always disturbed me in *Desert Hearts*, for example, that Kay is able to undress, fold her clothes, and arrange herself in bed during the brief time that Vivian is imagining her revenge on Kay's stepmother. Kay and the filmmaker both seemed so much in a hurry that they defy logic and stretch the bounds of verisimilitude.

In the love scene between Kay and Vivian, what is important is the looking, which serves as a viewer-inclusive brand of foreplay. The scenes of looking, then touching with hands are imaged from a me-dium distance, which retains the viewer's place in the scenario. The main coherent activity that governs the scene is seen in shots of the women kissing that both recall their earlier encounter and limit the depiction of most coherent sexuality to a familiar activity. When the women become more involved in touching other body parts, the camera shifts from its look at the looking to close-up shots of nipples, hands, hair, and tongues and slips in and out of point-of-view shots from the perspective of the lover—a technique used only in heterosexual scenes in soft-core porn films. This shift in distance and position signals the substitution of fetish objects for the pleasure of the look; when distance is lost, fetishized body parts come to stand in for a loss of scope. Where the scenes convey the two women together —scenes that threaten to reveal lack—something else is offered for the eye: a glint of sweat, a tongue, breasts, long, veiling strands of hair, and, particularly, isolated erect nipples that touch one another and stand in for the missing object. The sexuality is mainly conveyed by means of these isolated parts never spatially or temporally bound to either the women's bodies or their sexual activity.

As the camera moves closer, presumably to offer a better view, its use of extreme close-ups actually offers a less coherent view, both of the women's touching and of the trajectory of the sexual activity. The scene, already plagued by cause-effect ellipses that move by fits and starts toward images of sexual effect, begins to move even more rapidly toward a mystery orgasm in a series of ellipses masked by a lack of distance and coherence. After the initial set of looks, the sexual scene between Vivian and Kay can be seen as series of contextualized fetishes that heterosexualize an otherwise incomprehensible activity. What this mainstream lesbian sexuality becomes, then, is a series of fetish fixations that substitute for the missing phallus, something that rephallicizes lesbian sexual activity along the same lines that the women's looks are masculinized by the operation of the cinematic apparatus. The question "What do they do?" is defensively answered by means of the fetish: lesbian sexuality is a phallic sexuality that employs a substitute phallus. This is most comforting, since it subordinates lesbian sexuality to masculinity, making it again the pretender, the imitation of the "real" thing.

Reiterating the attachment to questions of knowledge, the sex scene in *Lianna* immediately follows the recognition kiss scene, but the postsex discussion centers on whether Ruth "knew" that Lianna was interested. The scene between Lianna and Ruth is even more temporally ellipted than the scene in *Desert Hearts,* and the stylized fragmentation of bodies becomes the major mode of Sayles' representation. The scene involves a series of low-light, slow-motion, partial images of the two women in bed, where their specific actions are barely detectable, though again the scene's coherent activity tends to consist of kissing. Like *Desert Hearts, Lianna* repeatedly positions the breast and strands of hair as fetish, images that stand out in the context of the otherwise mysterious flow of gray lines and shapes on the screen. The low-light, "artistic" style of the scene appears to be designed to leave an impression of sexuality rather than to depict graphic sex, a style we might applaud if we see the avoidance of cinematic scopophilia as a political act.[33] But the fragmentation and haziness of the scene actually merges the two bodies of the women into one large fragmented body, a practice that eliminates or masks the fact of an excess femaleness, while the camera's insistent focus on operative parts allows a voyeurism that both satisfies curiosity to a point and offers one large, many-nippled woman's body up as spectacle.

This style, which seems to imitate the fluid politics of a feminist notion of jouissance, is actually created through a tremendous and artful control located in the apparatus instead of in the scene. The fact that the scenes consist of two women engaged with one another is dissolved, subordinated to the unifying but indiscriminate scrutiny of the camera. This opportunity for control is also sustained by the lack of temporal logic and the absence of much of a sense of narrative progression in the scenes. This stylistic fragmentation functions only vaguely like the porn films' moments of disorientation. Though the image appears to be disorienting and frustrating, the editing, the slow-motion, and the lighting effects are signifiers of increased control by the apparatus. The confusion that is exposed in porn is occluded here by an overcontrolled construction of disorder. Already strongly marked by the fetish, the culminatory positioning of the scene in the narrative situates the scene itself as a kind of mastery—both the mastery of completion and consummation and the mastery of the appearance of a knowledge gained. In other words, in these films lesbian sexuality takes the place heterosexuality holds in porn films. Posed as mastery, the rhetoric of cinematic mastery takes over.

The control scenario enacted by the proliferation of fetishes is matched by a controlling sound track. While the eye rejoices in *Desert Hearts* at the lush garden of flesh and fetish, the scene's coherence is created by the sounds of the women's response, which sexualize and to a degree organize the fragments (both of bodies and of time). The sound organizes and interprets what is offered to the eye and fills in for what is not seen. In *Desert Hearts,* sound adds an additional, supporting layer to the combined voyeurism/fetish already present in the scene. The director likes to match sounds of jouissance with facial close ups, pinning the sexual weight of the scene mainly on Vivian's response. Without the sound, Vivian's expressions might be just as easily construed as pained or annoyed. Because the sound in *Desert Hearts* is almost completely linked to a visible sexual cause and effect, it operates as an analogue to the fetish, reinforcing for the ear that which the eye seeks, augmenting the presence of the invisible, providing another dimension to the fetishistic strategy used to deny the threat offered by the image of two sexualized women on the screen. This sound, which is also somewhat free-floating—that is, not entirely attached to visible cause/effect—tends to reinforce the overall spectatorial mastery of the scene, especially when there is nothing to see because the sounds of jouissance organize sexual pleasure in the absence of visual mastery. The sexual scene in *Desert Hearts*, then, might be described as overcompensated, overinvested, and overcontrolled. While this is presumably Vivian's "liberation," it is singularly comforting, circumscribing the women's sexuality within three lines of defense, mastering and containing cinematically a sexuality that threatens narratively to go outside the bounds of patriarchy.

Lianna presents a different case, since its sound track appears to be completely detached from the fragmented action of the scene. The voiced- or whispered-over sound track, though it gives the illusion of a fragmented, multivoiced chorus that seems to distract from scopophilic pleasure, in fact provides an increasing sense of mastery over the entire scene as words of sexual assent and desire become increasingly discernible. Like the breast, which remains a clearly visible part throughout, the sound, dislocated from the women, appears to speak directly to the audience in a kind of impassioned direct address to the mechanism—the camera—that produces the scene. In this way the women's sexual activity becomes subject to the apparatus, begging it to "touch" them. And the fragmented disorganization of the scene does not work so much to play with anxiety and mastery, as it is itself already overly subject to a mastered, stylized, and narratively fixed apparatus.

In both films, finally, the question of the configuration of lesbian sexuality is answered, oddly enough, within the same paradigm of immature penultimateness offered by the soft-core porn film. Although knowledge of lesbian sexuality is positioned as a culmination in both films, the governing moment of the depiction of lesbian sexuality resides in the kissing scenes—the penultimate and exploratory moments. Serving as matrices for the later representation of the bedroom scenes, the kissing scenes and the kiss itself serve as the main signifiers of sexuality between women. Other images of lesbian sexuality are governed by the kiss and by the same screen politics that characterize the kissing scenes. Lesbian sexuality is conveyed as "kisslike"—as a meeting of parts with limited interpenetration—as oral, as an activity whose nature is occluded and marked by the fetish just as the kissing scenes are. And that the kiss is both foreplay and one sexual practice common to lesbian sexuality and heterosexuality makes the kiss a safe model that retains, I think unconsciously, the position of lesbian sexuality as foreplay—as the unfulfillable prelude to desire.

That all of this occurs still within the veneer of a quest for sexual knowledge poses the fetish as the answer to questions about women's sexuality. If what Annette Kuhn suggests about the function of lesbian sexuality on screen is true, if it "side-steps the embargo on the image of the phallus," then in these scenes it does so by proliferating fetish images that compensate for the imagined lack of phallus in the scene, making the scene an occasion for a spectacular denial rather than affirmation of lesbian sexuality. What do women do together? By means of a multiplication of fetishes, they make a space for the phallus that should be there and, in fact, is there in the fetishes on the screen. This transformation also erases any implicit female license to view, since the fetishes in this sexualized environment seem particularly useless to a woman spectator except as that which contributes to an alienation from the scene. The woman's position as looker both as cinema audience and as lesbian on screen, as desiring subject, though still present, becomes objectified and indirect. In the sex scene, the lesbian becomes the looking woman, object for cinematic consumption instead of active viewer, a repositioning that negates her implicit authorization as active viewer in much the same way that the female spectator's implicit characterization as lesbian ultimately works to reinscribe her as masculine instead of lesbian. While the spectator is still asked to identify with a woman desiring a woman, the fact of the character's gender is to some degree erased by the fragmentation, the ellipses, the illogic, and the fetishes created by editing and imaging the scene. The transformation of the desire into spectacle has taken the scene from the realm of potential lesbian desire to the realm of the very masculinized trope of the fetish, which eliminates the female spectator from the circuit of looks.

Thus is the specter of lesbianism split, dislocated, and recuperated. Though it might be argued that the importance of sound replicates authentic experience (and it might), its function in lesbian scenes makes quite "visible" its operation within the entire convention of pornography: sound is a controlling device that both suggests a normative female response (lesbian and heterosexual) and masters any excess uncertainty posed by female sexuality. Set off in special genres of films—women's films and pornography—lesbian sexuality is paradoxically reduced to operation either in a politically authorized field (women's stuff) or within the licensed libertine dissipation of pornography. While positive women's films and pornography may be related to one another by the similarity of their positions on the margins of mainstream culture, I think their affinity points to a more insidious relation between them as different versions of containment strategies. In the way in which both genres freely feature female sexuality, they both might quality as pornography. And that specifically women's films have a status like that of pornography reveals both the nature of pornography as that which controls and images female excess and the nature of women's films, which present "obscene" images of excess female liberation. As a feature of these "segregated" genres, lesbian sexuality need not appear in or disturb other kinds of "sensitive" films not specifically designated as either "women's films" or pornography. Thus "dealt with" in films like *Desert Hearts, Lianna, Personal Best,* and others, the presence of "positive lesbian role models" belies the recuperative semiotics of mastery that reclaims lesbian sexuality as a fetishistic performance aligned with the conventions of mainstream cinema rather than soft-core pornography.

The appearance of this genre and in particular lesbian films in the early to mid eighties during the halcyon years of the Reagan administration illustrates the rule of overcompensation already demonstrated in the films' overly controlled style. Appearing within a mainstream women's genre, mainstream lesbian films represent the encapsulated fear of the women's movement, which must be kindly heard and dispensed with. The appearance of these films is consistent with a conservative politics of dissimulation, which takes credit for allowing dissonant visions while taking smug pleasure in the destruction visited by the form of the representation itself. At the same time, the production of women's films can be culturally rued and used as an exemplum of the dangers of feminism.

It is more than likely that none of this goes unnoticed, particularly by the female spectator of both pornographic and mainstream films who is disappointed by her continued discomfort with images presumable projected just for her. Though the female viewer is embarrassed and alienated, perhaps the source of her dilemma is brought into stark relief. The character of the investment that excludes the female viewer to begin with excludes her again, only this time without the occluding pastiche of a heterosexual narrative. The difficult and paradoxical politics of the feminist porn viewer are revealed as dependent upon the paradox that founds her viewing: the female spectator's alienation—that which makes her subject and object at the same time—is what enables both her critique and her captivation. The double-bind inscribed in the film is an impossible double-positioning that reveals itself, inviting critique, but also distancing and disimplicating us from it, making safe our investment in it. It is not us or our folly; it is someone else's. In effect, the same system continues to work in mainstream lesbian films, but in this case, it is presumably posed for the female spectator, at least for the lesbian spectator. Our spectatorial dilemma is redefined. We may still feel the distance created by the semiotic operation of the fetish, but we have difficulty disavowing the film because, like the heroines in the film, we have knowledge we want to see confirmed. Its false fulfillment of our knowledge blocks and contains us far more effectively than cultural opposition or disapproval ever could.

Siren Screen

> I do not think that they will sing to me.
> T. S. Eliot, "The Lovesong
> of J. Alfred Prufrock"

AS THE epitome of seduction, the mermaids of T. S. Eliot's poem lure the lover by means of an absence or a lack—in "Prufrock" through their lack of address to the narrator of the poem. What makes the mermaids' lack of address alluring is not a voyeuristic envy of voices heard elsewhere, but rather the sustenance of absence itself—the mermaids' continued lack of address, the unheard music that leaves open the desiring place their song doesn't occupy. Unlikely as it may seem, Eliot's aquatic chantresses provide a clue to how two films that represent lesbian sexuality, Diane Kurys' *Entre Nous* and Patricia Rozema's *I've Heard the Mermaids Singing*, solve the problem of depicting lesbian desire and sexuality without making it the spectacular object of a scopophilic consumption. In both films sexuality between women is an analogue to the mermaids, whose presence is acknowledged, whose song is heard, but who, unseen, never directly serenade the viewer. This aesthetics of indirect seduction provides a possible solution to two related problems: one is how to dismantle the oppositional, gendered alignments of viewer/subject/ active/masculine and image/object/passive/feminine that found the exploitive role of sexualized screen images of women and shape perceptions of film spectatorship. The other is how lesbian desire can be portrayed without necessarily being translated into the phallocentric terms by which sexuality in general tends to be depicted.

The problem of the expressibility of lesbian sexuality is suggestively delineated in Virginia Woolf's novel *Mrs. Dalloway*. Clarissa Dalloway, the novel's protagonist, struggles in her effort to verbalize certain feelings she has for women:

> She could see what she lacked. It was not beauty; it was not mind. It was something central which permeated; something warm which broke up surfaces and rippled the cold contact of man and women, or of women together. For *that* she could dimly perceive. She resented it, had a scruple picked up Heaven knows where, or, as she felt, sent by Nature (who is invariably wise); yet she could not resist sometimes yielding to the charm of a woman, not a girl, of a woman confessing, as to her they often did, some scrape, some folly. And whether it was pity, or their beauty, or that she was older, or some accident—like a faint scent, or a violin next door (so strange is the power of sounds at certain moments), she did undoubtedly then feel what men felt. Only for a moment; but it was enough. It was a sudden revelation, a tinge like a blush which one tried to check and then, as it spread, one yielded to its expansion, and rushed to the farthest verge and there quivered and felt the world come closer, swollen with some astonishing significance, some pressure of rapture, which split its thin skin and gushed and poured with an extraordinary alleviation over the cracks and sores! Then, for that moment, she had seen an illumination; a match burning in a crocus; an inner meaning almost expressed.[34]

Mrs. Dalloway can feel it, but she cannot say it, cannot pin it down except in heterosexual terms—"what men felt." Subject only for simile, her desire for women is as ephemeral and intangible as an illumination, a "pressure of rapture," an "extraordinary alleviation," as an "inner meaning *almost* expressed" (my emphasis). And yet Mrs. Dalloway's inability to specify paradoxically constitutes the narrator's expression of lesbian desire, an expression made in the form of a configuration created by accumulating approximations that ultimately fail to approximate in the very indirectness of the inevitable displacements of Clarissa's various metaphorical interpolations. The difficulty of representing lesbian sexuality, as Woolf illustrates, lies not in whether or not such desire exists or whether it is ultimately representable at all, but in an inability to recognize continual indirection or a failure of language as representation.

This problem of representing lesbian sexuality is the same as the problem of the representability of and from the female taken up by feminist aesthetic theorists. If we see lesbian sexuality as specifically engaged with females and with an explicitly female sexuality and if we see a relation, though not necessarily an essential connection, between femaleness and the feminine, then the difficulties of representing sexuality between women are related to the linguistic problems of expressing a distinctly female perspective. Perceiving that femaleness is representationally suppressed, philosopher/critics such as Luce Irigaray and Hélène Cixous demonstrate the implicit phallocentrism of theories and language about sexuality and link that phallocentrism to a systematic expression of the feminine as merely a version of the masculine. In the oft-cited "This Sex Which Is Not One," Irigaray broadly asserts that "female sexuality has always been theorized within masculine parameters" and is premised upon a phallomorphic conception of female bodies.[35] To counteract this phallomorphism— to engage in what Irigaray sees as a specifically feminine practice—one must expose phallomorphism by means of a conscious metacriticism and engineer a new way of thinking about and expressing female sexuality that is metaphorically founded on the specific morphology of female genitalia. Whether genitomorphism is a solution to phallocentrism or merely another version of it, Irigaray's discussion of the relation among bodies, language, and theories of sexuality reveals the extent to which sexuality, language, and theory have coalesced in a complementary relation to a masculine norm in Western culture. This same concatenation of sex, language, and theory is explored by Hélène Cixous, who theorizes a feminine writing based on the rediscovery of the connection among women, their bodies, and representation. Asserting that women have been culturally and libidinally alienated from themselves, Cixous sees writing as a way to return to femininity and its own suppressed, specifically heterogeneous erogeneity. Since for both Irigaray and Cixous the feminine is conceived of as a separately existing, distinctly different mode of experience, the aesthetics of representing the feminine and female sexuality are specifically related.[36]

In ways roughly parallel to Irigaray's and Cixous' analyses, feminist aestheticians also decry the suppression of a female voice by phallocentric and phallomorphic aesthetic theory and practice. Relying on perhaps a more essential relation between experience, gender, and language, Julie Penelope Stanley and Susan J. Wolfe find a specifically feminist aesthetic in what they empirically identify as tangibly different uses of language by women writers: "The relationship between consciousness and linguistic choice is confronted and articulated as the self expressing itself in and through a language remade, reordered: the feminist aesthetic."[37] This simple observation of a biologically based linguistic difference joins earlier attempts by other theorists to found a feminist aesthetic based upon a woman-oriented content. Both dominated initial formulations of a specifically feminist practice, though they were soon augmented and in part supplanted by more interactive theories of a politicized feminist aesthetic, still premised on the existence of a female cultural perspective, but detached from any essential relation between gender and language use. Judith Barry and Sandra Flitterman describe this later, more politicized aesthetic as an attribute of women's position in patriarchy, a position "which enables them [women] to play on the contradictions within it."[38] For Barry and Flitterman, "feminist art evolves from a theoretical reflection on representations: how the representation of women is produced, the way it is understood, and the social conditions in which it is situated" (44).

While it is clear in Stanley and Wolfe's concept how a feminist aesthetic relates to the representation of the female as content or product, later formulations such as that of Barry and Flitterman and those adduced by feminist film theorists concentrate on a textual practice—on an analytic, self-reflective, political practice that divorces a feminist political aesthetic from attempts to represent the female or the feminine. This has been the tendency in feminist film theory: to see representations of the female as inevitably bound up in an apparatus that operates primarily in a phallocentric field of sexual difference and which because of this, inevitably reproduces a phallocentric, and hence not female, vision. Theoretically, inscribing the cinematic apparatus as masculine makes dubious any possibility of representing a female perspective at all unless, as it might be argued, it is impossible to represent anything specifically female beyond a kind of textual practice consisting of a meditation on the nature of representation itself. Two practical responses to this have been to make feminist cinema 1) a form that denies vision—denies the eye and the scopophilic desire to see—or 2) a completely analytical, metacritical practice. But to make either denial or continual analysis a systematic aesthetic would still not be to represent a female or necessarily feminine perspective. They would merely be antipractices, dependent upon the dominant practice they seek to deny or debunk. This is perhaps why Silvia Bovenschen in her essay "Is There a Feminine Aesthetic?" finally answers her title question: "Certainly there is, if one is talking about *aesthetic awareness* and *modes of sensory perception*. Certainly not, if one is talking about an unusual variant of artistic production or about a painstakingly constructed theory of art."[39]

Rather than build on conceptions of antipractice, feminist film theorists interested in the question of feminist film production commence with Bovenschen's emphasis on awareness. While feminist film production is not limited to issues of expressing a feminine, the two questions—how to make women's films and how to express a female perspective—are related in much the same way issues of feminist aesthetics are related to the possibility of expressing something uniquely female. While both come to question the validity of separate gender categories, they nonetheless envision a specifically feminist praxis as somehow engaging with the relation between gender and representation. In a discussion about feminist aesthetics held among feminist film theorists and filmmakers in an issue of *New German Critique*, the participants consistently shift their attention from content or product to process and questions of awareness. Judith Mayne, for example, sees feminist film collectives as one form of alternative action that creates a new awareness by establishing "a different relationship with what's being filmed or who's being filmed," which she hopes will "necessitate a different relationship between who's watching the film and who's made the film."[40] Teresa de Lauretis continues this strain of argument in a later essay, stating that "the project of feminist cinema, therefore, is not so much 'to make the visible invisible,' as the saying goes, or to destroy vision altogether, as it is to construct another (object of) vision and the conditions of visibility for a different social subject."[41] De Lauretis goes even further, combining questions of vision, apparatus, and narrative to envision a feminist cinema bound up with questions of desire: "As I see it," de Lauretis says, the project is "to articulate the relations of the female subject to representation, meaning and vision, and in so doing to set out the terms of another measure of desire, the conditions of presence of another social subject. The problem is how to reconstruct vision from the contradictory—but not impossible—place of female desire, how to represent her double identification in the process of 'looking at her looking' and so to perform the contradictions of women in language, in imaging, in the social" (38).

That questions of cinematic desire depend not only upon vision but upon the shape of narrative has been convincingly demonstrated since the 1970s by critics such as Claire Johnston, Laura Mulvey, Stephen Heath, and de Lauretis herself. What we see on the screen is shaped and mediated by narratives that cajole our investments and empathy, that create multiple and sometimes conflicting identifications such as identifications with both the direction of the narrative, in its urge toward closure that tends often to guarantee a patriarchal victory that forecloses the possibilities for or destroys female characters, and specific characters who may be male or female. In light of the central importance of narrative form, de Lauretis redefines the project of feminist cinema as enacting "the contradiction of female desire in terms of narrative, to perform it in the figures of movement and closure, image and gaze" (40). In other words, a feminist cinema must make these contradictions and their gendered mechanism grossly apparent to configure and thus contain them.

De Lauretis writes that one way to perform this configuration is to "create narrative that is Oedipal with a vengeance," that stresses "the duplicity of the scenario and the specific contradiction of the female subject in it" (40). Oedipal in this context means a drive toward closure and completeness, a drive associated on one hand with the bringing together of oppositions, or heterosexuality, and on the other with a need to account for and finish off all parts. Feminist cinema must make the cooperative urge of desire, narrative, and image so apparent that their operation is exposed and we are no longer captivated. But does this vengeance simultaneously enact and reveal another measure of desire? Or how does it? The exposure of oedipal narrative and its process does not leave a blank or gapless self-cycling analysis. If the oedipal is exposed, then something is left, if Luce Irigaray is right in her observation that the whole does not equal the sum of its parts: there is something still unaccounted for. And this something else resulting from the exposure of the oedipal may have always coexisted: it might be the something else of another measure of desire connected to a female perspective. In this context the problem of representing lesbian sexuality becomes an exercise in manipulating the interdependent terms of image and narrative so that they reveal their operation and complicity and so that with their revelation something else emerges, something like Woolf's inner meaning almost expressed or something like a sense of the mermaids' song. But it is possible, too, that this works the other way at the same time, that representing lesbian sexuality is part of the means by which the operations of oedipal narrative might be exposed.

What is "oedipal with a vengeance"? How do we set the terms of what de Lauretis calls "another measure of desire?" Diane Kurys' *Entre Nous* enacts one solution.[42] Masquerading within the conventions of mainstream narrative cinema: attractive protagonists played by Isabelle Huppert and Miou-Miou, a slick photographic style accompanied by appropriate and pointedly schlocky music, and the obvious cross-cutting of parallel histories, *Entre Nous* appears to construct the typical matter for scopophilic consumption. Seducing by seeming to unite two very oedipal narratives with highly consumable, completely objective camera images, the film constructs a lure that entices viewers into a trajectory of desire that in its doubly oedipal course promises heterosexual completion, romance, and victory. In the first plot, Lena, doomed to an internment camp during WW II, is able to escape by marrying one of the camp's workers, Michel, and the film traces the couple's road to freedom and postwar prosperity. Intercut with this narrative is the story of Madeleine, whose young husband is shot by the Nazis during the war and who then marries Costa, an unsuccessful jack-of-all-trades. The two women meet at a school play where their children are performing and become good friends. The couples begin meeting socially. But at this point in the film something starts to go narratively awry. The women show too much of an interest in one another, an interest that is not at first specifically romantic or sexual. The oedipal gloss of the film is interrupted, yet apparently shifted onto the story of the two women, whose joinder we anticipate as we anticipated the weddings of the characters or the social intercourse of the couples.

Oedipal with a vengeance—that is both more oedipal than oedipal and also avenging the heterosexual thrust of completion that from the outset seemed to shape the narrative of the film—*Entre Nous* sets forth a new measure of desire by using its overtly oedipal gloss as a decoy whose progressive exposure reveals the nature of our spectatorial and narrative investments. The film rather self-referentially cues us into its own process by means of a series of figurative and narrative clues. The French title of the film, *Coup de foudre*, means both love at first sight and an unexpected blow: in this film both are true, the love revealed through the unexpected shift. That oedipal narrative is a mask in this film is prefigured by Lena's daughter's performance of a Chevalier song while wearing a Chevalier mask whose oversized masculinity does not fit her little girl's figure. Like the audience of interested parents, we complacently watch a narrative film whose other face is masked and whose movements are accompanied by the repeated playing of the song "I Wonder Who's Kissing Her Now," sung by the daughter. Like the daughter, the film's movements, though they appear to be intended to create an adultery scenario that fits nicely with the question of the song, have as little relation to adultery as the daughter's somewhat spastic and arrhythmic dance movements have to Chevalier's tune. The film also includes another cuing configuration, this one connected with the younger daughter. Though the film's conventions masquerade it as having been shot from a fairly objective omniscient camera, the end of the film reveals that in fact the entire story was told from the perspective of the younger daughter. Even our trust in convention is undermined, and we are invited to review the film from a new and more limited subjective perspective, one that undoes whatever reliability the apparatus had managed to retain. Not a scopophilic vision, the daughter's view is perplexed and perceptive; seen retroactively from her perspective, the narrative becomes more an exploration of the women's motives than an exhibition of their sexuality and the oedipal thrust toward closure is transformed into a circular meditation on continuing friendship and female bonding.

Narratively, *Entre Nous* also provides clues to the deployment of its decoys in the themes of disappointed hopes and misperceived and missed targets that touch all of the male characters except Madeleine's son, René. Michel attempts to purchase love or at least faithful gratitude by marrying Lena out of the internment camp; his faith in her appearance blinds him to the simple platitude that one cannot buy love. Costa's scheming has as its immediate focus the "decoy" of an object that will make him get rich quick, but the objects always turn out to be something other than what Costa anticipated—his Modigliani is stolen and the American shirts he plans to resell have only one sleeve. Just as they do not fit the measure of his desire (or any but one-armed human beings), neither does the film fit the measure of an oedipal desire.

Entre Nous defers and reshapes oedipal desire by successfully detaching image from narrative expectation. Urged on by the lure of what has become the promise of a lesbian joinder, this desire is ultimately undermined by the film's constant denial of an overt and direct imaging of lesbian sexuality. Whatever sexual desire exists between the women is put off in favor of affairs with art teachers, plans for dress shops, and groping with young men on trains. Although the preliminary clues, the glances, the touches, their absorbing interest in one another point to something more, physically, within range of the camera eye, the women remain pristinely apart. Only their emotional investment is made narratively apparent, an investment that finally undoes the heterosexual hegemony of the narrative masquerade. Their friendship, evidently strong enough for Lena's guilty deployment of the tombstone-in-Belgium decoy so she can meet Madeleine in Paris, has also become problem enough to arouse the jealousy of Michel and the defeated complacency of Costa. The film, however, or the camera, consistently misses all of the moments of sexual closure it appears to have constructed. The encounters of Lena and Madeleine are truncated the moment before anything can be seen, and we are never given any clear idea that there is anything that comes after. We are finally left with a dislocated desire represented by the absence of any consummation—an absence that belies the carefully constructed oedipal mask of the film.

That lesbian sexuality occupies the place of visual disappointment in *Entre Nous* suggests that the specific imaging of that sexuality configures another measure of desire. Lesbian sexuality and desire *are* portrayed in this film, but they are portrayed in the film's strategic deployment of a lack of direct image. Couched within the film's metatextual exposure of the politics of oedipal narrative and desire, performing in effect what is truly an "oedipus interruptus," the scenes in which the characters' lesbian sexuality is suggested but not depicted illustrate a practice that sustains rather than thwarts desire while engendering another kind of desire. Preventing the apparatus from objectifying and fetishizing the women's sexuality—preventing it from being translated into a consumable object staged for the scopophilic desire of the viewer—the film creates not voyeuristic pleasure, but a play on voyeurism that nonetheless exceeds that play and does become something else. What the camera does not show and what we cannot see can still be vividly sensed. But how?

Rather than presenting us with another version of nonvision, *Entre Nous* constructs lesbian sexuality as the moment that forces an absence in an urge toward visual mastery, enacting a literal lack that sustains desire, not necessarily sexual desire between the women or the fantasy desire of the audience for the imaged characters, but a desire analogous to that portrayed by Woolf in *Mrs. Dalloway*—it is the inner meaning almost, but not quite, expressed. While this appearance of a lack at the moment of completion is reiterated on different levels throughout the film, one specific scene may help make explicit the cinematic mechanism of this absence. The conversation in the scene is constructed from a series of comparisons and silences that occur while the women are looking at themselves and at one another in the mirror. During the only moment in the scene when Lena's breasts can be seen, Madeleine observes, "You have a wonderful body." The camera shifts angle slightly after that, blocking any view of breasts, while Madeleine continues her comparison: I have terrible breasts. You don't. [silence] I've always felt ashamed of my breasts." Lena appears to look in the direction of Madeleine's breasts, then at her own, and observes, "Mine are too small." Madeleine contradicts her, "They're adorable." All of this has been oblique: the women look at each other indirectly through the agency of the mirror; the conversation about breasts is also only an approximation, a metaphor for something else. A long silence ensues, during which Madeleine shifts her look from the mirror to a direct glance at Lena. This is a moment that is loaded with what is unsaid and focuses the desire of the scene. The shift in look signifies what isn't said, but only in the context of a series of already indirect looks. The scene ends with another approximation: "Why do I feel so at ease with you?"

A scene overtly about looking at fetish objects—breasts—this episode seems at first to construct a typically voyeuristic moment where, under the guise of a completely innocent viewing, bodies are offered for the cinema viewer's atavistic pleasure. That the women are comparing their breasts is a familiar trope descending from the patriarchal emphasis on size, but that the women are so dispassionately doing the comparing estranges the project of objectifying body parts from its typically fetishistic context. While the first part of this brief scene plays upon and exposes the investments of voyeurism and fetishism by de-contextualizing them, the second part of the scene frustrates voyeurism completely. As the camera shifts, the fleeting view of the breasts disappears while the women are still discussing them. Lena and Madeleine look at one another's bodies in the mirror, creating a circuit of looks at one another that implicitly includes but does not privilege the viewer, who can certainly watch the women look at one another but can no longer see what they are talking about. This lack of centered privilege in relation to the women's mirrored faces disturbs the fetish function by inscribing the women's bodies within another system of looks between the women. Their simultaneous discussion about feelings of closeness also poses another economy against the viewer's frustrated drive to see and know. They know, but we cannot; what we see is that we cannot know. What is made literally absent is the breasts the women look at, but the scene is about more than breasts. It is about what isn't breasts, what isn't sexual in an objectively driven and consumable way. What the scene conveys through the exchange of the women's looks beyond the breasts is a kind of desire that surpasses the breast, the kind of desire proclaimed not by what they say and look at, but by precisely what is not said in the scene, in the absence of contact, in the absence of any specific acknowledgement of mutual desire.

We can trace the recognition of the something else to Madeleine's direct look at Lena. At the moment Madeline looks at Lena, the circuit of indirect looks that has included the audience is broken. While we see Madeleine's look and it is silently eloquent, it is the first look aimed elsewhere; it does not "sing" for us. Her look becomes a literal and structural gap in the mirrored circuit of screen, viewer, and image—a circuit that emblematically reflects the cinematic apparatus itself. This gap or absence not only exposes the indirectness and voyeurism of the scene and our investment in it, but also conveys what is another measure of desire, a measure not for us. But like Eliot's mermaids, this desire is conveyed because it is not for us. It is neither absent nor present; it is represented by the configuration of indirection that results from the simultaneous exposure of voyeuristic drives and the moving awareness of something else contained in Madeleine's turn of the head.

This is neither an antivision nor the making visible of something invisible; it is actually an active depiction of something we do see, but our seeing is made different by Madeleine's shift from indirect to direct, forced into a different relation to the screen by the film's practice of breaking the circuit. The pattern of this one scene operates quite analogously to the film's overall narrative/image relation as it too breaks the oedipal circuit of desire over and over by directing it elsewhere, by interrupting us in midinvestment and giving us a glimpse of our misdirection while the cataclysmic gap between what we thought and what we see reveals both desire and an otherness, a something else—like the daughter's perspective and the possibility of Madeleine's look—that has been there all along.

Entre Nous thus suggests one operation of desire in relation to lesbian sexuality that seems to respond to or to embody theoretical formulations of a feminist cinema or at least operates within that economy. In some ways the film is not quite successful: it has been read as slick and cruel, dishonest, unrealistic, and disappointing, as not embodying either a realist or a politically focused feminist aesthetic. But the sense that the film is dishonest may be engendered by its very operation of oedipus interruptus, by its challenge of our viewing expectations.

Entre Nous was released in 1982. From 1987, Patricia Rozema's *I've Heard the Mermaids Singing* employs a similar strategy for detaching narrative and image, but it does so in a more overt, self-conscious, and self-referential way that signals where we've come but also shifts the debate from the relation of narrative, image, and desire to more pointed questions about the relation of image, desire, and sexuality.[43] Overtly alluding to Eliot's mermaid line, the film plays with the two lines taken together: "I've heard the mermaids singing, each to each. I do not think that they will sing to me." The film is as much about the first line as the second, as much about hearing the mermaids as it is about the lack of their address, playing out the aesthetics of lack and desire, not in relation to a narrative that is oedipal with a vengeance, but in the self-reflexive terms of representation itself. By conspicuously connecting art, desire, and sexuality both literally and figuratively, the film explores the relation between desire and image, where images quite literally embody desire and where desire may be satisfied through the creation of images.

The film beings with what appears to be the self-made video autobiography-cum-confession of the protagonist, Polly, an awkward, naive, but lovable "Person Friday" and amateur photographer. The videoed scenes of Polly talking directly into the camera, presumably addressing the audience, frame the narrative, gloss it with an air of authenticity, signal the apparent absence of tricky cinematic production values, and establish a subjective perspective. The videoed segments alternate with more omnisciently filmed scenes of Polly, the gallery curator Gabrielle, for whom Polly works, and Gabrielle's lover, Mary, which replay flashback portions of the story Polly tells into the video camera. These are also interspersed with black and white fantasy segments, clearly a part of Polly's imaginary vision, that present and elaborate upon her desire—her dreams of what she wishes to be. Subjects of each of these three filming techniques are the images that occupy the characters: the paintings Gabrielle collects and sells, the pictures Mary paints, the photographs Polly takes, even the video frame to the film itself. By layering and combining visual media and images of their production, the film not only draws our attention to the fact that all of the images in the film are produced, including the film itself, but it also plays upon our consciousness that the film's images can only be seen indirectly—that they are always mediated by something else. We see Polly's video through the agency of the film, her photos through the video and the film, the paintings through the film, Polly's wish fulfillments through her photographs, which come to life: all seeing is mediated, transformed, interrupted but never direct.

This indirection works as well for the film's narrative, which combines three stories of desire told indirectly through the framing medium of Polly's video. Polly, whose humble ambitions are altered by the surreptitious view of a love scene between Gabrielle and Mary, falls in love with Gabrielle. As she says, "I think I kind of fell in love with the curator. I know love is a pretty strong word when you're talking about another woman and she isn't your mother," and later: "Gosh, you know, sometimes I think my head is like a gas tank. You have to be really careful what you put into it because it might just affect the whole system." Gabrielle's desire is to be a great painter, an ambition she confesses to Polly in a drunken stupor after her birthday party. But in her confession it is clear that Gabrielle comprehends the mechanism of desire: she aches to do what she knows she can never do, a lesson Polly has not yet learned. Mary, who is able to create beautiful images, merely desires Gabrielle; she is the one who is successful, not because her desire is fulfillable, but because she understands best the value of unfulfilled desire, of settling for what pleases her. Art as the creation of beauty is what seems to satisfy all three. If Polly can be a good enough photographer, she can gain the admiration and even the love of Gabrielle, who admires beautiful images. If Gabrielle could create beautiful images, she would find meaning in her life. Mary knows that images are like the mermaids' song; because she would be content to listen, she understands the relation of image and desire. Perhaps the most important ploy connected to the play of image and desire is the film's consistent denial of the beautiful images. We see Mary's paintings as panels of light, certainly a wonderful metaphor for their quality, but also a configuration of the denial of our desire to see.

Even as the images are represented indirectly by the film's layered media, so their sources are also misattributed in the film's narratives, a misdirection that creates the conflict among the three plots. Polly sends samples of her photographs to Gabrielle under an assumed name; Gabrielle rejects them as "trite made flesh," an evaluation that wounds Polly's nascent ambitions. Gabrielle shows Polly Mary's paintings, but as her own. Loving Polly mistakes Gabrielle's guilt for shyness and steals one of the paintings to put on display at the gallery. By the time Gabrielle discovers that Polly has acted on her claim of authorship a review of the painting is in press. She is stuck with the false position of being the creator of Mary's paintings. Even the unraveling of the mistaken attributions creates another misperception. After Polly, eavesdropping again, overhears Gabrielle and Mary's discussion of Gabrielle's unwarranted celebrity, Polly angrily throws hot tea into Gabrielle's face. Polly says later, "How was I supposed to know it was hot tea?"

It is evident also that desire and image are imbricated with sexuality. The drive to produce images is connected to the desire for love and to sexual attraction. In one scene, as Polly and Mary discuss

Polly's rejected photo, Mary calls Polly's snide recitation of Gabrielle's original assessment "harsh" and says further, "What's good? What if it's a shot of someone this photographer just loves to distraction? Isn't that a good thing?" Polly replies, "Like you love the curator?" Like Mary's beautiful paintings imaged as panels of light, full-blown representations of overt lesbian sexual behavior are denied. In a metacommentary on voyeurism, what we want most to see is disallowed, cut off, evaporated the moment before we see it. The videoed scene of Gabrielle and Mary in the gallery is perhaps the clearest configuration of the relation between voyeurism and the imaging of lesbian sexual behavior.

Through the video camera embedded in the head of the statue of a woman, Polly is able to watch Gabrielle and Mary's discussion of what turns out to be their frankly sexual relationship. Indirectly imaged through the medium of the video, the scene is as much about Polly and her desire and discomfort in watching. While in the *Entre Nous* mirror scene our position as voyeur is comprehended by film convention, in this scene Polly's comical choice between curiosity and propriety points to the whole scene's construction of a voyeuristic moment and the conscious consumption of what the narrative promises will be a sexual image. Even from the beginning of the scene, however, our pleasure is thwarted. We hear only snatches of conversation; our view of the scene is interrupted by shots of Polly watching. The sexual moment of the scene is constructed by the increasing intensity of Mary and Gabrielle's conversation and by the gradual erasure of distance as the two move closer to the camera. Finally, even Mary's eyes are directed off-screen toward Gabrielle, who has walked out of the frame. When the culminating kiss comes, it is frustratingly off-screen, represented only by a shadow on Mary's face. Again left out of the circuit, disappointed at the moment all is to be visually fulfilled, we, like Polly, strain to the edges of the screen to see what has been denied. But that the screen cannot contain the image is a literal clue to how lesbian sexuality and beautiful images can be imaged in relation to desire. In this film they can only exist beyond the limits of the screen: extraordinary, they are literally off-screen, beyond the frame of film. What remains on the screen, as so eloquently happens here, is the image of denied desire conflated with seeing as Polly strains to see around the edge of the monitor.

The end of the *Mermaid* film reiterates this aesthetic playing with limits. The film itself seems to end. Credits begin to roll as Polly is finishing her video confession. But when she is done, she does not turn off the camera. We witness the arrival of Gabrielle and Mary, who admire Polly's photographs and accompany Polly out a door at the back of the scene, a door that opens up into the noncontiguous space of a beautiful autumn scene that has never been there before. We cannot follow. The film that has gone beyond its limits shows us the limits of cinematic representation, sustaining desire in the place where we can no longer see.

Going one step further than *Entre Nous*, *I've Heard the Mermaids Singing* dissects the alignment of image, desire, narrative, and sexuality, not by frustrating oedipal hopes, but by showing the mechanism of voyeurism on a grander scale, by exposing the nature of our investment in image, not just in images of sexuality, but in images—in representation—as the root of and answer to desire. That the film focuses on the narrative of a lesbian love triangle creates the parallel between its configuration of lesbian sexuality and the song of the mermaids to which its title alludes. Lesbian sexuality, like images of beauty and desire, though all are clearly present, sustains desire by giving us only the shadow, the hint of a kiss almost expressed and expressed in its almost-expressedness. Like Mary's paintings, whose impenetrable light is an indirect expression of incredible beauty, lesbian sexuality is made to configure what we understand because our vision is indirect, denied and not, suggested but not consumed. It is the mermaids' song. But perhaps unlike Eliot's rather oedipal poem, the song, this measure of desire, is all in the hearing rather than in the address.

What this suggests about questions of representation, feminist practice, and representing a female perspective is that our analysis has been limited to a rather monolithic notion of representation as direct and tangible in the same way that our ideas of sexuality and sexual difference have tended to be heterosexual. The closest we get to a kind of indirection or representation enacted by the interplay of presence, almost-present, and absent is the aesthetic of metacritical analysis and awareness. But such analyses, because they are premised on two terms: presence and absence—what's there and what's not— have difficulty taking a kind of shifting or secondary presence into account. This other measure of desire, though we know it is there, though it is conveyed, gets lost in our analysis or relegated to the category of paradox, the ultimate configuration of desire. In these films this other measure of desire is a desire for desire, not just a teasing titillation, but a desire enacted by the perpetual interplay of desire and lack.

The configuration of lesbian sexuality as immature and penultimate in soft-core pornography is transformed into a positive practice in these two films. Taking advantage of multiplicity, the films unravel investments to not only expose the relation between desire and viewing that constitutes scopophilia, but also to enact a different economy of desire. Following the configurations of lesbian sexuality through pornography, mainstream films, and more alternative films reveals the very defensiveness of the culture and the media that employ lesbian sexuality in vastly different ways but in relatively the same configuration. This tells us more about film practice than it does about lesbian sexuality as it reveals itself in the lesbian moments.

TWO

"This Is Not for You": The Sexuality of Mothering

*"T*HIS IS *not for you": the daughter's paradox of the sexual mother, the punch line of her narrative of identity and differentiation. "This," the mother's desire, "is" for a moment within your grasp, knowledge, experience, but passes on, over you, "not for you." Knowing it, you cannot have it. The story of your own desire generates theories of a barely remembered fusionary peace—preverbal, preoedipal, utopian, innocent—the paradoxical sexuality of genderless innocence swathing the threatened incestuous homosexuality of the mother-daughter bond. In the sanctity of remembered beginnings, in their representation, which is all we can ever know, "This is not for you" becomes "This was once for you," a way of admitting and denying the loss of the mother's desire, of living on with her, of fulfilling a continued wish with imagined traces of "already was" in the perpetual, impossible, illusive circularity of origins.*

• • •

But "This is not for you" also begets a lesbian story: the tale of desire for desire. Here "this" is, but you cannot have it; "this" is directed elsewhere. Its presence proclaims and defers the loss that generates desire; its persistent denial provokes the desire that would be extinguished by its fulfillment. The paradox of "This is not" is the wish fulfilled by its nonfulfillment, like

Freud's Witty Butcher's Wife's dream. While the wish for the mother is unfilled, the wish for an unfulfilled desire—the desire for desire—is sustained. Instead of evoking memories of edenic joinder, the second explication of "This is not for you" casts the daughter's dilemma as a perpetually present absence. The mother is both there and not, sighted but always out of reach.

The two previous parables are both stories of desire I distilled from heterosexual and lesbian narratives of mother-daughter relationships. In this chapter, I want to trace these stories of desire through their sources, first through presumptively heterosexually premised analyses: Julia Kristeva's various accounts of the psychosocial operation of the mother and Nancy Chodorow's *The Reproduction of Mothering,* and then through the two more or less typical contemporary lesbian novels, Rita Mae Brown's *Rubyfruit Jungle* and Jane Rule's *This Is Not for You.* The purpose of this comparison is to see, insofar as desire is imbricated in narrative, whether there is a difference between female heterosexual and lesbian narratives of the mother, what that difference is, and how that difference might help characterize mainstream representations of female heterosexual and lesbian desire.

To arrive at these parables of desire, I am making certain assumptions and choices. Since I am perplexed by what I see as a paradoxical relation between mothering theory as represented by Kristeva and Chodorow and the absence of the mother in lesbian novels, understanding that contradiction means comparing the dissimilar forms of argumentative analysis and fiction. I assume that despite their differences in purpose and style, both genres provide symptomatic narratives that reveal something about how the combination of the mother/daughter relation, desire, and sexual preference is represented. Even though Kristeva's and Chodorow's analyses are attempts to identify and explain broad cultural representations of the mother, they are also narrative depictions of the maternal phenomenon they are analyzing. Similarly, while portraying lesbian experience, Brown's and Rule's novels are also representations of a mother-daughter relation, though the mother is most often missing. Since narrative inscribes desire (another assumption) and since these narratives also overtly describe desire, these four narratives are double inscriptions of desire: the desire that shapes the narrative and the desire described by the narrative. I also assume that this narrative desire reflects sexual preference, though desire and sexuality are not coterminous. By comparing different inflections of desire as they operate in these two strains of narrative, we might understand why lesbian and heterosexual versions of mother-daughter history seem incongruous, what kinds of desire and self-perception are embedded in these two versions of mother-daughter history, and how they might help define the relation, if any, between sexual preference and narrative.

The Sexuality of Mothering

JULIA KRISTEVA and Nancy Chodorow confront and circumscribe the image of the mother to understand the mother's psychic and social functions. Starting from the imagined experience of the infant daughter, both Kristeva and Chodorow return to origins as the beginning of the story: to the infant's preoedipal maternal origin and to their own syllogistic source in Sigmund Freud's theories of infantile sexuality. Freud's hypothesis of an infantile sexuality eroticizes the mother-infant relationship, and like Freud, both Kristeva and Chodorow assert and deny this sexuality. Described by Freud as fragmented autoeroticism, infantile sexuality is aimed toward a self not yet formed, toward disconnected sites—oral and "sadistic-anal"—that are not yet " 'masculine' or 'feminine.' "[1] But this autoeroticism is not a solo performance: the mother (in Western culture, at least) is the primary source of the stimuli that produce infantile sexual excitation. The paradox of this infant sexuality is, however, that it develops *before* both identity formation and the infant's recognition of sexual difference; therefore, for the infant this is a kind of asexual sexuality, while the mother of the pair is a gendered, sexual being. For Freud, who views from the perspective of the male child, the mother's entry into the infant's fragmented world establishes around her the primal paths of adult sexuality. For Kristeva and Chodorow, who see from the mother's perspective, the lack of differentiation, sexual and not, is the safe place before the trouble starts.

The trouble is sexual difference, associated with the infant's growing capacity to differentiate itself. Sexual difference sexualizes sexuality, outlaws the incestuous mother/child duo, and begins to organize the infant's scattered autoerotic drives. At this point of differentiation Kristeva and Chodorow both diverge from Freud—at the point, not so coincidentally, of what Jacques Lacan terms "the mirror stage," the phase in an infant's development when it is able to begin to perceive its own illusory future mastery or integrated wholeness, the place where it can imagine its separateness.[2] In Lacan's formulation this period not only presages a concept of a separate self, it also initiates the child into history. The mirror stage is where perceptions of history begin—the child's, Freud's trajectory of human sexual development, Kristeva's psycho-semiotic investigations of motherhood, and Chodorow's theory of the circular reproduction of gender roles.

This mirror stage point of beginning—a second origin—is actually in the middle of a chronology, though it is the point from which we are able to see the first origin. The mirror stage thus defies chronology and becomes the origin of the origin. Operating in a temporal dialectic, the infant anticipates a future wholeness that enables a recognition of a previous chaos and fragmentation *as* chaos and fragmentation. The celebrated preoedipal lack of differentiation is actually a perceptual product of differentiation, both sexual and individual. The chaos only recognized by virtue of the passage through the mirror stage with its concomitant introductions to both sexual difference and castration/loss is the same as the utopian, nostalgic lack of differentiation seen by Kristeva as outside language—the chora, the semiotic—and seen by Chodorow as essentially feminine, clinging to the female throughout her adult life. Both Kristeva's and Chodorow's accounts of mothering, then, have the understandable but impossible impetus of a desire to return to a pre–mirror stage, preoedipal, pregendered world. Caught, as they inevitably and paradoxically are, in a post-mirror stage world, their ancient histories are actually generated from the misrecognitions of an inescapably gendered grid. While language and thought can only come from the point of the mirror stage forward, the third contradiction—that the origin of the origin is not original—inevitably and retrospectively revises representations of preoedipal chaos that becomes paradoxically and problematically gendered after the fact.

Their divergence from Freudian psychoanalysis and Lacanian psychoanalysis to gender the preoedipal at this point is telling; since both Kristeva and Chodorow premise their revisions of the maternal role upon psychoanalytic conceptions of identity, gender, and development, it is around this theoretical point of mirror stage separation from the mother that they too separate to devise what appear to be fuller, more attentive, less phallus-dependent accounts of the mother-daughter relation that make more operative the oft-ignored preoedipal. But the way their revised narratives diverge from more masculine-centered theory is also significant: both tend to assume, perhaps because of their reliance upon a preoedipal homosexual bond with the mother, a far more homogeneously heterosexual female identity than either Freud or Lacan. Paradoxically, this means both that the relative heterosexism of their narratives becomes all the more visible when read against the accounts of Freud and Lacan and that Freud and Lacan tend to represent more fully what might be read as a lesbian narrative. This is not to claim Freud and Lacan as lesbian revisionists, but it does explain why both, but particularly Lacan, better accommodate nonheterosexual positions in their formulations.[3]

That the preoedipal is transformed by the "trouble" of sexual difference generates the heterosexual structures that make the sexualized mother and the reproduction of mothering a problem. In *Revolution in Poetic Language*, Julia Kristeva essentially reiterates the temporal contradictions of this paradoxical structure by postulating these two points of origin—the preoedipal and post-mirror stage conceptions of history—as two coexisting, inseparable, metaphorical modalities. The first is the semiotic "chora," a concept borrowed from Plato, connected to the maternal body, and characterized by the same motifs of fragmentation and lack of differentiation attributed to the preoedipal. Kristeva describes the chora "as rupture and articulations (rhythm), preced[ing] evidence, verisimilitude, spatiality, and temporality" (26). The other modality, the "symbolic," chronologically succeeds the semiotic but, like the mirror stage, precedes all representation, including representations of the semiotic. Connected to law, syntax, and language, the symbolic "is a social effect of the relation to the other, established through the objective constraints of biological (including sexual) differences and concrete historical family structures" (29). Simply, the chora is the preoedipal, the prelinguistic, but like pre-mirror stage chaos, can only be recognized once the ideas of separation and wholeness have been imagined in a relation to another person perceived as separate. The chora reiterates the representational paradox of the preoedipal: it cannot be until it cannot be, but yet, according to Kristeva, it still is. Wanting to sustain the chora and its maternal matrix, Kristeva posits the simultaneous survival of both modalities, made possible by the chora's continued amorphous atemporality. The chora can have a place within the symbolic because by definition it is placeless.

Like Freud in his formulations of infantile sexuality, Kristeva connects this preoedipal phase with the mother and, via the mother, links the semiotic and the symbolic:

> Drives involve pre-Oedipal semiotic functions and energy discharges that connect and orient the body to the mother. . . . The oral and anal drives, both of which are oriented and structured around the mother's body, dominate this sensorimotor organization. The mother's body is therefore what mediates the symbolic law organizing social relations and becomes the ordering principle of the semiotic *chora*, which is on the path of destruction, aggressivity, and death. (27–28)

The mother, then, is the undifferentiated other around whom are organized the primitive paths of sexual excitation. But at the point of Kristeva's description where the mother meets the chora is a footnote that veils that which "situates" the mother "in space": the phallus. The transition point between semiotic and symbolic is achieved in metaphorically gendered terms; the mother becomes the phallic mother in an apparent gender paradox symptomatic of the symbolic's rendering of the chora. But in the symbolic process of depicting this breach in the symbolic—the chora—the mother fixes, hardens, becomes herself the site of the shift between semiotic and symbolic as well as the signifier of the daughter's inevitable path to a heterosexual conclusion figured by the transformation of the relationship from one between a mother and a daughter to one between a phallic mother and a daughter. This phallic mother is posed against the surviving non- or not yet phallic mother who is also associated with the chora and the preoedipal. For Kristeva, the mother, phallic and not, and her body, which "mediates the symbolic law" (27), becomes *the* location of the mirror stage temporal paradox, containing within motherhood more than one mother, extending her oscillating matrices from preoedipal to post–mirror stage, becoming the other of the mirror who ultimately injects sexual difference retrospectively back into representations of the semiotic. While the phallus can be construed as power rather than as a signifier of gender (or as both at the same time), Kristeva tends to slip into the terminology of sexual difference at this transitional point in the maternal matrix.[4]

This same system of interpenetrating gendered oppositions is politicized in Kristeva's other 1974 work, *About Chinese Women*. To characterize the "lens" through which she views Chinese culture, Kristeva reiterates in starker terms the tensions between the chora and the symbolic, the preoedipal and the oedipal, situating their paradoxical interplay as a symptom of the structural centrality of sexual difference in a monotheistic capitalist system. In her brief description of the function of sexual difference in Western culture at the beginning of her book, Kristeva pays disproportionate attention to female homosexuality, a preoccupation that seems unusual in light of the slim space devoted to lesbian sexuality in *Revolution*. Its greater presence is due to its configuration as political regression, as a practical enactment of limiting sexual binariness of the culture. According to Kristeva's description of the development of lesbians in Western culture, a woman can either identify with the mother, appropriate the father, and accede to "the vaginal *jouissance* of heterosexual woman" (28), or identify with the father and repress the vagina. While the heterosexual woman enjoys "a sort of fundamental homosexuality in this preoedipal identification with the mother," the homosexual woman is doomed to play out, in terms of sexual difference, the tragedy of failing to recognize such differences:

> In her fantasy, the girl obtains a real or imaginary penis for herself; and the fantasy penis seems here to be less important than the access she gains to the symbolic dominance which is necessary to censor the pre-Oedipal phase and wipe out the last traces of dependence on the body of the mother. Obliteration of the pre-Oedipal phase, identification with the father and then: 'I am looking, as a man would, for a woman': or else, 'I submit myself, as if I were a man who thought he was a woman, to a woman who thinks she is a man.' Such are the double or triple twists of what we commonly call female homosexuality. (29)

These "twists," which deny the preoedipal, wish, paradoxically, for the preoedipal; their "atemporality," characteristic of the preoedipal, contributes to their "apolitical appeal" (15). The desire for phallic power played out in their development is a political dead-end, creating "the totalitarianism which is the inevitable result of the denial of this [sexual] difference" (15–16) and becoming "theologians of an inverted humanism rather than its iconoclasts" (14). In this sense, then, lesbians become the configuration of revolution gone wrong, where the oppressed become regressive, power-seeking recreators of the status quo.

Contrasted to this rigidly binary logic of sexual difference that crystallizes in Kristeva's description of female homosexuality is the Chinese system, which Kristeva sees as a more fluid, more historically transmuted, less binary system. In her analysis of the historical changes in the relative cultural power of men and women in China, Kristeva credits a basic matricentrism with accession of both men and women to symbolic power. While women in Western culture cannot accede to the symbolic without also acquiescing to the phallic (and the lesbian is the worst case in point), in China an originary reserve of symbolic power enables Chinese women to avoid this phallicization. Chinese culture permits the coexistence of multiple genders and power in the same way that at one time it permitted the coexistence of heterosexuality and female homosexuality. Only during the twentieth century, when sexual difference has become a conscious basis for political action, does lesbian sexuality reemerge as the fleeting by-product of struggles premised, in part, on sexual difference. In this political context, the lesbian is the one who privileges sexual difference while denying it, the one who maintains the status quo and refuses the revolutionary potential of a de-gendered, and hence egalitarian, preoedipal. While this argument is finally explicit in her examination of the relation between maternity and feminist concerns in Maoist China, in the rest of Kristeva's work lesbian sexuality implicitly stands for the error of a separatist feminism gone wrong.

Kristeva continues her study of the semiotic in her essay "Motherhood According to Bellini," where she rereads the semio-symbolic functions of the mother in sociocultural terms as expressed in Italian Renaissance paintings of Madonna and child.[5] Prefiguring Kristeva's own path to the mystical conflation of psychoanalysis, religion, and the maternal that culminates in her 1987 collection of essays, *In the Beginning Was Love: Psychoanalysis and Faith,* Kristeva's notion of motherhood in "Bellini" turns out to be mother as "a thoroughfare, a threshold where 'nature' confronts 'culture.' "[6] At this threshold— this turning point—the "so-called 'Phallic' mother" is necessary because otherwise "every speaker would be led to conceive of its being in relation to some void" (238). Again, though the phallus is not exclusively a signifier for masculinity, Kristeva overphallicizes this phallic mother, who is additionally marked by the phallus in more literal ways—by the law of the father and by the male penis in order to bear a child and become the mother. This phallic mother is posed against that other "choric" motherhood that is "impelled *also* by a nonsymbolic, nonpaternal causality," a "spasm" of "pre-linguistic, unrepresentable memory" (239). What happens in this text is that this "spasm of memory" becomes gendered, becomes feminine, homosexual, lesbian:

> Such an excursion to the limits of primal regression can be phantasmatically experienced as the reunion of a woman-mother with the body of *her* mother. The body of her mother is always the same Master-Mother of instinctual drive, a ruler over psychosis, a subject of biology, but also, one toward which women aspire all the more passionately simply because it lacks a penis: that body cannot penetrate her as can a man when possessing his wife. By giving birth, the woman enters into contact with her mother; she becomes, she is her own mother; they are the same continuity differentiating itself. She thus actualizes the homosexual facet of motherhood, through which a woman is simultaneously closer to her instinctual memory, more open to her own psychosis, and consequently, more negatory of the social, symbolic bond. (239)

After her heterosexual marking, the "woman-mother" regresses into a homosexual facet, which, like the chora, is "a complete absence of meaning and seeing; it is feeling, displacement, rhythm, sound, flashes, and fantasied clinging to the maternal body as a screen against the plunge" (239–240).

In "Bellini" the lesbianism of the daughter-as-mother/mother bond takes the place of the preoedipal daughter/mother unity. It precedes chronologically the "symbolic paternal facet" that both enables the mother/daughter bond in the first place by making the daughter a mother, then permits the speaking of this bonded moment by alleviating the "feminine aphasia" that has afforded a metaphorical defense against "the image of the mother" put up in the place of psychosis, manifested, according to Kristeva, as this preoedipal "paradise lost but seemingly close at hand" (240). The conflation of preoedipal, feminine, homosexual with psychosis and schizophrenia is the effect of a preference for the semiotic in the face of the symbolic—is an effect of the daughter's impossible paradox of origins that can only be known when they are lost. The preoedipal location of this homosexual economy, which derives, again paradoxically, from the fruits—child-bearing—of the heterosexual moment, relegates the homosexual to a preverbal, autoerotic, undifferentiated phase that is seen as both a regression and a stage toward "normal" heterosexual maternity and acquiescence to the primacy of the father and the symbolic. This situates the homosexual economy not only in absence (the void, the nothingness asymmetrically opposed to the being of the phallic mother), but also in the sterile stasis of daughterhood and immaturity where the virgin daughter, again paradoxically, cannot effect the contact with the mother instigated by the daughter's maternity. In Kristeva's heterosexual rendering, the woman can become subject only when she accepts the phallus—both metaphorical and literal—only when she reproduces the image of man where contact with the mother is a phantasmic by-product.

Kristeva, however, is not yet done with the paradox of origins, the chora, motherhood. Reformulating once again the axes between which the pivotal, transitional maternal figure turns in "Stabat Mater," Kristeva sets forth simultaneously two sublime maternal histories: the personal, stream-of-conscious travails of a mother giving birth to a son, and the cultural, sacred history of the mother—the Virgin Mary.[7] Again, two registers—modalities—of the mother, these two stylistically different histories are spliced via the figure of the mother, who, in this essay, arrives at the full mystical paradox of her powers. Characterized by Kristeva as a "fulcrum," the mother has become both the point of separation and its compensation, the place of death and love: "Belief in the mother is rooted in fear, fascinated with a weakness—the weakness of language. If language is powerless to locate myself for and state myself to the other, I assume—I want to believe—that there is someone who makes up for that weakness. Someone, of either sex, *before* the id speaks, before language, who might make me be by means of borders, separations, vertigoes" (251). The mother is the mirror, the agent of separation, as well as the "shield against death. It is only 'normal' for a maternal representation to set itself up at the place of subdued anguish called love" (253).

On either side of the maternal hinge are aligned the familiar Kristevan sets of signifiers, now fully and universally drawn. On the one side are the choralike attributes of the "semiotic": femininity, the body, nonlanguage, the "return of the repressed," "the underhand double of explicit phallic power," the place of the undifferentiated group. On the other, the "symbolic," risen to new spiritual potency: masculinity, singularity, primary narcissism, revelations of God. Between these two modalities, containing both, at this place of the "commonality of the sexes," is the paradox of the mother, now expressed by the figure of the Virgin mother. The mother's paradox, formerly the paradox of chronology and gender, has become exclusively a patriarchal paradox. Part of what Kristeva has been addressing is the phallocratic primacy inherent to an idea like the mirror stage, which seems to privilege mastery and consciousness. Kristeva, however, reiterates the duplicity of this point by making the mother the mirror that sustains rather than subverts singularity.

While the figure of the mother is marked by the phallus, subject to law, virgin means sexually unmarked, but in reference to the same patriarchal grid. Her function is to go "against both of the two sexes," to mediate the two modalities, the two genders, on the level of fantasy, "by setting up a third person," a capitalized and italicized *"Him,"* the unknowable superpatriarch (256–257). This mediation between genders is also a denial of the very fact that makes such mediation impossible: the perception by a woman that another woman is a woman, which disturbs the balanced symmetries of gender. The Virgin Mary, by "suggesting the image of A woman alone as Unique," totally occupies the site of feminine singularity, checking female "longing for uniqueness" by conditioning that uniqueness on a patriarchally inflicted "masochism"—on being like the Virgin Mary (258). Outside of the inaccessible asexual conditions "embodied by the Virgin," outside of a definition in reference to patriarchal categories, there can be no singularity. Singularity is thus appropriated for the masculine side, and both singularity and sexuality become impossible except in reference to the masculine.

Kristeva's final and unarticulated shift to the side of the symbolic —signified even in her sidebar choric lyric of the birth of a son— creates problems for the daughter. Only able to achieve singularity through maternity, women, unless they acquiesce to the masculine, are entangled in the group indistinguishability of the semiotic. The daughter's story is omitted:

> Among things left out of the virginal myth there is the war between
> mother and daughter, a war masterfully but too quickly settled by

promoting Mary as universal and particular, but never singular—as "alone of her sex." . . . a woman seldom (although not necessarily) experiences her passion (love and hatred) for another woman without having taken her own mother's place—without having herself become a mother, and especially without slowly learning to differentiate between same beings—as being face to face with her daughter forces her to do. (261)

Though Kristeva leaves a slim opening in her parenthetical "not necessarily," the daughter cannot generally be separate or singular except as she is able to identify with the mother as same, *as* a mother, then differentiate herself though this face-off with the same, where same refers to gender. Sameness cannot be recognized unless the woman has encountered the difference intrinsic to maternity—the heterosexual encounter with masculinity. Thus armed, she can face off against other women and depart from the undifferentiated semiotic. Reverberating the paradox of the mirror stage yet again, the daughter is caught in a chronological paradox: before she can differentiate herself she can be marked by difference—by the masculine. Once marked by difference she differentiates herself from women. Only retrospectively does she become already a subject and only through phallic agency transmitted through the mother.

The woman who "repudiates" "the other sex (the masculine)" is the woman relegated to undifferentiated sameness where she cannot recognize an "other woman as such." Like the pre-mirror stage infant who cannot recognize chaos per se, without maternity the woman is either destined to a kind of figurative autoeroticism or is subject to the symbolic, linguistic mark of the phallus. Among women:

Women doubtless reproduce among themselves the strange gamut of forgotten body relationships with their mothers. Complicity in the unspoken, connivance of the inexpressible, of a wink, a tone of voice, a gesture, a tinge, a scent. We are in it, set free of our identification papers and names, a computerization of the unnameable. No communication between individuals but connections between atoms, molecules, wisps of words, droplets of sentences. The community of women is a community of dolphins. (257)

If Kristeva's woman should see differences among women—see difference as not necessarily the category of gender—she is marked with a gender difference that removes her from the community: "If the woman aspires to singularity—she is condemned, by other women—as masculine" ("Stabat" 258). Does this not doom the woman who wishes to be singular among women, recognize other women as such, and accede to the subjectivity that enables a nonautoerotic sexuality? Kristeva's use of the term *masculine* is tricky in this context; if masculine means a representational rather than a literal masculine, then she is insightfully observing the representational politics for the depiction of lesbians, as her second use of the term suggests. But her first meaning of masculine as the sex repudiated implies not representation, but biological difference. The woman-to-woman relation is erased in the transition from biology to representation.

A creature of representation, Kristeva's fulcral mother denies this third—this lesbian—possibility, resting as she does on gendered oppositions and differences that coalesce in the figure of the mother: the meeting ground of the sexes. The only way to individuation is through the mother—the figurative mirror stage. For the woman to pass through the mother, she must accept the law of the father—maternity, heterosexuality—or be condemned to a "countercathexis in strong values, in strong *equivalents of power"*: to psychosis, to a "disturbance of the libidinal relation to reality" ("Stabat" 261). The circle of paradox is complete: biology becomes representation becomes a psychotic lack of relation between biology and representation. The homosexual woman refuses to relate properly—heterosexually—to the maternal (hence patriarchal) system; therefore, her libidinal relation to reality is disturbed. She is mad. Discarded, she is omitted from the story.

In Kristeva's rendition of the mother the possibility of female singularity—of women recognizing other women as both singular and female—is what "is not for you." This relegates women to an undifferentiated group from which individuals can escape only via the paternal or the masculine. We can only understand singularity and gender once we have acceded to the symbolic law, both metaphorically and literally linked by Kristeva to the masculine. In the semiotic, the community of women relate, but they cannot recognize themselves as women. The story's nostalgia resides in this place of sameness among women: it is a nostalgia for a loss of individuation seen as the return to the fullness and fulfillment of the group. But a permanent stay in the preoedipal feminine is neither possible nor desirable for Kristeva, since there is specifically no place for difference—and hence any interrelationship—among the perforce homosexual females there. What is not, then, for the reader of Kristeva is the lesbian's story, a story Kristeva sees as a nonstory, the most impossible, extreme example of choric claustrophobia. But despite the impossibility of Kristeva's lesbian configuration, it is the necessary joint of her argument; the undifferentiated community is source and ground for the configuration of femininity that departs from and, postpartum, returns to it.

Nor might the reader of Nancy Chodorow's *The Reproduction of Mothering* find a lesbian story. Like Kristeva, Chodorow is interested in representations of mothering. But rather than examining psychocultural representations of motherhood as Kristeva does, Chodorow explores how the mother herself represents gender and mothering to her daughter, thereby reproducing attitudes about gender and inculcating mothering roles in the daughter. Whereas Kristeva's mother is the turning point, embodying the mirror stage paradox of plenitude and loss, love and death, the mediation between genders, Chodorow's mother is an active messenger to the preoedipal, conveying gender codes to an as-yet-undifferentiated infant. These gender messages and the mother's differing perspective toward sons and daughters operate asymmetrically on them, producing in the son the "masculine" characteristics of independence and creating a longer-lasting, more ambivalent bond with the daughter in ways that reproduce exactly the gender ideologies of the culture. And for Chodorow gender is clearly the primary factor inflecting both psychological and social development: "Because they are the same gender as their daughters and have been girls, mothers of daughters tend not to experience these infant daughters as separate from them in the same way as do mothers of infant sons" (109).

Chodorow's mother as agent of gender quite literally reiterates the mirror stage retrospective genderment of the preoedipal. Via the mother the infant is always already gendered, its psychological trajectory determined primarily by the fact of this gendering. Chodorow assumes that infants will automatically internalize their mother's gendering of them, even before they can perceive themselves as differentiated from her. This "always already" gendered self helps Chodorow account for the asymmetries in male/female development via the Oedipus complex:

My reading of the psychoanalytic account of the feminine oedipus complex suggests that the asymmetrical structure of parenting generates a feminine oedipus complex with particular characteristics. Because mothers are the primary love object and object of identification for children of both genders, and because fathers come into the relational picture later and differently, the oedipus complex in girls is characterized by the continuation of preoedipal attachments and preoccupations, sexual oscillation in an oedipal triangle, and the lack of either absolute change of love object or absolute oedipal resolution. (133–134)

In her reading of the Oedipus complex, Chodorow introduces the issue of sexuality, occulting, however, all sexual variations except heterosexuality as the inevitable culmination of the daughter's "oscillations." On the one hand mother/daughter sexuality, suggested as one side of this oscillation, is dangerous, leading to a threatening incest: "Given the organization of parenting, mother-son and mother-*daughter* incest are the major threats to the formation of new families . . . and not, equivalently, mother-son and *father*-daughter incest. Mother-daughter incest may be the most 'socially regressive,' in the sense of a basic threat to species survival . . ." (132). On the other hand, because she assumes that mothering—conceiving a child—is the act of a heterosexual woman (instead of the heterosexual act of a woman), she limits her examination of mother-daughter relations only to the reproduction of heterosexual daughters. She is concerned "with the kind of social and intrapsychic relational situation in which . . . heterosexuality and . . . identifications get constituted" (113). The effect of this limitation, of course, is the creation of another circular reproduction of the reproduction she is exposing.

And the dangerous spot in this, the blind spot of Chodorow's "dream of asymmetry," is the implied homosexuality of the mother-daughter bond, an implication she symptomatically omits. The lesbian daughter is the one example that does not prove her case, and yet the lesbian daughter is an obvious result of the psycho-social structure she elaborates. Because in her model the mother injects gender into her relationships with her children, any sexuality between mother and child shifts from the autoeroticism of Freud's undifferentiated infant to the potentially incestuous relation between two gendered beings. In the case of the daughter, Chodorow describes these erotic investments as "bisexual" and further avoids any lesbian implications by defining this bisexuality as the daughter's "emotional, if not erotic, bisexual oscillation between mother and father—between preoccupation with 'mother-child' issues [presumably the homosexual side] and 'male-female' issues" (168).[8] The few times Chodorow raises the issue of the mother as a primary love object for the daughter, her elaborations follow Freud's torturous path to the father, the vagina, and "normal" heterosexuality. As in Kristeva's work, the daughter's path is triangulated through the father; her love for mother coexists with and is made safe by a competing love for the father. What is dangerous in Chodorow's account, and what she studiously avoids, is not so much mother-daughter incest, but the possibility of its exclusivity, the possibility that such exclusivity might prevent the reproduction of mothering.

In fact, Chodorow deliberately has very little to say about those who escape being reproduced as heterosexual women. In her account, mother-daughter sexuality is clearly part of the path toward heterosexuality. She discounts that both mothers and daughters may not be heterosexual. In a note, she confesses that she ignores the possible effects of a lesbian mother, since her scenario is completely dependent on the "fact" of heterosexuality: "Part of what I am talking about also presumes a different kind of cathexis of daughter and son deriving from her [the mother's] heterosexuality" (110*n*). Though her reference to a specific "cathexis" deriving from the mother's heterosexuality suggests that there may be other possible cathexes that obtain from a mother with a different sexuality, Chodorow's conception of mothers assumes a dominant heterosexual notion of maternity that necessarily takes place within clearly patriarchal organizations. For Chodorow the term *mother* refers to father, even if father is absent and even if mother has no relation to him. Maternity is unquestionably the site of the merging of sexual differences, even if that merging occurs only as an exchange of genetic material. In this patriarchal scenario, heterosexuality (conflated with heterogeneity) creates maternity, which is then the effect of a paternal cause. If, however, the mother were not predefined as heterosexual, if her maternity were not necessarily created by paternity, then the cycle by which heterosexual maternity is endlessly reproduced may be stopped. If we detach maternity from heterosexuality, it also disengages from the strictly familiar versions of the oedipal complex, leaving not chaos, but a repositioning of maternity outside the nuclear, familial, patriarchal organization with which it has been inevitably associated and by which it has been defined as a position and a relation more than as an activity. Conceiving mothering as an activity makes it a function rather than the fate of a gender. And if it is a function, then mothers can be (and are) lesbian, adoptive, unmarried, celibate, sterile, grand-mothers, aunts, hired nannies, or males. In any case, heterosexuality may well reproduce the mother rather than the other way around.

Chodorow also rarely acknowledges that lesbian daughters are gen-erated in this heterosexual paradigm, a fact that might bring the whole model into question, or at least her insistence on a heterosexual effect. The only time she uses the term "lesbian," she dismisses the relationship with an evasive reference to social pressure:

> Deep affective relationships to women are hard to come by on a routine, daily, ongoing basis for many women. Lesbian relationships do tend to recreate mother-daughter emotions and connections, but most women are heterosexual. This heterosexual preference and ta-boos against homosexuality, in addition to objective economic depen-dence on men, make the option of primary sexual bonds with other women unlikely—though more prevalent in recent years. (200)

This passage reveals the paradox of Chodorow's own reproduction of mothering. Dependent upon sexual difference as a preexistent con-struct, women are already what they are destined to be. Already heterosexual, daughters strain against the imprisoning exclusivity of their bond with their mothers, who because of gender sameness keep their daughters locked in a more dependent bond that results in the daughter becoming a mother like the mother—what the mother has already seen her to be. And all of this is somehow dependent upon the lesbian nature of the bond between mother and female infant, the survival of which is prevented by the mother's reproduction of moth-ering.

What kinds of desire reside in these circular and paradoxical narra-tives? Both Kristeva and Chodorow set up contradictory, interreliant wishes: a desire for differentiation enabled by encounters with sexual difference and a nostalgic wish for preoedipal unity with the mother. The coexistence of these wishes, like the coexistence of the semiotic and the symbolic, enables the illusion of a potential wholeness and fulfillment dependent upon an oscillation between preoedipal memory (the dream of the mother) and sexual differentiation (becoming a mother). The paradox that founds this oscillating structure is the temporal paradox of the mirror stage, where the nostalgic wish for unity with the mother can only be realized when it is no longer possible. Nostalgia for the mother becomes an unfulfillable desire that is nonetheless fulfillable via memory and representation—through Kristeva's chora. This fulfillable unfulfillable wish is displaced into a fulfillable wish—the desire for a child. And this wish for maternity encapsulates the mirror stage paradox: by becoming a mother, the daughter can simultaneously identify—rejoin—with her mother, enjoy the differentiation endowed by her patriarchal marking, and enjoy a placental unity with her own child. Maternity has it all. Or does it?

Desire here is a circular wish that is desired, then fulfilled, then desired, then fulfilled in a cycle of deprivation and illusory gratification, very much like what Lacan, in an analysis of desire, defines as "neither the appetite for satisfaction, nor the demand for love, but the difference resulting from the subtraction of the first from the second, the very phenomenon of their splitting."[9] In the narratives of both Kristeva and Chodorow, the figure of the mother occupies the point of this splitting, figuring, in fact, desire itself. What is split by the mother is the "appetite for satisfaction" or the fulfillable desire to become a mother and the "demand for love" or urge to return to the mother. When the desire to become a mother is subtracted from the desire for the mother, an unfulfillable wish—the nostalgic desire for preoedipal unity with the mother—remains. This leftover desire is what Kristeva answers with her hypothesis of an identificatory unity between daughter-as-mother and her own mother, which asserts a projected memory of mother/daughter unity in the place of desire. The paradoxical presence of the past drives the cycle of desire, which flirts with fulfillment, circling from current sexual difference to past sameness, touching base with the phallus in order to go back.

Kristeva celebrates this cycle, but Chodorow critiques it, seeing it as an imprisoning desire generated by the mother.[10] In her doubts about mother/daughter interdependence, Chodorow seems to want to remove the unfulfillable wish for the mother and replace it completely with maternity itself as the site of daughterly independence and the place of the fulfillable wish. Denying the desire for desire in favor of an illusory dream of heterosexual fulfillment, Chodorow fixes finally on the father instead of the mother. She wants to break the cycle of the reproduction of mothering by redefining mothering as parenting —by inserting the father into the frustrating, desire-generating mother/ daughter duo. With this solution, Chodorow displaces the nostalgic "demand for love" and its unfulfillable desire for the mother entirely into marriage, making both disappear into a heterosexuality that promises the illusion of fulfillment. But unable to get rid of the desire "remainder," that desire, repressed, returns in her constant celebrations of the preoedipal moment. While her analysis places the mother/ daughter preoedipal relation as the source of the reproduction of mothering, it also constantly returns nostalgically to this moment as one of peace and harmony. For Chodorow, as for Kristeva, the memory of the mother stands in the place of desire.

The Absent Mother, or the Desire for Desire

IF HETEROSEXUAL scenarios of maternity play on an illusion of maternal fulfillment, many lesbian novels focus on the remainder—on the desire for desire. Lesbian protagonists in a number of lesbian novels have no mother, nor are they likely to be mothers. The absence of a biological mother in a remarkable number of lesbian novels (Rita Mae Brown's *Six of One*, Jane Rule's *The Desert of the Heart*, Colette's *Claudine* novels, Isabel Miller's *Patience and Sarah*, Alice Walker's *The Color Purple*, to name only a few) denies from the start the nostalgic wish and maternal fulfillment of Kristeva's and Chodorow's stories, since from the very beginning there has been no mother. Lack of mother means lack of origins and vice versa. Beginning, instead, in media res, after mirror stage differentiation, lesbian novels avoid a mirror stage temporal paradox in favor of confounding post–mirror stage history itself, by denying the importance of origins, even as the protagonists seem to return to them.

This Is Not for You (1970) and *Rubyfruit Jungle* (1973) are prototypical lesbian novels, characteristic of a genre that typically recounts more or less realistic fictional histories of the development of a lesbian protagonist or the course of lesbian relationships. *This Is Not for You* is a chronicle of the relationship between the first-person narrator, Kate George, and her beloved but difficult friend, Esther Woolf. Borrowing from the literary conventions of autobiography and epistolary novel, *This Is Not for You* is a retrospective account of why a romantic, sexual relationship between Kate and Esther never occurs. Kate explains the failure as the triumph of her own self-denial and her unwillingness to take advantage of the compliant but naive Esther. Beginning after Esther has cloistered herself in a convent, Kate begins to recount their history from the start of their association as college roommates to trace their fifteen-year friendship, ostensibly because she likes "to remember" (4). The ensuing narrative does more than merely reiterate history; while recording the relationship between Kate and Esther, it also reveals the fruitlessness of looking to the past for answers to questions of character and motivation. Only in the most limited sense are either character's antecedents—Kate's American mixed white and Native American ancestry and Esther's wealthy lapsed Jewish one—relevant to the aesthetics of self-denial that rule the novel.

Rubyfruit Jungle is a bildungsroman, the first-person history of the life of Molly Bolt, who, like Kate George, is an illegitimate child of mixed ancestry (French and American) living with adoptive parents. The chronicle of a lesbian's gradual self-discovery, *Rubyfruit* follows Molly through childhood moves from Pennsylvania to Florida, her first high school loves, her truncated Florida college career, her adventures in New York City, and her final return to Florida to film her adoptive mother. While the chronicle leads away from and back to Molly's origins, like *This Is Not for You*, *Rubyfruit* ultimately reveals their meaninglessness as any explanation for anything other than Molly's physical attributes. Instead, the novel focuses on the exploits of the assertive, inventive Molly, whose personality is a given rather than something to be analyzed.

In both novels, the paradox of the lesbian story begins with the novels' adoption of the mode of personal history. These lesbian novels represent the lesbian character as an orphan, as illegitimate, with mixed parentage, no original relationship with a biological mother, and no link to a patriarchally blessed beginning. Because, however, lesbian novels are posed as histories or bildungsromans, the lack of origins posited at the outset in the protagonist's orphan status would seem to make the answer to the mystery of that origin a partial explanation of the character, as it does in *Jane Eyre* and *Bleak House*."[11] But in both *This Is Not for You* and *Rubyfruit Jungle*, while genetic origins seem to be important, they turn out to be irrelevant. The lesbian narrative severs the connection between present and past and eliminates the past—the origin—as any useful explanation for the present. Sexual preference is thus detached from origins, either biological or psychological; no implicit or explicit connection is ever made between the lack of biological mother and the protagonist's sexual preference except by Molly's adoptive mother. These lesbian fictional histories thus exist in a paradoxical relation to any notion of history; origin denied or useless, the lesbian novel traces a history with no beginning urged by a desire for a total picture already defined as unfulfillable. The failure of origins to answer the questions of history in lesbian novels suggests that origins themselves are lures away from the "key" or solution to the character, which exists some-where else—perhaps always already there. On one hand, the novels trace history; on the other, they declare that history finally cannot explain either character or sexuality.

The uselessness of—and ambivalence about—origins threads its way through both novels. In Rule's story, Kate's particular brand of self-denying self-sufficiency might be read psychologically as her re-sponse to her lack of origins, though Kate claims that her origins were made irrelevant: "I had my own stories to tell, being the illegitimate child of an Indian woman and a white man, a half-breed, adopted by an Episcopal minister and his wife who had already raised their own daughter. . . . My background was never mentioned to me by my adoptive parents on the theory that I was to be made to feel no separation from them. And I half forgot it myself, growing up in the world given to me" (11). Only half-forgotten by the "half-breed" Kate, this anonymous and illegitimate background might seem to incite Kate to an overcompensatory solitude, as if her background exists to make her feel separation rather than no separation at all. She almost but never quite hints that it is a factor in her behavior. In the end, Kate does not link her background or lack thereof to her lesbi-anism or to her moral choices or to the particular quirk in her person-ality that enables her to delight in an unfulfilled wish.

Molly Bolt also tantalizes us with a suspiciously nonchalant attitude about her lack of parents. She begins the novel in an apparently defensive analysis of the importance of origins: "No one remembers her beginnings. Mothers and aunts tell us about infancy and early childhood, hoping we won't forget the past when they had total control over our lives and secretly praying that because of it, we'll include them in our future. I didn't know anything about my own beginnings until I was seven years old . . ." (3). Her cynical denial of memory is suspect, especially since the novel traces Molly from childhood to adulthood, when she returns home in what appears to be a quest for own history. For Molly, origins are false harbingers; the novel itself both parodies and critiques the ultimate importance of those things "no one remembers." One clue to this parody is that the event that elicits mention of her origins is Molly's thriving business exhibiting her friend's odd penis. Her adoptive mother credits Molly's behavior to her illegitimacy, offering, in her simplistic way, the theory of "like mother, like daughter" in the category of sexual behavior. With her adoptive mother so obviously wrong in her estimation of the effects of heredity, Molly perceives herself as self-created, taking only the genetic advantage of her unknown parentage. Even when Molly returns to discover that her father was a French Olympic athlete, we find that heredity has made no difference in her choices, behaviors, or personality and that ultimately it is her own determination and fortitude—her "self-madeness"—that has made the difference.

But while the protagonists have no memories of their biological mothers and though the identities of these mothers provide only superficial antecedents to their daughter's physical attributes, in both novels the daughters either are told or know about the rudimentary facts of their birth mothers' circumstances. Kate's and Molly's biological mothers are both heterosexual outlaws; Kate's Native American mother bears a child begotten with a white man, and Molly's mother, an unruly, rebellious girl, conceives Molly, out of wedlock, with a "foreigner." In each case, the mother's sexuality is suspect; indubitably heterosexual, these mothers break patriarchal rules of propriety. The disappearance of these overly sexed mothers and the absence and distance of adoptive mothers does break any cycle by which mothering (and heterosexuality) is reproduced. Posed not as causes of their daughters' lesbian sexuality, but rather as reasons for their motherlessness, the mothers' active sexuality and patriarchal transgressions are remote precursors of their daughters' lesbian desire.

This paradox of history and origins in lesbian novels is related to and perhaps creates and sustains a similar paradoxical structure of desire that typifies lesbian accounts. While the drive of conventional history is to know, lesbian fictional histories frustrate the possibility of total knowledge and define the desire for mastery as unfulfillable from the start. Not fulfilling the desire to know sustains desire, continues it so that desire, like history, is a paradox: to desire is to desire not to have a desire fulfilled; it is the desire for an unfulfilled desire.

This Is Not for You is replete with paradoxes: the paradoxical desire for an unfulfilled desire, the protagonist's desire for Esther, and the protagonist's depiction and sustenance of desire in her writing. As the history of an unfulfilled relationship (as opposed, for example, to the story of unrequited love), Kate's account embodies a desire for Esther that is never explicit, but assumed almost from the beginning. This desire is textual, created and sustained by a narrative shaped in the quest to understand this desire, which is not directly depicted. For example, near the beginning of Kate's retrospective, she explains what she is not explaining by describing how she could not confess her feelings, which remain unnamed: "If I had been a little older, a little less frightened, I might at least have been able to sit down, let my feet dangle over the edge, send you a rueful whistle through my teeth, and then, say, little dog, listen. What I had to confess was no more than ordinarily grotesque. That as the trouble for me. I suffered so uncommonly from such common fears" (11). There in its absence, this unnamed desire piques the reader's desire to see and know the protagonist's desire, but like the absence of origins, this desire remains unanswered and unspecified, though it operates throughout and though Kate clearly has sexual relationships with other women.

The connection between the desire to know, the desire to see, and the desire of the text is embodied in the title, which operates as a paradox on all of these levels. "This" refers to the text itself, to the explanation offered the reader, to the lesbian love felt by Kate, to the manner in which Kate was decided to live this love. What is offered both is and is not; the text is not for Esther, the lesbian love Kate has for Esther is not for Esther to share, Kate's self-denial is not the way Esther should live, the history provides the reader with few answers, the desire it embodies is not named or described, yet in each case the opposite is equally true. The paradox: "This is not for you" is the paradox of a desire fulfilled by its unfulfillment, by remaining a desire, a question. Paradoxically, then, in its nonfulfillment the desire for desire is fulfilled.

Like Kate George, self-sufficient Molly Bolt has a series of lovers, all of whom are rejected because of either Molly's career or her sense of personal morality. Unlike Kate, however, Molly has no single love like Esther to catalyze her desire for an unfulfilled wish. She quickly loses interest in the lovers she does have; when her desire is fulfilled, it fades as desire or the lover is removed through some extraordinary circumstance. Instead, Molly's dream is for a career as a film director, a singular impossibility that remains as her unfulfilled wish at the end of the novel. In her final summation—a wish list—Molly says: "I wished I could get up in the morning and look at the day the way I used to when I was a child. I wished I could walk down the streets and not hear those constant, abrasive sounds from the mouths of the opposite sex. Damn, I wished the world would let me be myself. But I knew better on all counts. I wish I could make my films. That wish I can work for" (246). While Molly accepts the impossibility of going back, of returning to origins, signified by her use of the past tense "wished," her unfulfilled desire remains in the present, potentially fulfillable, and important because it is a desire that is currently unfulfilled. In this way Molly sustains desire. Both Kate and Molly are self-sufficient women who place careers ahead of love, but who are left with a wish for a wish, a "this is not for you" that is a future rather than a past they know they cannot return to.

Structured around a desire for a desire, both novels lead to an absence: In *This Is Not for You* the absence is Esther, who signifies Kate's desire. In *Rubyfruit*, Molly's desired filmmaking career stands for absence in two ways—not only is she unlikely to achieve it, but making film has already led her back to the mother and the story of her origins: the place of absence. Both novels begin with this absence, a lack in the place of the mother, and the importance of this originary lack is consistently denied. Their descriptions of the maternal reveal the structuring absence located in the place of the mother. Kate describes her adoptive mother as "old enough to be my grandmother," knowing "too little about the world to discover the promises to exact" (9). Though this mother is depicted as distant and kind, for most of the novel she is suffering from the effects of strokes and is quite literally not all there. And in *This Is Not for You* there is no memory of a biological mother evoked to fill the space. In *Rubyfruit*, Molly's adoptive mother constantly reminds Molly that she is not, in fact, her mother and complains to her husband, "I'll never know what it's like to be a real mother" (40). And even at the end of the novel when Molly returns to reclaim her origins, she finds that her biological mother, Ruby, looked and was nothing like her: "You don't look a whit like Ruby except you got her voice, exactly" (235). With nothing but her mother's voice, Molly's presence, bravado, athleticism, and artistic fervor all come from her father, a French Olympic athlete.

Even though Molly makes peace with her adoptive mother, the resolution constitutes the film that begins Molly's career and ends her childhood. When the film is shown, it is greeted with silence.

The insistent appeal to absence in these novels suggests the real importance of the missing mother as the original model for unfulfilled desire, as hovering behind the characters' denials of their desire and of their beginnings. If we see the relationship to the mother as one of lack instead of a nostalgia for plenitude suggested by Kristeva and Chodorow, if these lesbian stories privilege the moment of separation from the mother rather than the time of unity with her, we can see the genesis of a ironically heterogeneous desire as opposed to the nostalgic desire that characterizes heterosexual accounts of mothering.

Hidden within lesbian stories is the moment of separation from the mother and its effects, whose dynamic is similar to the scenario Lacan describes in his psychoanalytic version of the loss of the mother: "What we meet as an accident in the child's development is linked to the fact that the child does not find himself or herself alone in front of the mother, and that the phallus forbids the child the satisfaction of his or her own desire, which is the desire to be the exclusive desire of the mother."[12] The infant is denied desire by the symbolic phallus characterized by Jacqueline Rose as the signifier of rupture and by Lacan as the signifier of desire: in either case the phallus in this story of the mother becomes the signifier of both lack and its fulfillment. If we read the function of the phallus back against lesbian narratives, this does not mean that the lesbian desires a literal phallus in a penis-envy scenario as is often assumed; instead, the phallus, like Esther and like filmmaking, stands in for the lack—the remainder—that constitutes the desire for desire. This desire exists beyond what either Kate or Molly needs and beyond their sexual desires, which both of them satisfy in various ways. It is like the dream of the Witty Butcher's Wife in Freud's *Interpretation of Dreams*, a dream that elaborates the desire for desire in terms of a woman's identification with the desire not for a phallus, but for a woman.[13]

In Freud's analysis of the Witty Butcher's Wife's dream, the Witty Butcher's Wife, knowing Freud's theory that dreams are wish fulfillments, comes to Freud with a dream that she thinks specifically denies the fulfillment of the wish. In her dreams she wants to give a supper party and serve smoked salmon, but she has no smoked salmon and it is Sunday, so she cannot give the party. In discussing the dream with her, Freud elicits several additional facts: the Witty Butcher's Wife has a thin friend her husband is interested in, though he usually prefers more full-figured women, her friend likes smoked salmon, and the Witty Butcher's Wife likes caviar but asks her husband not to give her any. Freud then interprets the dream in two ways. The first is that "the non-fulfillment of one wish meant the fulfillment of another" (148). By not giving the party and thus not feeding her friend smoked salmon, the Witty Butcher's Wife was preventing her friend from becoming fatter and more attractive to her husband. The second interpretation is that the Witty Butcher's Wife identified with her friend through the mechanism of the renounced wish: the Witty Butcher's Wife's self-denial of caviar was combined with her desire to deny her friend the smoked salmon. The salmon takes the place of the caviar, and she takes the place of her friend in her husband's eyes.

Lacan comments further on Freud's second interpretation in ways that bring the Witty Butcher's Wife's dream close to lesbian novels' narratives of unfulfilled desire.[14] Lacan reads the caviar/salmon as the signifier for an unfulfilled desire, a desire that is gratuitous, a desire for desire, since the Witty Butcher's Wife is supposedly satisfied by her husband and doesn't want the caviar. But suggesting yet another identification, Lacan also brings in the husband, the man who desires the thin friend but cannot be satisfied with her since she is not the type to attract him. The wife, again through the desire for an unfulfillable desire, identifies with her husband's desire for the other woman: "How can another woman be loved . . . by a man who cannot be satisfied by her?" (262.) This would seem then to be a hint of lesbian desire, mediated through an identification with the husband. But Lacan takes the case one step further and equates their unfulfillable desire for the friend with the friend's desire for the smoked salmon, which Lacan sees finally as a phallus, a signifier of desire. The Witty Butcher's Wife identifies with the salmon as a signifier of the desire of the Other. Her desire, then, is to be the object of desire of the Other.

The Witty Butcher's Wife's dream suggests not only that the desire for desire manifested by both Kate and Molly is an identification with another woman via the medium of denied desire, but that this desire is really the desire to be the desire of the Other. But who is this Other? If we trace back the metaphorical chain of displacements tracked by Freud and Lacan in interpreting the Witty Butcher's Wife's dream, we return to the impossible mother, the one whose desire we can never be. By combining a desire for unfulfilled desire with a literally absent mother, these lesbian novels recreate the scenario of maternal loss whereby the daughters cease to be the desire of the mother. But the absence of the mother is a displacement of the loss of the mother's desire, which is displaced again into the daughter's desire for an unfulfillable desire. Kate has no mother. In the novel she displaces this loss into her love for Esther, whom she chooses not to have. Molly has no mother; she displaces this loss into her desire to make films, the first of which attempts to capture the mother. In both novels, this displacement is simultaneously a way of recognizing loss and of recognizing the nature of desire itself as an identification with the desire of another women where that woman either is the salmon/phallus as Esther is or Molly Bolt's somewhat narcissistic self-image accessible only through the reproductive qualities of the salmon/phallus of the film equipment.

Where in Kristeva and Chodorow's stories of the mother the mother figure is the fulcrum, the place of the split that creates desire, in these lesbian histories the absent mother is equated with the absent and inaccessible phallus, which works figuratively as a signifier of desire. Whereas the heterosexual accounts privilege the illusion of a desire fulfillable via maternity, lesbian stories situate desire as fulfillable only by desire itself. These different emphases reflect not radically different structures of desire, but rather different positions within the same structure. The difference in position between heterosexual and lesbian accounts has to do with their different placement of the mirror stage and the ensuing problem of individual and sexual differentiation. Kristeva and Chodorow reproduce a mirror stage dialectic, seeking a predifferentiated state from a post–mirror stage position. The lesbian accounts erase the preoedipal and focus instead on an already differentiated and very independent protagonist daughter where the lack represented by the absent mother is displaced into the lack constituting desire itself. The heterosexual accounts' oscillations around the mirror stage result in a notion of difference defined as sexual difference; woman are different from men, but not from one another, because in those stories femaleness is located before the mirror stage in the place of sameness and maleness is located after the mirror stage in the world of differentiation. Lesbians' post-mirror stage concentration avoids the female gendering of preoedipal unity and assumes a post-mirror stage differentiation that occurs both as sexual difference and as differences among women.

This dissimilarity in concepts of difference explains both how it is that lesbian sexuality is not preoedipal and why lesbian accounts omit preoedipal origins as irrelevant. While heterosexual accounts of quasi-incestuous, quasi-sexualized relations between mother and infant daughter can only exist as an immature stage in the trajectory toward difference and heterosexual fulfillment, the lesbian omission of the mother removes the threat of mother/daughter incest and perceives woman-to-woman sexual relations as relations between different individuals. Since the specter of fulfillable maternal desire does not exist, lesbian desire fulfills itself by making desire the fulfiller of desire. This parallels Lacan's psychoanalytic observation about lesbian sexuality that "such a love [female homosexuality] prides itself more than any other on being the love which gives what it does not have, so it is precisely in this that the homosexual woman excels in relation to what is lacking in her." [15] While "pride" may not be the word for it, the lesbian novels do "excel in relation to what is lacking in" them, that is, both origins and fulfilled desire.

The varying shapes of female heterosexual and lesbian desire suggest that the differences in the narratives and their interpretation have to do with differing perceptions of the locations of the sexualities in relation to one another. While clearly the two are not, in fact, completely separate, in heterosexual scenarios lesbianism is depicted as immature—as a stage, as preoedipal, undifferentiated, and therefore unsatisfiable—while heterosexual relations are seen as mature, with potential promises of fulfillment. In this convention lesbians are portrayed often as crazy, self-destructive, unfulfilled, and/or travesties of masculinity. Lesbian narratives portray lesbianism as the act of a completely independent, self-defined, but marginal woman whose fulfillment comes in the understanding that there is no such thing, that desire perpetuates desire. These same narratives depict heterosexuality as a difficult deception that ends in a fairly peaceful acquiescence to a status quo of nonfulfillment.

These differing depictions of desire have finally to do with questions of the operation of desire in narrative. If, as Teresa de Lauretis observes in *Alice Doesn't*, narrative is shaped by an oedipal desire for completion and mastery, only female heterosexual narratives would come close to fulfilling that narrative desire, while lesbian narratives would thwart it.[16] But just as humans rarely exhibit purely heterosexual or homosexual desires, so narratives might inscribe conflicting and inconsonant desires. The mixture of heterosexual and lesbian desire in many novels by women may account in part for the kind of undecidable tension in women's writing that prevents it from easily adhering to oedipal expectations. Instead of reflecting "pure" theoretical trajectories derived from heterosexual or homosexual texts, these narratives represent a confused mixture that reproduces not only the varied tensions of desire/fulfillment or desire for desire, but also a tension among these two and the variants that fall between them. The interplay of these desires in such novels as Virginia Woolf's *Mrs. Dalloway*, Gloria Naylor's *The Women of Brewster Place*, Djuna Barnes' *Nightwood*, and Toni Morrison's *Sula* may help account both for their fascination and the difficulties in characterizing them as they mix different patterns of desire or different stages in the same pattern.

It is also true that not all lesbians or all heterosexuals will operate within the parameters of one or another desire; cross-desire identification permits a wider, more dynamic interplay of desire and narrative than the models imply. If desire is shaped differently according to gender and sexual orientation, then it may differ in respect to other criteria as well. As the terms multiply, so do the operations of desire. This possibility complicates any simple correlation between gender and sexuality and reading identifications, either with characters or trajectories of desire. The reader's desire in relation to the desires that shape the narrative also complicates economies of desire as they weave through text and reader, producing, rather than harmony, a discordant tension between reader and text that produces yet another level of desire—the reader's desire for the text and the reader's desire to change the shape of the narrative to reflect or inscribe other desire. All of this suggests that insofar as narrative is driven by desire, the idea of a standard, monolithic oedipal narrative is too narrow to understand narrative adequately. Given the possibility that there are many different shapes of desire, the fact that the oedipal trajectory is often so dominant—the only one recognized—reveals the cultural hegemony of the heterosexual and the patriarchal. We need to recognize the multiple shapes of desire that drive and shape narrative in order to read differences themselves, and by reading those differences, we may escape the oedipal to new scenarios of desire.

■ T H R E E
Beginning with L

*L*ESBIAN SEXUALITY *as the erotic relation among women is the origin of this project, though it is now difficult to tell how much my initial idea of the lesbian has changed through the process of writing this book. I begin this chapter with the observation that something that appears to be lesbian sexuality is used rhetorically to found feminist theories of writing and reading. The idea of women together is the rationale, motivation, metaphor, or question that founds and supports investigations of women's writing and what it means to read as a woman. French feminist theories of écriture féminine are premised upon the metaphor of an eroticized economy of woman-to-woman relations and primarily American formulations of feminist reading theory center almost obsessively around the question of Emily Dickinson's illusive sexuality. That these continentally bifurcated theories of writing and reading should both appeal to lesbian sexuality indicates not only their affinity and necessary correlation, but also the way lesbian sexuality is configured in association with notions of origins, identity, and essential femininity.*

I noticed this common lesbian thread when I read the works of Luce Irigaray as deliberate expressions of a lesbian economy. Her evocations of feminine morphological metaphors are remarkably similar to fictional accounts of lesbian sexual behavior. While I feel empowered by her trenchant analyses of patriarchy and at home with the somatic aspects of her inquiry, as

I read more carefully I am disturbed by her rejection of the nominal lesbian. How can she both appeal to and deny lesbian sexuality? How can I identify with and be rejected from the same text? How do I become coterminous with a sexuality? How do I know what that sexuality is?

The lesbo-centric approach employed in this book assumes a definition of lesbian that is even now shifting, difficult, contradictory. How can I begin from a point if I don't know, except from personal experience, what that point is? And even if my own personal bodily experience of erotic interchange with another woman qualifies me to "know" what lesbian sexuality is, how do I disentangle that experience from my distanced rendering of it or from what has already been culturally defined as lesbian? My understanding of lesbian is politicized, reactive to the many doctrinal do's and don't's of a feminist academic community. Identifying as lesbian already requires a circle where experience and representation define one another. There is no "pure" place unaffected by language and culture that tells me what sexuality or identity are in the first place; any concept of sexuality I have is necessarily a composite of social imperatives, theoretical deliberations, and various philosophical, emotional, and libidinal choices.

Even if I don't know precisely what lesbian is, I look for the lesbian in the text, for what happens rhetorically to eroticized relations among women, finding, perhaps narcissistically, their catalytic function in feminist theories of writing and reading. I begin with this perspective probably because reading, even academic reading, is stimulated, at least for me, by a libidinous urge connected both to a sexual practice and to the shape of my own desire.

I began the original manuscript of this book with an analysis of Cixous and Irigaray, though this chapter turned out to be the last to be finished. I thought if I could understand feminist ambivalence about lesbian sexuality, then I might understand something more about the position of lesbian in culture and about the relation between the rhetorical lesbian and women who perceived themselves as lesbians. I don't think I am where I began, but it seems I've always been here.

The Lure of Origins

I am a woman
who understands
the necessity of an impulse whose goal or origin
still lie beyond me. . . .

"Artemis"
Olga Broumas

Reliance upon the projection of an ideal, archaic, and inherently female locus as source of an "impulse" necessary to undo the status quo characterizes a feminist cultural praxis ranging from accounts of mothering to feminist theories of writing and reading to the terms of a feminist aesthetic. This female locus is a species of origin that appears to constitute a point from which culture can recommence, promising the possibility of reconfiguring human relations without reiterating the dismal hegemony of endlessly monolithic binary oppositions. Through appeals to multiple, female, and/or joyful origins in the form of the preoedipal, the body, a great goddess, or an essential, biological gender identity, these various theories attempt to found or describe a disparate "feminine" economy consisting of the free interplay of differences and the fruitful coexistence of multiple perspectives. In definitions of these origins, emphasizing the "archaic" matriarchal and multiple instead of the "more civilized" patriarchal and singular provides an imaginary authority for a different order and explains, via the fictional reenactment of a prehistorical scenario of gender conflict, the evolution of sexual difference and the oppressive character of an usurping patriarchy. At the place of this origin is the lesbian, admitted as model, denied as position.

As we have seen, Julia Kristeva and Nancy Chodorow seek familial origins to account for the cultural function of woman as mother, both unearthing a species of origin when they assign the preoedipal mother-child relation an originary status in human and cultural development. Though both describe this preoedipal estate nostalgically, both also attribute the daughter's preoedipal relation to the mother with causing difficulties when the daughter enters a patriarchal system. Locating a similar kind of prepatriarchal origin, Hélène Cixous' theory of a "writing said to be feminine" and Luce Irigaray's postulate of a feminine "syntax" situate the body as an originary locus catalyzing a writing that exceeds and evades the discourse shaped by phallocentric oppositions of difference introduced by language and culture. The body's presumably divergent relation to discourse is modeled on edenic paradigms of women together—mothers and daughters, lesbians. Likewise, feminist theories of reading offered by Adrienne Rich, Judith Fetterley, Bonnie Zimmerman, Jean Kennard, Catherine Stimpson, Dale Bauer, and Jane Gallop originate with questions raised by the reactions of women to women; reading is premised on an identificatory process that relies on an originary experience of biologically and/ or culturally constructed gender. In the poetry of Olga Broumas, writing, the body, sexuality, and questions of origins converge to suggest a feminist aesthetic that posits an interrelation among desire, writing, and the body as a central source of creation. At the core of all of these formulations of feminist practice is the catalytic, dangerous lesbian who configures both the utopian joinder of women that promises a basis for profound change and the sterile and dangerous homogeneity that stifles progress and creativity.

This quintessentially feminine something ambivalently linked to a lesbian sexuality seen as preceding patriarchy also echoes more traditional accounts of origins. Appeals to a prehistorical, precursory, preoedipal state like Kristeva's "semiotic," Cixous' and Irigaray's references to a multifarious, plenitudinous body, or Judy Chicago's use of antique foremothers and great goddesses are similar to some folk myths of origins.[1] Akin to representations of the preoedipal or the pre–mirror stage, mythical origins are also visions of fragmented chaos coupled with a jubilant integrity that combines the singular and monolithic with a preexistent plurality, ordering it. "In the beginning, Euryome, the Goddess of All Things, rose naked from Chaos, but found nothing substantial for her feet to rest upon, and therefore divided the sea from the sky, dancing lonely upon its waves . . ."[2] In this Pelasgian creation myth, both the goddess and the chaos from which she arose are original, the goddess arising from but not created by the chaos, the chaos predating the goddess. The beginning is the first moment of an organization of singular and plural that commences the binary division of the world.

These origin myths create their own narrative. A chaos or shapelessness always precedes some kind of intervention that organizes it. Like Lacan's "mirror stage," origin myths depend upon the creation of a more cognizant consciousness that supplants a formlessness. The connection of primitive myths of origin to water, birth, resurrection, and a suspension of profane time creates a historical progression from chaos to order. Like feminist impulses to recreate the preoedipal or the matriarchal, primitive originary moments heal: "It is through the actualization of the cosmic Creation, exemplary model of all life, that it is hoped to restore the physical health and spiritual integrity of the patient. . . . The cosmogonic myth is also recited on the occasion of birth, marriage, and death; for it is always through a symbolic return to the atemporal instant of primordial plenitude that it is hoped to assure the perfect realization of each of these situations."[3] In feminist myths of origins and theoretical accounts of female space, the feminine is originary—the healing model of life. Patriarchy becomes the alien and alienating force that separates woman from herself. For this reason, goddess myths are particularly appealing, since by changing the gender of the intervening force, one might hope to change the effects of alienation.

Inherently same-sexed (or homogeneously asexual, since gender appears only at the organization of chaos) and suggestively but "innocently" erotic descriptions of origins, particularly feminist representations of the preoedipal and the female body, evoke a homogenous and feminized sexuality.

> Nourishing takes place before there are any images. There's just a pause: the time for the one to become the other. Consuming comes before any vision of her who gives herself. You've disappeared, unperceived—imperceptible if not for this flow that fills up the edge. That enters the other in the container of her skin. That penetrates and occupies the container until it takes away all possible space from both the one and the other, removes every interval between the one and the other. Until there is only this liquid that flows from the one into the other, and that is nameless.[4]

Describing a mother-daughter relation, Luce Irigaray conjures an originary sensual, bodily relation between two females where the borders are dissolved, interchange is free and uninhibited, and the economy of exchange is liquid. Cultural preconceptions of the erotic as a bodily intermingling define this metaphor of symbiotic joinder as sexual, and cultural configurations of lesbian sexuality as erotic relations between female bodies render it suspiciously homosexual. Not surprisingly, Irigaray's mother-daughter passage echoes fictional descriptions of lesbian sexual activity such as Violette Leduc's depictions in *La Bâtarde:* "The sea monster in my entrails quivered. Isabelle was drinking at my breast, the right, the left, and I drank with her, sucking the milk of darkness when her lips had gone. . . . As we melted into one another we were dragged up to the surface by the hooks caught in our flesh, by the hairs we were clutching in our fingers; we were rolling together on a bed of nails."[5] Or the narrator's portrayal of Clarissa Dalloways' feelings for other women in *Mrs. Dalloway:* "She did undoubtedly feel what men felt. Only for a moment; but it was enough. It was a sudden revelation, a tinge like a blush which one tried to check and then, as it spread, one yielded to its expansion, and rushed to the farthest verge and there quivered and felt the world come closer, swollen with some astonishing significance, some pressure of rapture, which split its thin skin and gushed and poured with an extraordinary alleviation over the cracks and sores!"[6]

The parallels between accounts of origins and descriptions of lesbian sexuality bespeak their paradigmatic association. Sharing attributes of an economy situated as preeminently feminine, feminist constructions of origins and lesbian sexuality are both characterized by images of fluidity, female genital morphology, multiplicity based on erotogeneity, and what Cixous calls "an economy of giving." The liquid character of origins recalls Irigaray's observations in "The 'Mechanics' of Fluids" that there is no systematic science of fluids. In the dialectical opposition maintained between the theoretically solid and the relatively unknown liquid, physics, according to Irigaray, reflects the dichotomy between the rational, linear, and hierarchical solidity of science and reason and the nonrational, unknown plurivalency of fluidity. She links the absence of a physics of liquids to a definition of women as excess: *"Since what is in excess with respect to form—for example, the feminine sex—is necessarily rejected as beneath or beyond the system currently in force."*[7] Cixous and Irigaray link liquids with images of breast milk, blood, and other fluids exchanged between women— mother and daughter, woman and woman. The source of these fluids is the female body, whose morphology, perceived as myriad and diverse, configures an excessive uncountability that parallels the theoretical ungraspability of the liquid and provides a pretext for the originary fragmentation of polymorphous erotogeneity seen as characterizing feminine sexuality. The apparent lack of anatomical complementarity among women (at least from a phallocentric perspective) also enables the interpenetration and dissolution of boundaries that removes both the mother-daughter relation and female erotogeneity from the masculine realm of possession and acquisition associated with the penetration of one by the other. Instead this "feminine" supports a "riskier," "more adventurous" libidinal economy of open giving or "spending" "on the side of the body" that, according to Cixous, circumvents property, commodified exchange, and singularity.[8]

Feminist representations of origins diverge into two economies that reiterate the singular/plural tension of folk myths and predict the splitting of the lesbian into acceptable plural and phallocentric forms. The predominant singularity of the great goddess maternal figure represents the essentially female, and the preoedipal body embodies multiplicity; the relation of these two categories repeats the inevitably binary organization such imaginary origins seek to evade, incarnating the self-contradictory posture of an essential female multiplicity. Each category, though emphasizing a singular or plural aspect, also embodies a dynamic consolidation of singular/plural that yields the illusion of a peaceful settlement. Governed by a dominant single figure, matriarchal economies premised on sharing, equality, and the nourishment of differences provide the mythical basis for a feminist aesthetic patterned after the projected attributes of the culture or goddess. The matriarchal as a single source is parallel to feminist aesthetic theories that posit a feminine experience of the "real," the "authentic," or the material body as the source for their shape and inspiration. Finding this real, a process that requires or locates a singular consciousness, results in a recognition that language does not reflect this experience and attempts to reform language so that it does.[9] Even specifically matriarchal aesthetic theories, such as that constructed by Heide Göttner-Abendroth, refer to a "universal" matriarchal organization as the source for aesthetic practice that is designed on principles of multiplicity.[10] The hypothesis of the matriarchal or the great goddess also engenders, via an imaginary historical precedent, theories of female superiority and essential sexual differences. Embodying the singular/plural contradiction, this plenipotentiary figure reigns by virtue of her endless ability to give, to split herself into multiple fragments that both reflect and found politicized endorsements of maternity as an exclusively female source and pattern of power.

Evocations of fragmented multiplicity characteristic of theories dependent upon the body or the preoedipal found the highly valued aesthetic of diversity that either coexists with the idea of a singular figure or underwrites and/or reflects feminist philosophical arguments rejecting singularity and authority altogether. Emphasizing the plural and the lack of boundaries, ideas of feminine multiplicity relocate the singular of the mother/goddess figure into the category female, which sustains a singularity otherwise rejected, or into a female consciousness that becomes a space from which patriarchy can be read. Claiming multiplicity as a quality inherent to femininity, however, paradoxically renders multiplicity a singular trait within the exclusive frame of the female.

These two patterns, though divergent, are interdependent, superimposed, playing through and against one another in a productive tension figured by the mother and daughter and/or by the lesbian. The contradictory relation between the singular and the plural displayed in originary narratives is crucial to a feminist deployment of origins and actually characterizes feminist theories of writing, reading, and aesthetics that propose a divergent and politically effective feminist praxis. This self-contradiction would seem desirable, especially in a politic that wishes to reject notions of authority. The problem with it is that such tension is rarely identified as a productive dynamic; instead it is displaced into and subsumed by notions of origins such as the body or essential gender traits that serve as masking authorities in an ironic return to binary oppositions. It also resides in and is contained by the two emblematic configurations: the mother-daughter relation embodies the benevolent but ambivalent tussle between dependency and fusion, between a drive for individuation and the paradise of unity resolved, as in Kristeva and Chodorow, by the fiction of a cyclical return to preoedipal merger in the oscillating pulse between illusions of independence and joinder. The lesbian is represented as both singular/phallic and feminine/multiple, working to configure the self-contradictory point where a binary economy apparently fails to account recognizably for relations among women, providing an opening for analysis, but where, simultaneously, the heterosexual representational tactics by which lesbian sexuality tends to be perceived return evocations of multiplicity to the binary of masculine/feminine —a point of failure and return for both phallo- and matri-centric systems.

The tension basic to feminist theories that seek origins as paradigms for an ensuing practice shares in the paradox of impossible origins. Origins are at best only a lure, mimicking and standing in the imagined place of something else, decoys of a return to the prerepresentational made impossible by the very conditions that enable us to conceive of it. Any concept of origin necessarily comes, as is suggested by Lacan's notion of the "mirror stage," only through a historical retrospection that makes any subsequent experience of an origin itself impossible, since what enables the perception of an origin—a sense of separation, the "armour of an alienating identity"—is what disenables any further participation in the fragmented world of pre-oedipal unity.[11] And our very concept of an origin is itself a representation, an act that necessarily adds to and alters whatever is represented, removing it irrevocably from its source. As Jacques Derrida posits: "What can look at itself is not one; and the law of the addition of the origin to its representation, of the thing to its image, is that one plus one makes at least three."[12] Even trying to conceive of an originary origin represented by the concept of origins is to be lured into mistaking the representation for the represented, signifier for signified, of believing in the possibility of a pristine source not subject to the inevitable alienation of representation. The paradox of origins, then, is that to perceive them *as origins,* one must be inaccessibly beyond them, just as to perceive an ab original plurality and loss of a singular self one must experience an irreversible individuation or to perceive something as "real" one must be already one step removed from it. And even arguments that claim that maintaining the inaccessibility of origins is a phallocentric or "postmodern" position premised on a dominant consciousness of the one who cannot relinquish singularity or comprehend such a borderless and propertyless economy reiterates the binary singular/plural, them/us, masculine/feminine structure within which such originary tales operate. In any case, consciousness—representation itself—is always the problem, both for feminist attempts to regain origins and in attempts to conceive of them. This is not to deny the mirror stage's inherent sense of chaos; the point is that consciousness is what perceives chaos.

Paradoxical origins function as a lure, occupying the impossible place of that which appears to fulfill desire, thus masking the paradox of a desire sustained only by the impossibility of fulfilling it.[13] Concepts of origins appearing to embody the desirable attributes of a re-formed culture are lures that distinguish an originary cause, then confuse that cause with its effects. In this focus on cause/effect, a consciousness of desire as a driving force tends to be subordinated to the seductive mirage of the impossible but ideal object. Even the quest for origins is a paradox, since it is the search for that made impossible by the conditions that enable a search for it. A version of the desire for desire, the quest for origins reflects the urge to have what one cannot have that sustains desire in a tension between the threat of lack represented by no more desire and the specter of power promised by its fulfillment. Origins are alluring because their imagined pattern of joinder and multiplicity opposes the alienating singularity that enables the operation of binary oppositions—because they promise both fullness and the power to change all representations beyond the origin itself. Origins configured as women together appear to be the place of difference without sexual difference, difference without opposition. And within the parameters of desire illustrated by the mother-daughter politic in the previous chapter, the desire for desire enacted by a feminist search for origins is related both to the appearance of the lesbian configuration at the origin and the constant theoretical oscillation between lesbian and mother-daughter configurations. The fact that this materno-lesbian precursory space obsessively reappears in feminist theoretical writing about both writing and reading, even when the writers are consciously aware of the impossibility of an originary moment, confirms the allure cast not only by the potential power promised by origins, but also—and perhaps more poignantly—by the imagined edenic economy of women together.

Body Integrity

OLGA BROUMAS, a writer in what Mary Carruthers calls the "lesbian poetry" movement, is concerned with refashioning originary myths in her collection of poems, *Beginning with O*.[14] Removing the masculine from mythology in her "archaeology of an excised past," Broumas not only seeks traces of a buried primordial time, but also explores how and if that time can be regained or reconstructed. While the idea of myth structures part of Broumas' collection, the process of writing as a rediscovery, as an archaeology of lines already inscribed, positions language and writing as never original, as a process of returning to one's own lines. Focusing, thus, on desire and writing rather than on an origin sustains the productive tension of the interplay of singular and plural:

> I work
> in silver the tongue-like forms
> that curve round a throat
>
> an arm-pit, the upper
> thigh, whose significance stirs in me
> like a curviform alphabet
> that defies

decoding, appears
to consist of vowels, beginning with O, the O-
mega, horseshoe, the cave of sound.
What tiny fragments
survive, mangled into our language.

"Artemis"

"Beginning with O," with the "O" at the end of the line that begins "O-mega," the word for end whose beginning "O" ends one line and whose last two syllables begin the next, with that which returns on itself, perpetually, paradoxically, that no-beginning beginning that recycles recursively, Broumas merges writing and images of the body, circling one around and through the other, losing where one begins and the other ends, making a "curviform alphabet that defies decoding." The writing on the body from the body exists around itself in "fragments" that "survive, mangled into our language." The point of origin, the specific source of writing or body is unlocatable, its vestiges overwritten by self-generated lines that trace the body, selecting what to trace, "throat," "arm-pit," "thigh," representing curves on the body, but already a step away, already performing a representation on top of a representation—a body—defined by its named fragments, parts already subject to the parsing of language. The source of the writing is evasive and circular like the "O," empty and full, beginning, end, middle, playing the paradox of the body as the source of the writing: the concept of the body already defined by representation, the body that generates language in its model that represents the body that generates language. . . .

Hélène Cixous' metaphor of the orange in *Vivre l'orange* echoes Broumas' recursive metaphor of the "O" as starting point: "I asked: *What have I in common with women?* From Brazil a voice came to return the lost orange to me. *The need to go to the sources. The easiness of forgetting the source. The possibility of being saved by a humid voice that has gone to the sources. The need to go further into the birth-voice.'* "[15] Suggestive of her birthplace, Oran, the orange configures exchanges among women as well as a notion of source or origin that exists within a specifically female economy linked to origins, a community of women, and an economy of giving. The roundness of the form already associated with the female body, the "shape of the orange, the O," suggests, mimicks, the route to origins. As Annette Kuhn comments, the orange, in its "sound association with Oran, . . . implies a return to

sources, but the shape of the orange, the O, tells us that the route
will not be a linear one" (38–39).

Cixous' route may not be linear, but neither is it as perpetually
circular as Broumas'. Reflected in Cixous' shifting between plural and
singular forms or "sources" in the passage—"sources," "source,"
"sources," "birth-voice,"—is her symptomatic alternation between
single and multiple, arriving at a singular source: the "birth-voice"
located at the site of the female body. Oscillating between women
and the mother, the group and the body, the body's multiple erogenous zones and the singular, gendered consciousness that experiences
and records them, Cixous' overt appeal to origins shifts the tension of
desire to the contradictory interrelationship of singular and plural
reminiscent of Kristeva's and Chodorow's alterations between daugh-
ter/individual and mother/preoedipal. While Cixous takes pains to
avoid any definitive appeal to a single locus, constructing the foundations of her theories within the circulating and interconnected parameters of women/writing/body and a theory of inherent bisexuality that
avoids even a singular essential gender, still her plurals work only in a
tension with the occluded but omnipresent singularity of the idea of
the body—the voice—as a prerepresentational, prepatriarchal source.

The passage from *Vivre l'orange* typifies Cixous' method of connecting language to the "source," to the "birth-voice" evoked by her
query about her relation to women: "What have I in common with
women?" The question not only begins the circulation of orange,
voice, origins, and salvation that describes in brief Cixous' *écriture
féminine,* but it also situates the relation among women as the catalyst
for this circulation, as the origin of the impetus to return to the sources
—the "birth-voice," the body—from which the writing comes. In
"Laugh of the Medusa," Cixous asserts that "it is by writing, from
and toward women, and by taking up the challenge of speech which
has been governed by the phallus, that women will confirm women in
a place other than that which is reserved in and by the symbolic, that
is, in a place other than silence" (251). Configured within a communal
body of women, writing, for Cixous, becomes the imperative to "write
your self. Your body must be heard" (250). Writing the "self" for
women is writing the body and the body in turn comes from the self:
"By writing her self, the woman will return to the body . . ." (250);
"women are body. More body, hence more writing" (257). A community of women, women's bodies, and writing become interchange-

able parts of a circuit, one succeeding the other in a revolving interchange of cause and effect.

Cixous' formulation of the body in "a writing said to be feminine" is quintessentially multiple: "What strikes me is the infinite richness of their individual constitutions: you can't talk about *a* female sexuality, uniform, homogeneous, classifiable into codes" ("Medusa" 245–246). The body's plurality is defined primarily as multiple erotogeneity: "To write. An act which will not only 'realize' the decensored relation of woman to her sexuality, to her womanly being, giving her access to her native strength; it will give her back her goods, her pleasures, her organs, her immense bodily territories which have been kept under seal" (250). The singular location of the trait of erogenous plurality that serves as the model for that "place other than silence" women's writing will produce, the body is discovered by means of a literal and metaphorical self-reflexive masturbatory writing: "You write and make an extremely bizarre and relatively auto-erotic gesture while others are behind closed doors and wait until you are done" (Conley 140–141). The prediscursive body underwrites writing by means of its autoerotic search for itself:

> A world of searching, the elaboration of a knowledge on the basis of a systematic experimentation with the bodily functions, a passionate and precise interrogation of her erotegeneity. This practice, extraordinarily rich and inventive, in particular as concerns masturbation, is prolonged or accompanied by a production of forms, a veritable aesthetic activity, each stage of rapture inscribing a resonant vision, a composition, something beautiful. ("Medusa" 246)

This accord between body and writing premised on a mimesis of a woman's experience of her body is the source of a means to overcome the systemic oppression of a binary system of sexualized oppositions: "I shall speak about women's writing: about *what it will do*. Woman must write her self; must write about women and bring women to writing, from which they have been driven away as violently as from their bodies—for the same reasons, by the same law, with the same fatal goal" ("Medusa" 245). While language and culture imprint phallocentrism and alienate the woman from herself, the woman's body, seen as repressed and silenced, functions as a reserve source of a potentially different economy. The result is an endless and excessive inscription interweaving writing and the body: "A feminine textual body is recognized by the fact that it is always endless, without ending; there's no closure, it doesn't stop, and it's this that very often makes the feminine text difficult to read" ("Castration or Decapitation" 53).

This relation between writing and the body presumes, or course, that the ultimately autoerotic and self-circular process by which this writing is generated comes from an experience of the body that occurs in a prerepresentational state. How else does the body escape the appropriation and marking of a propertied, patriarchal system? Somehow the woman's relation to her body, even if that relation is an analogy, must precede the discourses that alienate the woman from her body, discourses that supercede an originary language to which the woman has access via her body. Unlike Broumas, who sees even writing on/from the body as "surviving" "mangled into our language," Cixous' writing/body relation necessarily appeals to an origin or source of nonalienation that is prelinguistic, preoedipal, presymbolic, and seen as physical and concrete cut which, nonetheless, can be itself represented in its generation of a different, feminine discourse.[16]

But while the body is the ground figure of this autoerotic, self-reflexive economy, the body, via the metonymic equation of body/writing/women, becomes a communal, explicitly multiple space that operates on principles derived from the relation of woman to her own body. This autoerotic relation constitutes a microversion of a singular/plural circulation in its endless reflexivity while configurations of women together occupy a macroversion of that same economy. Appearing to pose multiple sources, Cixous reiterates the body model in her appeals to two different communal analogies to the body as the singular site of multiple possibilities. Cixous' linking of body and community brings together the inspirational notions of community or "civitas," to which both Virginia Woolf and Audre Lorde gratefully allude, with a physical, almost material reflection of that community existing on an individual plane.[17] For Cixous, women/writing/body as a circular source for action both leads toward and comes away from a larger metaphorical body figured by the mother on the one hand and the singularly multiple conjoinder of women on the other:

Everything will be changed once woman gives woman to the other woman. There is hidden and always ready in woman the source; the locus for the other. The mother, too, is a metaphor. It is necessary and sufficient that the best of herself be given to woman by another woman for her to be able to love herself and return in love the body that was 'born' to her. Touch me, caress me, you the living no-name, give me my self as myself. ("Medusa" 252)

Rather than serving as two discrete, opposing, or alternating models for feminist practice, the maternal and the lesbian shift and coalesce in Cixous' writing in a way that more symptomatically uncovers the resident heterosexism and oppositional thinking related to her covert reliance on origins.[18] "In women there is always more or less of a mother who makes everything all right, who nourishes, and who stands up against separation; a force that will not be cut off but will knock the wind out of the codes. We will rethink womankind beginning with every form and every period of her body. The Americans remind us, 'We are all Lesbians': that is, don't denigrate women, don't make of her what men have made of you" ("Medusa" 252).

Because the sexuality of the woman's autoerotic search for her own body haunts the premises, groups of these autoerotic women suggest a sexualized rather than a politicized (where the two are seen as mutually exclusive) source. While groups of autoerotic women exchanging writings among themselves threaten to suggest a lesbian interchange, the mother-daughter configuration acts as an antidote to counteract and neutralize suggestions of lesbian eroticism.[19] The term *lesbian* is brought into the discussion at the point where Cixous calls for a politicized rediscovery of differences among women; led off by a search for "every form and every period of her body," the lesbian steers her discussion back to woman's relation to patriarchy. The lesbian's connection to eroticism is delicately excised by the constant appearance of sexually "innocent" maternity and Cixous' appeal to a completely politicized (and curiously de-sexed) version of Adrienne Rich's "we are all lesbians."[20] While relegating the lesbian to America, Cixous takes Rich's paradigm one step further, cleansing the lesbian of all but a fairly lame, vaguely protesting message.

In an economy of interfemale relations premised on an autoerotic experience of the physical/sexual female body, why does Cixous labor to avoid any sexual lesbian identification? She does hypothesize a bisexuality that threatens to hint at lesbian sexuality, but hers is a bisexuality quickly defined so as to exclude any such suggestion: "I do not believe in sexual opposition nor in a sexuality that would be

strictly feminine or strictly masculine, since there are always traces of
originary bisexuality" (Conley 136). This "originary bisexuality" does
not mean homosexual with the tendency one may think" (131). In a
note added to the English translation of "Castration or Decapitation,"
Cixous remarks: "Bisexuality" is "this being 'neither out nor in,'
being 'beyond the outside/inside opposition' that permits the play of
'bisexuality.' Female sexuality is always at some point bisexual. Bisexual doesn't mean, as many people think, that she can make love
with both a man and a woman, it doesn't mean she has two partners,
even if it can at times mean this" (55n). Typical of the position of the
lesbian throughout Cixous' writing, lesbian sexuality is symptomatically omitted from the body of the text of "Castration or Decapitation" as "a position tangential to the central interest" of her work. As
this is a text about cutting women off from their own bodies and
sexuality, Cixous' exclusion of her comments about lesbian sexuality
is noted by the translator, who announces that the material was omitted from the "main body of the text" at the request of the author.

Cixous seems to use this concept of bisexuality to avoid any single
sexual preference, though bisexuality, too, *is* a sexual preference. But
she also invokes bisexuality to mask any suggestion of homosexuality.
While bisexuality would seem consistent with the multiple pleasures
of the female body, her way of defining it eliminates a lesbian possibility in favor of a heterosexuality seen as an encounter with differences on the one hand and autoeroticism on the other. That *the lesbian*
is the consistently missing and/or denied term in this context indicates
both a conscious, politicized avoidance of lesbian sexuality and an
unconscious repression of the obvious applicability of the term to her
own writing scenario.

Like Kristeva and Chodorow, Cixous ceases analysis of institutions
at that point where a reliance upon a heterosexual assumption blinds
her to both the recuperative operations of a phallocentric representation and the possibility of differences within gender. The "endless, feminine textual body" does end, stopping at the lesbian, who
otherwise serves as an obvious analogy for the women/writing/body
circulation. Circumspectly avoiding such oppositions throughout her
theory, at the point of the lesbian they resoundingly return in her
perception of the lesbian as a patriarchal imitator and as a structure
that mimics binary gender oppositions. In "Rethinking Differences,"
she characterizes the lesbian as "the latent man-within, a man who is

reproduced, who reappears in a power situation. Phallocracy still exists, the phallus is still present in lesbianism. . . . There is a homosexuality which is entirely feminine and has nothing to do with heterosexuality, and which leaves no room for man such as he is."[21] Merging the term *lesbian* with power, Cixous splits lesbian sexuality into two categories, phallicizing it on the one hand and making it homogeneously feminine on the other, reproducing her gendered binary opposition. This may, as Diane Crowder points out, reiterate a French cultural distinction made between lesbian and female homosexual, but Cixous' splitting of the term *lesbian* from *female homosexual* not only reveals an ambivalence and the reproduction of gender binaries among women, but also reserves for her system the purely feminine, which "leaves no room for man."[22]

This parsing of lesbian sexuality is a point of failure in Cixous' concept of bisexuality. Relying upon the very gender categories she wishes to reject, Cixous encourages a mingling of aspects of both genders while disavowing gender itself, mixing masculine and feminine in a liberated multiplicity. If, however, only the nonphallic female homosexual is appropriate for her system, and because bisexuality incorporates the same cross-gender elements as her "phallic" lesbian, Cixous eliminates bisexuality and multiplicity in favor of a very homogenous femininity. The only difference between bisexual and phallic lesbian seems to be in their organization—the lesbian is centered as phallic, and the bisexual randomly incorporates multiple traits of both genders.

Even in Cixous' own terms, the distinction between lesbian and female homosexual is artificial, reflecting positions in her system rather than any neat categorization of lesbian women. *Lesbian* refers not to a sexuality, but to an acceptance and enactment by women of a phallocentric economy tantamount to masquerade. By defining lesbian as phallic, Cixous is able to use the category as a banner under which she can eject all patriarchal impurities while retaining an idealized, eroticized female homosexual space. Even though she seems to accept the female homosexual, that term, though never used in direct relation to Cixous' female writing communities, refers to the kind of mutual autoeroticism that already founds her theory of writing. By defining the lesbian out of the realm of the feminine, Cixous rejects not just the phallic, but also differences among women and anything other than an autoerotic sexuality. But female homosexuality—still lesbian—remains. While the connotations of the term *lesbian* shift from culture to culture, configurations of sexualized relations among women are still lesbian, female homosexual, sapphic.

Cixous' neutralization of potentially overt lesbian content is necessary for her to differentiate the edenic community of women to which she appeals as a prime context for her theory of writing from what she sees as a phallicized sexual practice. Her edgy stubbornness about lesbian sexuality is premised upon the same logic by which she denies the possibility of origins. Both are impossible because representationally they return to the phallocentric singularity that Cixous is trying to supersede. Despite her constant return to the question of a source, Cixous declares that origins are really irrelevant—evidence of a linear hierarchy she identifies as phallogocentric. Like the lesbian, origins are masculine:

> The origin is a masculine myth: I always want to know where I come from. The question "Where do children come from?" is basically a masculine, much more than a feminine, question. The quest for origins, as illustrated by Oedipus, doesn't haunt a feminine unconscious. Rather, it's the beginning, or beginnings, the manner of beginning, not promptly with the phallus in order to close with the phallus, but starting on all sides at once, that makes a feminine writing. A feminine text starts on all sides at once, starts twenty times, thirty times, over. ("Castration" 53)

The distinction between origin and beginning seems to be the difference between the kind of passive inheritance of the individual's biological birth, identity, and antecedents, all presumably marked by the phallus via the question of paternity on one side and an active and multiple "starting," the quality and location of an action that avoids phallic singularity on the other. Trying to posit beginnings as a way to escape the singularity of gendered binaries, the distinction Cixous makes recreates them: masculine, singular, possessive origins versus feminine, multiple beginnings.

Their circularity hides a very real singularity behind Cixous' evocation of multiplicity: "Rather it's the beginning, or beginnings, the manner of beginning, not promptly with the phallus in order to close with the phallus, but starting on all sides at once, that makes a feminine writing." Performing even in the sentence her inadvertent return to the singular as she did in *Vivre l'orange,* Cixous begins the sentence three times, shifting from the singular noun to the plural to a participle, multiple beginnings, but not from all sides at once. The distinction she would like to make—origin versus beginning*s*—is not so clear as it is qualified as multidimensional, slipping from the apparently mistaken singular of its first enunciation to a corrective plural and back to the singularity of "manner" and "starting" that unite the process under a single verbal regime.

As Cixous slips from the plural to the singular, she enacts the impossibility of multiplicity in language rather than the "writing said to be feminine" she formulates. Employed and denied, both lesbian sexuality and origins occupy the ambivalent status of the repressed— of those things that, though consistently denied, still shape the unconscious Cixous seeks as the prerepresentational locus for a different symbolic structure.[23] The origins she denies are simply displaced from the mythical to the body, which becomes equally mythical. Sharing the same attributes, lesbian sexuality and origins promise knowledge in Cixous' system—promise a new way out from an old system. While her circular economy halts at the point of origins and the lesbian, they become decoys, drawing attack and denial that leads away from the essential homogeneity of Cixous's main project, which is to found an ab original economy of writing premised upon sexualized configurations of women together.

Like her rejection of the lesbian, Cixous' denial of origins lures us away from the importance of a concept of origin to her formulations. Arguing for the political and metaphysical impossibility of origins masks her rhetorical appeal to them. There are, then, really a series of lures in Cixous' idea of a "writing said to be feminine," beginning with the allure of implied lesbian sexuality and origins, then the lure of Cixous' denial strategies, which provide the seduction of a sophisticated deconstructive comprehension of patriarchal systems—origins are impossible—while disassociating Cixous' project from the patriarchal taint she perceives in both. With this denial Cixous can have the best of both worlds: the illusion of multiplicity, an origin that evades all of the patriarchal traps by which her delicate economy of giving might be recuperated, and the lesbian without the lesbian.

In comparison to the economy of Broumas' poem "Artemis," Cixous' circularity is essentially an oscillation rather than a real circulation where each term, in perpetual metonymy, stands in for infinite other terms that return, not to a beginning, but to a reiteration of the circle, which thus multiplies itself indefinitely:

> I am a woman committed to
> a politics
> of transliteration, the methodology
> of a mind
> stunned at the suddenly
> possible shifts of meaning—for which
> like amnesiacs
>
> in a ward on fire, we must
> find words
> or burn.
>
> > "Artemis"

While the "goal or origin" of "an impulse" still may "lie beyond" the poet, sustaining a desire to continue, the urgency of "a politics of transliteration" catalyzed by "possible shifts of meaning" forces the continuation of another circle that courses among layer of signifiers, some more, some less inscribed within the realm of bodily experience by which the poet knows her own desire.

Broumas' writing economy is not self-sustaining, as Cixous' economy of giving threatens to be. While Cixous locates an "economy of giving" in the prepatriarchal origins of the feminine libido, Broumas' body must be fed: "White wine eases the mind along the slopes of the faithful body, . . ." Cixous defines a feminine libidinal economy as "an economy which has a more supple relation to property, which can stand separation and detachment, which signifies that it can also stand freedom—for instance, the other's freedom" (Conley 137). The feminine libido must thus be able to stand alone, presignificant, since for Cixous assuming language begets the proprietariness of a propertied economy. The feminine libido becomes the starting point without starting point, sufficient unto itself, self-generative. "How does one give? It starts in a very simple way: in order for a gift to be, *I* must not be the one to give. A gift has to be like grace, it has to fall from the sky. If there are traces of the origin of the *I* give, there is no gift—there is an I-give" (Conley 159). Again, here denial of an origin is a decoy away from the origin, which resides in the self-sustaining character of the feminine libido. Avoiding the first person pronoun attempts to avoid singularity and identity, even her formulation of the question is "How does *one* give?" (emphasis mine). Cixous' giving denies the operation of desire. There is a point in Cixous of no desire, of a cessation of circulation, whereas in Broumas desire, like language, is perpetual. It cycles repeatedly because it takes in, feeds, incorporates, and is not trapped in the narrow paradox of self-denied origins.

Broumas' poem "Artemis" suggests a slightly different politic of writing. While Cixous ultimately posits a prerepresentational space, Broumas suggests that such a space is neither possible nor necessary. Instead, a recognition of "transliteration" requires the coexistent recognition of multiple systems, translated, transmuted, and not intermingled in differences. The tension of this system resides in a recursive desire: the desire to write over, a tracing that simultaneously moves through the past and the future. Origins "excised," writing becomes an archaeology, a present tracking of a past there and not to forge a future like and not like what was.

> Let's not have tea. White wine
> eases the mind along
> the slopes
> of the faithful body, helps
> any memory once engraved
> on the twin
> chromosome ribbons, emerge, tentative
> from the archaeology of an excised past.
>   "Artemis"
>   (lines 1–8)

"ONE PLUS ONE"

Echoing Broumas' description of the "mangled" survival of female experience in discourse, Luce Irigaray analyzes the phallocentric paradigm by which that experience is transliterated. *"Why,"* Irigaray asks, *"are mother-daughter relations necessarily conceived in terms of 'masculine' desire and homosexuality?"* "Female sexuality has always been conceptualized on the basis of masculine parameters."[24] Considering the question of how to envision relations among women, Irigaray analyzes the psychoanalytical and philosophical discursive systems that reduce the feminine to a position complementary to masculinity. While Kristeva and Chodorow go back to a maternal origin to relocate the space of woman-to-woman relations and Cixous returns to the body, Irigaray comes at them from what she sees as the discursive level of their impossibility: the "hommosexual" economy of a patriarchal culture that disenables the articulation of the relations among women except as they are mediated, translated, and transformed into expressions of a masculine economy. To Irigaray, relations among women cannot be expressed: "In this economy any interplay of desire among women's bodies, women's organs, women's language is inconceivable."[25]

Irigaray's analysis of representational impossibility is accompanied, not surprisingly, by the assumption of an "other" space—something physical and experiential that exists prerepresentationally. Like Cixous, Irigaray supposes an ab original site located in the woman's experience of her own body, relying on that site to locate and formulate a "feminine syntax" and to serve as the perspective from which phallocentric biases of psychoanalysis and culture might be clearly identified and analyzed. But while Cixous asserts an originary bisexuality, formulates an economy of giving, and denies origins to avoid essentializing that feminine space, Irigaray is suspicious of the position of the feminine itself. Though part of Irigaray's project is to open up the phallocentric singularity of sexual difference to "secure a place for the feminine," she is also aware of the contradictions that inhere in formulating a feminine space within a patriarchal model.[26] According to Irigaray, simply paying attention to or asserting a feminine is naive, since that feminine is precisely what has been constructed within a phallocentric system of selfsame: "For woman it is not a matter of installing herself within this lack, this negative, even by denouncing it, nor of reversing the economy of sameness by turning the feminine into *the standard for 'sexual difference,'*; it is rather a matter of trying to practice that difference" ("Questions" 159).

Practicing difference for Irigaray depends upon the emergence of "some other mode of exchange(s) that might not obey" the logic by which woman is a commodity in the "hommosexual" exchange among men. Like Cixous' economy of giving, Irigaray's notion of exchange defines property, proprietariness, and authority as phallocentric, but it also involves refusing the mirrored economy of binary gender that represents and obscures the essentially phallocentric singularity of discourse, fixing exchange within an exclusive masculine parameter. Reshaping the economy of exchange is, for Irigaray, "the condition for the emergence of something of a woman's language and woman's pleasure" ("Questions" 158). To challenge not just the relation of gender binaries but also the singularity of the system is to alter the position of the feminine, to liberate it from its dependent mirroring function, and to enable it to speak for itself.

Shifting the economy to avoid reiterating binary oppositions thus frees up the woman's relation to her own body inhibited by phallocentrism. Irigaray asks:

> For how can a woman be forbidden to touch herself? Her sex, "in itself," touches itself all the time. On the other hand, no effort is spared to prevent this touching, to prevent her from touching herself: the valorization of the masculine sex alone, the reign of the phallus and its logic of meaning and its system of representations, these are just some of the ways woman's sex is cut off from itself and woman is deprived of her "self-affection." ("Questions" 133)

And like Cixous, Irigaray posits the woman's experience of her own body as crucial to any change in signifying and/or social systems. The basis for a "feminine syntax," the morphology of the female body simultaneously defines a new writing and a different economy:

> What a feminine syntax might be is not simple nor easy to state, because in that "syntax" there would no longer be either subject or object, "oneness" would no longer be privileged, there would no longer be proper meanings, proper names, "proper" attributes. . . . Instead, that "syntax" would involve nearness, proximity, but in such an extreme form that it would preclude any distinction of identity, any establishment of ownership, thus any form of appropriation. ("Questions" 134)

Evoking qualities she elsewhere attributes to the body, Irigaray locates the best example of such a syntax "in the gestural code of women's bodies" ("Questions" 134). But that space and its syntax are very tenuous, threatening always to revert to or be dominated, obfuscated, and silenced by a masculine economy. Irigaray finds it difficult to enact such a syntax: "I tried to put that syntax into play in *Speculum,* but not simply, to the extent that a single gesture obliged me to go back through the realm of the masculine imaginary. Thus, I could not, I cannot install myself just like that, serenely and directly, in that other syntactic functioning—and I do not see how any woman could"

("Questions" 134–135). Much more suspicious than Cixous of any quintessentially female economy modeled on the relations among women, Irigaray questions whether women "speaking-among-women" may not still be a "speaking (as) man." Despite this danger, Irigaray's "speaking as a woman" still provides the possibility of another discourse, which appears, as it does in Broumas, intermittently, through the mesh of another system, not as its dialectical opposite or as an enactment of the gaps or an unconscious, but as a different syntax whose expression is a struggle because of the way the dominant economy operates always to return difference to binary phallocentric terms.

The context of other women—the homogeneously feminine community—provides, however, still the most likely site for the emergence of a "feminine syntax":

> It is certain that with women-among-themselves (and this is one of the stakes of liberation movements, when they are not organized along the lines of masculine power, and when they are not focused on demands for seizure or the overthrow of "power"), in these places of women-among-themselves, something of a speaking (as) woman is heard. This accounts for the desire or the necessity of sexual non-integration: the dominant language is so powerful that women do not dare speak (as) women outside the context of nonintegration. ("Questions" 135)

Like Cixous, Irigaray proposes the circular interrelationship among a feminine syntax, "women-among-themselves," and the body, but she emphasizes the need to shift the contextual, representational economy itself, making this economy a cause rather than simply another circulating term. Positing a cause/effect relation between a new system and feminine syntax where the system enables the syntax by permitting the discovery and expression of a woman's relation to her own body and to other women, Irigaray appears to situate the system as a kind of switch that either represses or permits expression. The body is not, as it is in Cixous' theory, the source for this shift but rather becomes the model for a feminine syntax that is allowed to emerge. While this chain of causality leaves open the question of the motive for shifting the system in the first place—the question of original impetus—it also seems to avoid conflating economy with syntax and syntax with content. The difference an emphasis on system makes for Irigaray is that she seems thus more aware of the danger of reiterating the original phallocentric economy in formulations of a feminine syntax.

For this reason, Irigaray is well aware of the dangers of substituting feminine for masculine: "For to speak *of* or *about* woman may always boiled down to, or be understood as, a recuperation of the feminine within a logic that maintains it in repression, censorship, nonrecognition."[27] And mistaking style as evidence of a shift in economy: "Its [the writing of women's] 'style' resists and explodes every firmly established form, figure, idea or concept. Which does not mean that it lacks style, as we might be led to believe by a discursivity that cannot conceive of it. But its 'style' cannot be upheld as a thesis, cannot be the object of a position" ("Discourse" 79).

Avoiding the valorization or "fix" on any aspect of a feminine syntax creates a perpetual circulation and de-centering that enables the operation of a different economy—not as an economy of circulation that implies points of exchange, but rather as a system where a lack of boundaries and discretion makes notions of exchange irrelevant.

> We would still have to ascertain whether "touching oneself," that (self) touching, the desire for the proximate rather than for (the) proper(ty), and so on, might not imply a mode of exchange irreducible to any *centering*, and *centrism*, given the way the "self-touching" of female "self-affection" comes into play as a rebounding from one to the other without any possibility of interruption, and given that, in this interplay, proximity confounds any adequation, any appropriation. ("Discourse" 79)

In this economy Cixous' autoeroticism implies a centrism, a reiteration of the old economy, an economy Irigaray avoids by always implying a plurality of indefinite dimension in her bodily analogies.

But even if systems are distinct from feminine syntax in Irigaray's analyses of discourse, when she comes back to such economies from the perspective of a feminine syntax, syntax and economy merge. For Irigaray, the body and relations among bodies no longer experienced as separate from one another is a central model for the shape of a new system, as well as for the consciousness that constitutes the basis of a feminine syntax, not just in its morphology, but also in its relation to dominant discourse. Relating language directly to an imaginary experience of the body, Irigaray posits the body/syntax's plurality: "Her sexuality, always at least double, goes even further: it is *plural* (*This Sex* 28). And this plurality premised on Irigaray's assertion that *"woman has sex organs more or less everywhere"* (28) effects its new economy not via the fact of plurality, but rather by means of proximity:

> Woman always remains several, but she is kept from dispersion because the other is already within her and is autoerotically familiar to her. Which is not to say that she appropriates the other for herself, that she reduces it to her own property. Ownership and property are doubtless quite foreign to the feminine. At least sexuality. But not *nearness*. Nearness so pronounced that it makes all discrimination of identity, and thus all forms of property, impossible. (*This Sex* 31)

Economies and writing are linked to configurations of female sexuality whose shape is determined by bodily parameters. As in Cixous, writing is an extrusion of sexuality, and in both cases it is a homosexuality, where differences have been absorbed and/or experienced as part of a feminine plurality. Assuming the identity of writing and sexuality as a different economy (even if the dominant economy is itself a version of writing and male sexuality) positions sexuality as a prerepresentational or potentially prerepresentational locus that can generate simultaneously a different economy and a different syntax. This echoes Cixous' situating of the body as an originary, prediscursive site and reiterates the problem of how one gains an unmediated experience of the body in order to fashion such a new syntax. The distinction Irigaray makes between economy and syntax breaks down, syntax becoming paradigmatic of the economy that permits it and the body serving as paradigm for it all. Irigaray's originary narrative follows a plot of an economic alienation that distances woman from herself, but a shifting economy allows syntax and system to merge and return to a prediscursive unity that removes this alienation in another version of a return to origins.

The reliance on the body as both model and location and the necessarily sexual nature of writing is, in Irigaray's work as in Cixous', linked both to lesbian sexuality and to mother-daughter relations as the context within which this syntax can be discovered. But Irigaray's analogy is of a borderless sexuality that is multiple because individuality and singularity are meaningless. This version of plurality fixes more on what appears to be a primary lesbian sexuality rather than on an oscillation between the poles of autoeroticism and mother-daughter relations effected by Cixous. Borderless plurality occupies a middle ground, incorporating within its homosexual intercourse all possibilities among women and rejecting the familial titles that import appropriation and identity. "We—you/I—are neither open nor closed. We never separate simply: *a single word* cannot be pronounced, produced, uttered by our mouths. Between our lips, yours and mine, several voices, several ways of speaking resound endlessly, back and forth. One is never separable from the other. You/I: we are always several at once."[28]

The actual entanglement of sexuality and writing, the body and language, reiterates Broumas' theory of writing on the body, but establishes this feminine syntax in an imaginary zone that pretends to be before representation and marking by any phallocentrism. Defining labels or positions seems to be what imports the repressive phallocentric economy into the otherwise ab original scenario: "I love you childhood. I love you who are neither mother (forgive me, mother, I prefer a woman) nor sister. Neither daughter nor son. I love you— and where I love you, what do I care about the lineage of our fathers, or their desire for reproductions of men? or their genealogical institutions? What need have I for husband or wife, for family persona, role, function?" ("Lips" 209.) Rejecting labels and positions, Irigaray strives to maintain the purity of both feminine syntax and the economy of nonappropriation that enables it. Curiously, this passage is often interpreted as a declaration of a lesbian relation, particularly in the parenthetical "forgive me, mother, I prefer a woman" phrase.[29]

In the context of Irigaray's redefinition of discourse, "forgive me, mother, I prefer a woman" rejects the familial, patriarchal position of mother in exchange for the common denomination woman, a shift that removes the patriarchal marking incident to maternity. For Irigaray, as for Cixous, lesbian sexuality does not liberate women from patriarchy, since the lesbian is a position within a phallocentric economy, one that reiterates power relations and possessiveness. In *This Sex Which Is Not One*, Irigaray warns:

> But if women are to preserve and expand their auto-eroticism, their homo-sexuality, might not the renunciation of heterosexual pleasure correspond once again to that disconnection from power that is traditionally theirs? Would it not involve a new prison, a new cloister, built of their own accord? For women to undertake tactical strikes, to keep

themselves apart from men long enough to learn to defend their
desire, especially through speech, to discover the love of other women
while sheltered from men's imperious choices that put them in the
position of rival commodities, to forge for themselves a social status
that compels recognition, to earn their living in order to escape from
the condition of prostitute . . . these are certainly indispensable stages
in their escape from their proletarization on the exchange market. But
if their aim were simply to reverse the order of things, even supposing
this to be possible, history would repeat itself in the long run, would
revert to sameness: to phallocratism. It would leave room neither for
women's sexuality, nor for women's imaginary, nor for women's language to take (their) place. (32–33)

In this analysis, female homosexuality becomes a stage rather than
either an end in itself or an essential pattern for women's writing.
Irigaray's description regards the category of lesbian as primarily political, separatist, and ultimately phallocentric, as distinguished from
the sexualized interaction of female bodies that underlies feminine
syntax. Like Cixous, Irigaray retains what might be identified as a
lesbian configuration, overtly rejecting the nominal lesbian who is
defined as selfsame and inevitably phallocentric.

Irigaray also appeals to both female homosexual and mother-daughter paradigms. "When our Lips Speak Together" is often characterized as her essay on woman-to-woman relations, one that "heralds" a
later essay, addressed to the mother, "The One Doesn't Stir Without
the Other." [30] This oscillation or shift between relations among women
and mother-daughter relations parallels the work of Cixous. "When
Our Lips Speak Together" celebrates the sexualized relations among
women, while "The One Doesn't Stir" mourns a previous ab original
time, while describing the daughter's alienation and attachment. The
point in Irigaray's essays is that mother-daughter relations are like
other relations among women; the problem with maternity is precisely
the possessiveness it imports from patriarchy.

The mother-daughter relation in Irigaray, however, enjoys a fate
similar to that of the lesbian. Like lesbian sexuality, the mother-
daughter relation is characterized as a lack of separation, but this lack
becomes more a problem of identity than a positive model for a new
economy: "There is no possibility whatsoever, within the current
logic of sociocultural operations, for a daughter to situate herself with

respect to her mother: because strictly speaking, they make neither one nor two, neither has a name, meaning, sex of her own, neither can be identified with respect to the other" ("Questions" 143). This lack of differentiation is a symptom of patriarchy: "'When I speak of the *relation to the mother*, I mean that in our patriarchal culture the daughter is absolutely unable to control her relation to her mother" ("Questions" 143).

While Irigaray tries to define a new economy/syntax, like Cixous, she relies on a notion of a prediscursive, female homosexual space. Though she positions this space somewhat differently, she still recreates the same original story in which the woman's relation to her body can serve as a source for an economy that has already and will continue to escape the markings of a phallocentric representational system. Described in the same multiple, borderless terms as Cixous' body, accounts of original chaos, and the preoedipal, this original feminine space is repressed by a phallocentric economy that supersedes and dominates it. Only the analysis, identification, and rejection of that phallocentric economy will enable a return to the ab original, the place before labels, positions, possessions, and singularity.

Irigaray openly acknowledges the importance of sexual libido, but in her work as in that of Cixous, lesbian sexuality as an expression of libido plays the same ambivalent role. Female homosexual relations serve as a paradigm for writing, but must be denied as a communal or political possibility. Libido, specifically a female libido in a female context, drives discourse in Irigaray's system. Writing that enacts a new syntax is driven by a libido or by a desire attached to sexuality— to an instinct seen as originary—a necessary condition of human existence rather than an urge conditioned by culture. And looking to the body as the source for such a libidinous language and economy creates, if one believes in the transparent transformation of flesh into word, a language that reflects or conveys femaleness, to be understood by others with similar bodies.

Whether or not this configuration is specifically labeled lesbian, it is lesbian if we define lesbian as sexualized relations among women. But while fashioning a syntax around a feminine libido, Irigaray rarely, except as already noted, directly addresses the question of lesbian sexuality, though occasionally she employs it as an example of Freud's masculinism, as she does, for example, in "Psychoanalytic Theory:

Another Look." In her brief analysis of the lesbian as a victim of a phallocentric imaginary, in "Commodities Among Themselves," Irigaray observes: "The dominant sociocultural economy leaves female homosexuals only a choice between a sort of *animality* that Freud seems to overlook and *the imitation of male models*. In this economy any interplay of desire among women's bodies, women's organs, women's language is inconceivable" (196). Three choices: "animality," masculinity, or invisibility, define lesbian sexuality in a phallocentric market, but it is precisely this interchange among women that Irigaray sees as creating a different "kind of commerce" directly linked to lesbian sexuality and consisting of "exchanges without identifiable terms, without accounts, without end . . . Without additions and accumulations, one plus one, woman after woman . . . use and exchange would be indistinguishable" ("Commodities" 197).

"Utopia? Perhaps. Unless this mode of exchange has undermined the order of commerce from the beginning . . ." ("Commodities" 197). "From the beginning," from the origin, exists an economy derived from a feminine libido in exchanges among women. Finding this economy requires an archaeology; women's desire, like "the beginnings of the sexual life of a girl child," is buried, "submerged by the logic that has dominated the West since the time of the Greeks" (*This Sex* 25). Reiterating myths of origins, Irigaray's metaphorical placement of a female desire puts it at an ab original time. But unlike Cixous, Irigaray doesn't reject this origin as phallic; instead, she sees it as the place of a challenging, different economy linked to desire and to lesbian sexuality: "We are women from the start" ("Lips" 212). Returning lesbian sexuality to the realm of maternity, however, Irigaray links origins, sexuality, and the mother-daughter relation: *"Why are mother-daughter relations necessarily conceived in terms of 'masculine' desire* and homosexuality? What is the purpose of this misreading, of this condemnation, of women's relation to her own original desires, this nonelaboration of her relation to her own origins?" ("Psychoanalytic Theory" 65). The alluring female economy, preoedipal at its source, is lesbian and not, mediated by the permissible maternity that in Kristeva, Chodorow, and Cixous has veiled the lesbian and embodied the deep-seated ambivalence about origins and lesbian sexuality. But perhaps Irigaray permits this ambivalent nexus to exist as unresolved, unabashed sexuality at the foundations of a different economy of desire, never quite returning to a singularity that renders this "other" economy the same.

The Lure of Identity

> . . . she suddenly began again. "Then it really *has* happened, after all! And now, who am I? I *will* remember, if I can! I'm determined to do it!" But being determined didn't help her much, and all she could say, after a great deal of puzzling, was: "L, I *know* it begins with L."

> Lewis Carroll
> *Through the Looking Glass*
> (quoted in Irigaray,
> *This Sex Which Is Not One*)

THE ONLY answer to Alice's puzzle of "Who am I?" is that it "begins with L." Like Alice, feminist theorists of reading focus on the question of identity, specifically, the identity of female readers as they encounter "alien" texts or as they identify with more sympathetic texts written by women. And like Alice, such theories seem to "*know* it begins with L" as pioneering critics center their investigations around the question of Emily Dickinson's enigmatic sexuality. What I shall call feminist reading theory is theory and criticism that pose the act of reading as a gendered problem and a political strategy. Identifying gender bias in texts, and as it necessarily plays through the reading and interpretation of texts, has created a substantial corpus of feminist theories of readers and reading that take as their starting point the work of Emily Dickinson. While developing a feminist reading practice, feminist theorists' concerns about reading also focus on the ways assumptions about gender have alienated women readers, deformed definitions of "good writing," and institutionalized gender bias in the literary canon. Encompassing the pioneering work of Adrienne Rich and Judith Fetterley, the reader-response theory of Patrocinio Schweickart and Jean Kennard, Bonnie Zimmerman's lesbian "double vision," Dale Bauer's Bakhtinian approach to reading and community in *Feminist Dialogics*, and theories of the encodement of lesbian-feminist writing, feminist reading theories illustrate the lure of identity as that which, like origins, can overcome a patriarchal hegemony.

Though rarely overtly connected, theories of women's writing and feminist reading theories share the same idea of an originary female space behind a superimposed, alien patriarchal gloss. Dependent upon identity as a species of origin, feminist reading theories tend to attribute a fixed feminine identity to the female reading subject, making this identity the site of readerly consciousness and subjectivity upon which a female experience of reading is based. As Freud's derailed readings of lesbians exemplify, the act of reading is inseparable from a subjectivity that includes not only the reader's narcissism and other psychic processes and by-products—those mechanisms often perceived as unconscious—but also the complex interrelation between this unconscious and the reader's position in culture, both as internalized and as conscious, which is affected by and affects the reader's assumptions about and alignment and identification with distinct positions within such categories as gender, class, race, sexual orientation, parenthood, and age. While the ab original space within which female writing can be produced posited by Cixous and Irigaray tends to conflate identity, subjectivity, and a homogenized experience of gender related to bodily metaphors, reading theories appeal to a female identity premised upon the more political, material gender bifurcations of Western culture as well as questions of sexual orientation.

THE EMILY ENIGMA

Beginning with *L*, feminist theories of reading have germinated around Emily Dickinson, whose (possibly) lesbian poetry presents a notorious example of a woman-identified text that has been consistently underrated and misunderstood by a masculinist academic establishment, but which is read very differently if heterosexist assumptions are cast aside. Dickinson's enigmatic poetry functions as a text that disturbs certainties about the singular nature of gender and identity and of binary oppositions altogether, catalyzing questions about the possibility of any monolithic subject position. Since her poetry can be read as both male and female, heterosexual and homosexual, reading Dickinson reveals as much about the assumptions and investments of the reader as it does about Dickinson. Thinking about how we read her poetry makes us reevaluate assumptions about gender and sexual preference.

Theoretical writing about reading Dickinson reiterates the tension between singular and plural resident in the work of Cixous. The disturbance represented by Dickinson's poetry, characterized as a sudden fanning into a vision of multiplicity, is in the theoretical process folded back into a monolithic reading position that has simply shifted to another place—another gender. Insofar as a possible lesbian reading of Dickinson plays through reading theory, she seems to stand for a disturbance of theory itself as any cogent system, suggesting a kind of heterogeneity that is recuperated by an almost inevitable recourse to the homogeneous necessities of theory itself. This creates an oscillation between multiplicity and singularity at the point of the lesbian that cycles between the multivalent lesbian figure and the singular drive to define how we read her, engendering theories about the role of gender in reading.

The tension between singular and plural is reproduced not just in readings of writing, but also in the project of theorizing those readings. The relation of necessarily multiple reading positions to theories about reading and of uncertainty and certainty in relation to feminist theory creates this oscillation, as Elizabeth Flynn and Patrocinio Schweickart observe in the introduction to their collection of feminist reader-response criticism, *Gender and Reading:*

> The exchange between Schweickart and Kennard illustrates a problem inherent in feminist theory. On the one hand, it is important to convey the multiplicity of interests and experiences that make up the female perspective and, more importantly, to avoid the repressive assimilation of perspectives of more vulnerable groups. On the other hand, generalization is essential to theory formulation: if we wish to examine the implications of gender, we must assume that there is some common ground in the experiences and perspectives of different kinds of women that sets women apart from men.[31]

The "one hand, other hand" metaphor of the counterposition of multiplicity and unity suggests a juggling or interplay between multiple positions and a unified "theoretical" reading subject, where multiplicity is implicitly aligned with "the female perspective" and unity with theory—with setting "women apart from men." Starting from

Emily, feminist reading theories are subject to an attempt to sur-
mount this problem.

At the beginning of much of this, Adrienne Rich's candidly lesbian
feminist work forms the basis for Fetterley's, Schweickart's, Kennard's, and Zimmerman's later formulations of feminist reading. Rich's
1975 essay on Emily Dickinson, "Vesuvius at Home," is prefaced by
a retrospective introduction that poses pithy questions of a lesbian/
feminist reading.[32] Beginning with Toni McNaron's call for "a lesbian-feminist reading of her [Dickinson's] poetry and her life," Rich
proposes a "lesbian/feminist criticism [that] has the power to illumi-
nate the work of *any* woman artist," asking "questions hitherto passed
over" such as "how she came to be for herself and how she identified
with and was able to use women's culture, a women's tradition; and
what the presence of other women meant in her life" (157–158). By
posing such questions the reader will be able to identify "images,
codes, metaphors, strategies, points of stress, unrevealed by conventional criticism which works from a male/mainstream perspective"
(158). Like Cixous, Rich appeals to a female communal space as the
source for a knowledge beyond the patriarchal, but Rich is unafraid to
define that space as metaphorically lesbian. With a lesbian perspective
as starting point, Rich employs a model of a woman-to-woman relationship, a kind of metaphorical lesbian encounter between reader
and author to find a better way to read women's writing.[33]

Rich's practice of reading Dickinson is a "re"-reading akin to her
proposed "re-vision:" "the act of looking back, of seeing with fresh
eyes, of entering an old text from a new critical direction" (35). What
this does is pose a different set of assumptions derived from a female-
centered community analogous to Cixous' and Irigaray's bodily metaphors, but not so radical as their exhortations to completely altered
economies. In its simplest terms, Rich's "fresh eyes" read back through
Dickinson's poetry from the vantage point of Rich's estimations of
Dickinson's life experience, from an imagined empathic identification
with the "reality" of Dickinson's daily existence as reconstructed
from text, biography, and history in confrontation with sexist and
heterosexist presumptions. Replacing mainstream assumptions about
Dickinson with a set of sympathetic suppositions enables an insight-
ful, fresh reading of Dickinson's poetry, and Rich's pinpointing and
rejecting of mainstream conjectures about the power of heterosexual
fulfillment (or lack thereof) as poetic inspiration provides a different

and more positive exegesis of Dickinson's poetry and the relation of her poetry to her female life experience.

Rich's metaphorically lesbian practice, while it unsettles conventional readings of women's texts, remains a mode of reading that is reliant upon a subject who has simply been transplanted and unified on the feminine rather than the masculine side. Her reading strategies assume a close correspondence between Dickinson's poetry and her life, a version of biographical criticism and its assumption of a unified intentional subject. And Rich, while overtly acknowledging her investment in Dickinson, doesn't seem to be aware of the degree to which her act of reading itself reflects and is affected by this investment—she is not retrospectively aware of her own unconscious processes of reading or of her own split subjectivity that she recontains within the single categories identification and woman. Establishing a singular female position enables Rich to appeal to the historically authentic—the ability to imagine and empathize with material existence through history—as the way to knowing an authentic personality. Identity, including her own, stays intact. Matching the correlation between poetry and life with a parallel affiliation between the cultural position of the poet and the reader, Rich suggests that, among other considerations, affinities between reader and author lead to better understanding of texts, another kind of unification. This is the identity version of an *écriture féminine* premised upon the common enjoyment of a bodily experience. Differences between reader and text as well as unconscious processes became a kind of feminist solidarity that crosses the lines of difference in an appeal to identity and transposes female differences and differences among women into the category of female singularity.

Once Rich shifts reading position via a negotiation of historical differences to a position more like that of the poet, she is concerned with rereading what has been previously glossed as heterosexual desire in Dickinson's poetry, revealing, from a woman-identified perspective, the masculine mask of Dickinson's own texts and resituating Dickinson's use of the masculine pronoun as self-protective and natural: "Since the most powerful figures in patriarchal culture have been men, it seems natural that Dickinson would assign a masculine gender to that in herself which did not fit in with the conventional ideology of womanliness" (166). Rich perceives the grammatical masculinity assumed by Dickinson as a mask for the unconventional woman underneath; this mask can then be consciously reread as a revelation of Dickinson's unconventionality. To some extent, then, reading for Rich is a process of stripping both patriarchal and masculine masks from the female reader and text to discover extant affinities between reader and author, to discover the woman—the lesbian—underneath. In many ways, this parallels Cixous' and Irigaray's desire to locate an ab original feminine economy existing before patriarchal marking. But Rich's unsettling lesbian reading again returns to the singular and the monolithic; the quest for the lesbian that has brought the notion of multiple or masked identities to light has turned into the search for the more authentic female under the mask. The question of the lesbian in the text becomes a certainty about *the* lesbian behind the text. Rich's empathy with the historical persona of an author individualizes reading, drawing attention on the one hand to the infinite variety of individuals and historical, material conditions under which they write and we read. But those multiple possibilities are reintegrated in her reliance on identity as that which is discoverable and knowable.

Rich's notions of identity should be analyzed: the idea of a knowable identity informs the way feminist theory displaces patriarchal mastery and unity into an appeal to a parallel feminist mastery and unity. One assumption about identity Rich relies on is that identity is both historically constructed and transhistorical; in Rich's reading of Dickinson, historical context actually becomes a frame that leads to a better comprehension of identity, as Rich, the moth, flutters against it. But this also assumes that identity itself is something that can be apprehended; it survives history if history is correctly probed and the ensuing dialogue is a model of stability that reaches through text and time. Rich also assumes that identity is related to both gender and a gendered perspective, which is in turn related to a consciousness of the political effects of gender. A shift in consciousness/identity of gender also necessitates a shift in perspective that creates a retrospective consciousness of gender. We read from the perspective of identity. But while in reading the reader gains a new identity or emancipates an underlying repressed identity by means of a consciousness of the political effects of gender, this consciousness or new perspective also comes *from* an identity that is already there, suggesting an interplay or circularity between two superimposed identities: a superficial mainstream identity and an underlying feminist identity that can provide the consciousness to shed the former. The unified consciousness that results then helps to prevent a return to the alienated and split feminist subject under patriarchy. Rich maintains in "When We Dead Awaken" that "until we can understand the assumptions in which we are drenched we cannot know ourselves. And this drive to self-knowledge, for women, is more than a search for identity: it is part of our refusal of the self-destructiveness of male-dominated society."[34]

But even though there seems to be an interplay of identities— Rich's with Dickinson's—inherent to Rich's approach, finally Rich's lesbian/feminist reading practice rests on the discovery of an underlying lesbian feminist identity in the reader, a stability that is politically useful, transhistorical, individual, and unified. The lure of identity in Rich's theory is that it provides the knowledge of a more authentic lesbian self. Curiously, however, while the multiplicity of lesbian and feminist tend to disappear into the singular position of reader identified as lesbian/feminist, the heterogeneity of the text is preserved: "Wherever you take hold of [Dickinson], she proliferates" (183), so that without recognizing it as a reading strategy (it may merely be inherent to Dickinson), Rich's model of the relation between reader and text in reading Dickinson retains a place for indeterminacy, multiplicity, and uncertainty in Dickinson's possibly lesbian text.

Rich's dialogue with Dickinson is tremendously suggestive in its combination of readerly identity and textual ambivalence. Ensuing feminist reading theorists borrow and often simplify pieces of its interactive model, its notion of a second, hithertofore hidden, more authentic female self, its connection between identity and perspective, and its hinge to the texts of Emily Dickinson, who remains a central figure in the discussion. Building upon Rich's notion of a hidden female identity "drenched" in patriarchal assumptions, Judith Fetterley in *The Resisting Reader* envisions both text and reader as entrapped behind malign masks of patriarchy in a sort of forced drag.[35] While this idea seems akin to Cixous' and Irigaray's formulations of a prerepresentational female space dominated by patriarchy, Fetterley treats gender as a fixed, essential position in a binary system she employs rather than questions. For Fetterley as for Rich, gender, identity, and consciousness are aligned, though Fetterley, perhaps because she is concerned with how women might read texts written by men, simplifies the reading formula, equating literature with the gender of its authors ("American literature is male" [xii]), reading with identifying ("To read the canon of what is currently considered classic American literature is perforce to identify as male" [xii]), and consciousness with political power ("Consciousness is power" [xix]).

Again evoking Emily Dickinson, Fetterley chooses the figure of the "Prince cast out" from Dickinson's Poem 959 as the operative metaphor for her proposal of a feminist counter practice: "The condition of woman under patriarchy is precisely that of a prince cast out. Forced in every way to identify with men, yet incessantly reminded of being woman, she undergoes a transformation into an 'it,' the dominion of personhood lost indeed" (ix). For Fetterley, the woman reader is "immasculated," dressed as a prince, but not allowed to act as one, alienated from her real, female self. Fetterley's use of the prince metaphor is an interesting choice, designed to illustrate the nature of alienation experienced by many female readers of American literature in precisely the gendered terms in which she sees this alienation operating. But the woman in drag also evokes the stereotypical image of the lesbian as the masculine pretender, which creates an odd interplay between the woman forced to don a masculine mask and the lesbian, who is often depicted as desiring that mask. What is conveyed by the image above all is an uncertainty about gender that disturbs clear gender lines, but Fetterley breaks the image down into clearly defined gendered parts. Thus passing over Dickinson's potential disturbance of gender and sexuality—through what Rich sees as Dickinson's understandable appropriation of the masculine pronoun—Fetterley relies instead upon a certainty about gender and a desire for a unified subject. Cross-dressing becomes a kind of bondage that stands for an imprisonment in masculinity. While Rich's reading of Dickinson's masculine personae preserves the sense of a lesbian radical challenge, Fetterley reduces it to an adversarial estrangement.

Fetterley's theory of reading follows this princely but adversarial suit. Recasting in starker contrast Rich's lesbian/feminist model of consciousness and resistance, Fetterley proposes a more singularly defensive and oddly heterosexual scheme. Driven by a feminist consciousness of the political effects of gender, the woman reader can shed her patriarchal "immasculation"—her princely clothes—and thereby gain a new perspective, a consciousness of this immasculation that brings with it the power to resist further immasculation. This resistance is the tactic Fetterley recommends as a strategy for reading male texts, resulting in a two-step process that includes, first, a refusal to assent to immasculation and, second, by means of this refusal, the beginning of a process "of exorcising the male mind that has been implanted in us" (xxii). The gender uncertainty of the woman as prince, a flexibility evident in Rich, has been reduced to detachable and defined positions. The nonplayful posture of the woman as a "prince" who cannot exercise power and the use of the metaphor of implantation suggest that Fetterley's process actually relies upon a more basic, very heterosexual phallic model of rape and castration. Women readers are raped—implanted in—but at the same time they are "princes," a combination that suggests a male homosexual model rather than immasculation. Or the "Prince" is a really a dildo, a deception, an immasculation that hides emasculation. Fetterley's model proposes to turn the rape/castration table; a refusal of "immasculation" by the female reader causes the emasculation of the "male" text"— it can no longer "implant" itself in us.

This system bypasses the suggestive sexual instability of the cross-dressed Prince figure who implies a stereotypical lesbian paradigm, an instability that imports a wealth of potentially disruptive strategies connected to uncertainty about gender and sexuality. Instead, Fetterley recreates the circular relation of consciousness and identity enacted in Rich's model. Consciousness of "immasculation" provides a new perspective—a new identity—which in turn enables one to become conscious of and exorcise one's "immasculation." Both a mask and something "implanted in us," external and internal, this "immasculation" hides the true female identity that exists somewhere in between. The authenticity of this hidden identity can lead to a more genuine reading in which "we can accurately name the reality [works of American literature] do reflect and so change literary criticism from a closed conversation to an active dialogue" (xxiii). While Fetterley seems to want to open up a dialogue, the relation between the text and reader depends finally on a notion of a stable, unified, gendered identity whose perspective is thereby more reliable—no longer masquerading as the Prince and no longer unwillingly "implanted" in.

Both Rich's and Fetterley's recourse to a unified female identity as participant in a dialogue ignores or makes superficial any psychoanalytic comprehension of the internalization of patriarchy, of the split subject and the impossibility of this stable female identity. Both see this patriarchal mask as something that can be shed, removed from another intact identity, Rich locating multiplicity in Dickinson's text and Fetterley healing the wounds created by masculine intrusion and displacing the whole exchange into the realm of critical discourse. While Rich allows the continuation of a kind of play among gender, sexuality, author, text, reader, and writer, at least for the lesbian/ feminist reader, Fetterley's unquestioned certainty about gender and sexuality closes down the interplay between reader and text even as she wishes for a more open exchange. The complete heterosexuality of Fetterley's model—woman reader, male text—requires the suturing of intrapersonal splits and multiple possibilities (such as a woman actually identifying with a male author's depiction of desire for a female character) on the side of the female reader and displaces them into a gendered, masterful discourse of criticism.

Fetterley's resistance strategy, however, does suggest a politicized combination of gender consciousness and reading—of consciousness as a tool for feminist revolt and subversion in a way that reenvisions the critical, interpretive task. When gender becomes a mode of perception, the lines are drawn in such a way that we can no longer assume a masculine subject or a unified reception of texts. This recognition of the differences inherent to reading is crucial to the political nature of feminist criticism. If Fetterley is perhaps too certain of gender lines, her delineations expose the extant erroneous certainties upon which reading itself has been premised.

This first generation of feminist reading theories introduces two interrelated paradigms taken up in the work of theorists who follow. The model of the mask that hides, alienates, and/or oppresses an authentic, stable, female identity becomes central to the work of Patrocinio Schweickart and Jean Kennard and encodement theories. In these the lure of identity is the enticement of a singular self-knowledge that leads to an empowerment. Identity is a lure in the same way that origins are: a single stable identity is an illusion produced by a nostalgic wish for mastery. This is not to say that individuals don't have identities: they do; but these identities are flexible, contradictory products of multiple intersecting conditions. They change through time and are capable of occupying more than one position simultaneously, and if we accept psychoanalytic accounts of subjectivity, identity is an illusion of wholeness constantly undermined and destabilized by an unconscious beyond the control of the individual and not necessarily consistent with the identity individuals believe they have. The lure of identity is often a political requisite: without identity, the monolithic identifications necessary to spark political empathy and action might be missing, unless notions of identity change to accommodate individual plurality.

The second paradigm, suggested by Rich's understanding of the uncertainty of Dickinson's texts, is a model of multiplicity and destabilization that takes the flexibility of both identity and texts into account. This takes up as well the subversive qualities suggested by Fetterley's use of the prince metaphor, qualities linked, through Dickinson, to the question of lesbian sexuality. Bonnie Zimmerman proposes a double vision that might break away from the need for a unified reading subject. Dale Bauer tries to account for the multiple frames of community and split subjectivity through the development of a gender-cognizant Bakhtinian model of feminist reading. Jane Gallop enacts a feminist psychoanalytic model of reading premised on an unstable or shifting identity that allows a conscious roving between uncertainty and mastery located both in the reader and in the text.

IDENTITY POLITICS

In "Reading Ourselves: Toward a Feminist Theory of Reading," Patrocinio Schweickart builds upon the dialectical aspect of both Rich's and Fetterley's approaches.[36] Splitting her project into gendered divisions that reflect the different targets of Rich's and Fetterley's readings—Rich's reading of a woman and Fetterley's strategies for reading male authors—Schweickart defines Rich's "dialectic of communication" between reader and the author as "subjectified object," a dialectic that enables differences and multiplicity. This is posed against Fetterley's resistant reading, which Schweickart characterizes as a "dialectic of control."

A major portion of Schweickart's article is devoted to reading Rich's essay on Dickinson, a project she defines as "close contact with an interiority—a power, a creativity, a suffering, a vision—that is *not* identical with her own" (52). What Schweickart stresses and stresses beyond Rich's own emphasis is the existence of difference in Rich's model, of the necessity for a consciousness of difference and an emphasis on multiplicity that takes place in the context of a lesbian reader of possibly lesbian texts. It is not so much that the differences

Schweickart sees are not intrinsic to Rich's reading, but that Schweickart chooses difference itself as the crucial essence of Rich's enactment and locates that difference in the relation between Rich as reader and Dickinson as text. Reading affinity as like, but not like, and for a moment valorizing that uncertainty, Schweickart then displaces this self-contained contradiction into a series of dialectical reader/text splits. The divisions in the reader in Schweickart's scheme, developed to account for an "awareness of the double context of reading and writing" (53), translate potential multiplicity into more rigid and dialectical positionalities in a reader/text relation, more reminiscent of Fetterley's "resisting reader."

Schweickart's plan recuperates potential differences present in Rich's work into a dualistic difference, breaking the process of reading into "three moments." The first moment displaces into an otherwise singular subject the difference between reader and author: "Because reading removes the barrier between subject and object, the division [the duality of reader and author] takes place *within* the reader. Reading induces a doubling of the reader's subjectivity, so that one can be placed at the disposal of the text while the other remains with the reader. Now, this doubling presents a problem, for in fact there is only one subject present—the reader" (53). Schweickart proposes that the text gains a subjectivity via the projection of the reader in the process of interpreting the text. This projection of the reader occupies the place of the absent author, and the reading subject becomes the receptacle for this complex splitting.

Since the absence of the author disenables "safeguards against the appropriation of the text by the reader," Schweickart's "second moment" recertifies the singularity of the reading subject by displacing any divisions, projective selves, or introjective processes into a separate "readerly" consciousness similar to the consciousness of an underlying gender identity evoked by Rich and Fetterley. But Schweickart goes beyond a consciousness of gender to recognize that reading involves a broader consciousness; the subject must recognize that "reading is necessarily subjective" (53). The increased awareness of subjectivity retains what is for Schweickart a troublesome duplicity. Consciousness of subjectivity splits the subject. This second splitting is cured by Schweickart's "third moment," where the reader's split is relocated to the context of reading and writing. This displacement moves the question of split identity away from the reading subject and envisions differences as the natural results of history and reading rather than as an effect of intrasubjective splits that undermine the mastery of the reading subject.

This contextual resolution both explains and erases differences by situating them as objects to be comprehended by a singular subject: "Reading becomes a mediation between author and reader, between the context of writings and the context of readings" (54). "Mediation" is a settling of differences. Who accomplishes the mediation? The reader—the subject—occupies the "monistic" position of theory and has become a figure wielding consciousness that replaces theory itself. From Rich to Schweickart, consciousness is the primary tool that endows control, combats immasculation, and provides a paradoxical certainty of a feminist identity achieved through the consciousness it is also responsible for creating. This circularity reflects another circularity: the underlying certainty of a feminist identity that reads Emily Dickinson to produce a feminist identity. The lesbian or uncertain text provokes a very certain feminist reader. The (possibly) lesbian text results in the evocation of a feminist reader's consciousness as the site of control. Consciousness and identity stand in for theory and reassimilate the differences that generate it.

The strength of a singular subject strategically wielding consciousness is also evident in Jean Kennard's "Ourself Behind Ourself: A Theory for Lesbian Readers," which using a line from Dickinson: "Ourself behind Ourself," as the operative metaphor of a reading strategy, constructs a theory for lesbian readers premised upon a unified, lesbian self.[37] Picking up Rich's and Fetterley's idea of a real self behind another, less politically conscious self, Kennard breaks apart the notion of a single *woman* reader in a recognition of the sexual differences among women. In this search for self, the question of definition becomes important, since in order to posit a lesbian self, we need to know what a lesbian is. Kennard scans the possible definitions for a lesbian reader, seeing multiple possibilities: lesbian sexuality as innate, lesbian as a social or political category, lesbian sexuality as a choice selected from a possible range. Arriving at an impasse between an innate lesbian predisposition and lesbian existence as a chosen posture—at the problem of multiple, contradictory stances—Kennard shifts the problem of lesbian (and ultimately of female) multiplicity into her theory of reading, which attempts to accommodate differences in a multipurpose approach. She defines her project: "What I wish to suggest here is a theory of reading which will not oversimplify the concept of identification, which will not subsume lesbian difference under a universal female, and which will be applicable to all texts, including those written by men, heterosexual women, and self-hating lesbians" (66). Like Schweickart, Kennard hopes theory itself can accomplish the mediation among differences that for her exist among texts and people rather than within them.

Kennard's specific strategy for wielding consciousness is within what she defines as a "polar" model of reading. Based upon Joseph Zinker's Gestalt psychology, the multiple intrapsychic differences of the reader are realigned into polarities—good/evil, hard/soft—which in turn contribute to a single identity, established by means of a repression or denial of the unacceptable, or "bad," traits on one side of the opposition. She organizes multiplicity into an identity that can then do what Kennard, borrowing from Zinker, calls "leaning into" the text. By consciously accepting a "repressed" trait, which turns out not to be repressed but merely part of an oppositional pair—in the case of the lesbian, identifying with/as a heterosexual—the reader allows "the polarities to co-exist" (70). But this coexistence of oppositions works ultimately to reinforce, to "redefine aspects of ourselves through contrast with the opposite aspects in a fictional other which we have temporarily experienced" (70). In other words, experiencing polarities (which are already artificial oppositions) enables the reader to arrive at an even stronger sense of self and permits the reader to experience or pass through conflicting possibilities by only temporarily engaging them. Paradoxically, this turns out to be a way of ignoring differences not by recognizing and containing them, but by putting them in the service of a "real" self. "Ourself behind Ourself" turns out to be a better-defined self instead of split or multiple selves.

Implicit in this approach, in her title even, is the same notion of a masked consciousness proposed by both Rich and Fetterley and reminiscent of Cixous' and Irigaray's preoedipal female space. But Kennard suggests a new and crucial twist. While Rich and Fetterley assume a mask already in place that must be shed, Kennard empowers the reader by suggesting that masks can be deliberately assumed and removed, a process that both allows the reader flexibility and range and suggests multiple layers or conditions of consciousness itself. Kennard's proposition of multiple consciousnesses and of conscious role-playing, though proffered within a rather fixed dialectic carefully moored to a certain identity, enables a controlled multiplicity that is but a short (albeit a difficult) step from allowing for multiple, coexistent, contradicting splits both in the subject and in texts. In other words, she is but a step away from relinquishing the theoretical necessity for identity and singularity even as she posits more strongly a notion of individual control.

Kennard ends with Rich's reading of Dickinson, suggesting that Rich has anticipated this polar reading practice:

> So Rich's insight into Dickinson allows her to affirm her own values through polarizing aspects of her "real" self. It is not coincidental that Dickinson finally teaches Rich what Rich has taught us: 'More than any other poet Emily Dickinson seemed to tell me that the intense inner event, the personal and the psychological, was inseparable from the universal; that there was a range for psychological poetry beyond mere self-expression' [p. 168]. (77)

The self becomes powerful, goes beyond itself, becomes universal. The overtly lesbian reading practice, or the practice Kennard proposes *for* lesbians, is a practice that tries to accommodate differences among readers, but can only do so by appealing even more strongly to the sense of a singular self constructed from oppositions that are really versions of the same. Even so, in the vicinity of the lesbian the potential for multiplicity emerges.

This series of texts centered around Dickinson—centered precisely around the intersection of questions of gender, sexuality, reading, and writing—raises an important question about the relation of multiplicity to singularity in reading practice and about the relation of multiplicity and theory played out in the return of the lesbian's text to a singular position of empowered readerly consciousness. Among these theories, there is a curious reiteration of the prefix *re*; these strategies result in a *re*-vision, a *re*sisting, *re*reading, *re*inforcing of the self behind the self who first comes to life in Dickinson's poetry. The repeated *re* is related to consciousness; the *re* stands for the wielding of consciousness—the moment where the redefined feminist subject encounters the text—the entry point into the circular and self-reflexive trading between (self)-definition and consciousness. The structure proposed is both multiple and singular at the same time. Two selves coexist, one under the other or one in opposition to the other, but the various reading strategies—the rereadings, resistings, revisings—ultimately refer to, rely upon, and veer toward the "real," good, female self behind some other, outer self constructed by and in patriarchy. Posed in this context as an identity, the real female self occupies a position analogous to the female ab original spaces proposed by Cixous and Irigaray. Identity and origins constitute the same kind of lure, while the multiplicities and differences initially posed as a problem with readers that must be surmounted are reinterpreted and displaced in this process as differences in the perception of texts. Difference is located away from subjectivity in the place between, in the place of the transaction between reader and text, and away from the reader, who regains her singularity and a more authentic identity.

By finding a mediation point or a transactional location, the sticky political problem of intrapsychic or intratextual contradiction and inconsistency does not have to be addressed. Feminist resistance requires a strong female subject, especially when the battleground is drawn between genders instead of among and within individuals. Privileging consciousness is a version of this strengthened feminist self, and when facing the task of reading, the feminist self seems to ignore or deny the operation of any unconscious. While the question of the lesbian seems to bring up the possibility of a split or self-contradictory subject in that each of these essays initially poses the problem of multiple selves raised by Dickinson's texts, they all end up closing that off by an appeal to a wholeness represented by an integral subject in conscious control. Perhaps of all of them, Rich leaves open the most possibility for contradictory existence, as she is less insistent finally on the method—on a monocular theory—than on experiences of differences themselves.

The idea of a feminist identity that exists under a patriarchal mask appears in a slightly different form in two additional feminist arguments about reading: encodement theories and "reading as a woman." The textual version of theories of a masked readerly feminist identity, encodement theories postulate that certain works by lesbian authors such as Gertrude Stein and Djuna Barnes are written in a code that, nonsensical or superficially heterosexual, masks an underlying lesbian meaning. As Catherine Stimpson formulates it:

> [Stein] takes certain lesbian or quasi-lesbian experiences and progressively disguises and encodes them in a series of books. I would speculate that she does so for various reasons. Some of them are aesthetic:

the need to avoid imitating one's self; the desire to transform apprentice materials into richer, more satisfying verbal worlds. Other reasons are psychological: the need to write out hidden impulses; the wish to speak to friends without having others overhear; the desire to evade and confound strangers, aliens, and enemies.[38]

Beginning again with lesbian sexuality, encodement theories envision the text as a translation of an identity and experience that will be recognized by readers who share that identity and experience. As Stimpson comments, "Whatever the motive, literary encoding does what Morse Code does: it transmits messages in a different form which initiates may translate back into the original" (499). This necessarily assumes a very certain and monolithic lesbian identity that correlates with the encoded lesbian meaning of the text. Not only, then, does encodement rely on a notion of an essential lesbian identity, but it also tends to define the text in terms of the "true biographical identity of the author, inadvertently limiting textual interplay and contradiction in favor of a correct translation.

While encodement theories propose one kind of masquerade, the idea of "reading as a woman" offers another. Far less dependent upon a stable identity, "reading as a woman" suggests that readers can deliberately and consciously assume a gender identity to read. Appealing to consciousness as a tool, "reading as a woman" is essentially a masquerade dependent upon the flexibility of identity and the ability of readers to either call up similarities within themselves or empathize from positions different from their own. "Reading as a woman" derives from the split identity that disturbed Schweickart. Peggy Kamuf describes this split as "the differential meaning which has always been at work in a single term."[39] Discussing the problem of "a woman reading as a woman," Kamuf points to the "repetition of the 'identical' term" which "splits that identity." While identity here is related to gender—is a gender—to think of any identity splits it, makes identity not identical to itself. The split in identity creates a kind of consciousness of the first identity so that the repetition of identity becomes a kind of conscious assumption of identity or a masquerade. So that what might be perceived as an authentic identity or position—"reading as a woman"—is always, paradoxically, not an authentic position (if there can ever be such a thing), but the masquerade of one, i.e., at least two positions, one playing itself. If the same identity is repeated, if for example we read as a woman reading as a woman, the duplication tends to be disguised as different levels of self-consciousness confused with critical practice itself.

"Reading as a woman" became the subject of debate among Elaine Showalter, Jonathan Culler, and Terry Eagleton. The danger of such formulation to feminist theory is that with it anyone—including men —can theoretically read as women. This bothers Showalter. In "Critical Cross-dressing; Male Feminists and the Woman of the Year," Showalter critiques the work of male critics who claim some part of the practice of feminist criticism, questioning the authenticity and validity of a man dressing, reading, writing, looking as a woman.[40] Though she lists a number of critical issues, the essay is primarily focused on the problems and possibilities of cross-gendered critical practices—reading, writing, looking—on a "critical cross-dressing" she aligns with "both radical chic and power play" (120). What Showalter questions is whether a man can read as a woman and the extent to which the idea of the split woman reader might enable that idea is the degree to which men can become women. In rejecting woman as an essential identity, it would appear that Culler is making a place for the male reader in a feminist project; if woman is a construct, then why can't a man construct himself in that position just as easily as a woman?

This discussion clearly reveals what is at stake in the fixed gender identity that underwrites so much feminist reading theory. While a conscious manipulation of gender might seem to be one way of escaping phallocratic hegemony based on gender, permitting the free play of gender identity deprives feminists of any power premised upon gender identity. While the idea of cross-dressing plays its way through the tradition of feminist reading theories—in Fetterley, in encodement theories—it is most acceptable when it is the performance of a certain gender identity taking on or shedding an obviously false identity. The idea that gender and identity themselves might be unstable threatens the basic identity presumptions of this strain of feminist theory.

The lure of consciousness and identity that persists in feminist theories of reading is linked to the problem of self-definition—to the problem of knowing self. Appeals to consciousness and certainty about feminist identity are attempts to establish a locus, a place from which one can begin to sort out differences and gain a politically efficacious consciousness, intra- and interpsychically, inter- and intratextually. But of course, consciousness and definition of necessity create a circularity, a kind of self-referentiality: how do you know where to start unless you know where to start to start? Seeking *a* definition pits a singularity—a definable persona—against the complex multiplicities encountered in reading that this singular consciousness wants to control, resulting in an even better *re*definition of self, a better consciousness of self that leads to a more cohesive self in a better position to define self. This methodology could be seen as primarily defensive, as a way of mustering an armor of self to face the attacks upon self threatened by the alienating, sometimes patriarchal or heterosexist other of the text. An identity-oriented version of Cixous' and Irigaray's paradigms of an ab original female space, consciousness, too, plays *ab origine,* even though according to this series of accounts, the self must be found or created prior to the act of reading and the self is a creature of consciousness.

Part of the lure of identity, definition becomes a critical preoccupation. The problem of lesbian definition that underlies a substantial portion of Kennard's argument (as it must, since this certain identity wields dangerously multiple differences) reflects a feminist critical preoccupation with self-definition as a starting point of perhaps unachievable clarity about the subject of discourse. This "problem of definition," as Bonnie Zimmerman calls it, is another version of the problem of theory mentioned by Flynn and Schweickart and reflects the allure of knowledge and certainty that underwrites identity.[41] For feminism in general, definition is a political tool linked to the self and to consciousness; the urge to define is in part a politically motivated desire for *re*definition, which is an often subversive attempt to wrest the subject of woman from the language of patriarchy, but which is also part of a desire to name, possess, own, resingularize positions within the realm of feminist control—it is thus also a stabilizing and/ or defensive activity.[42]

Multiplicity and difference catalyze a desire for differentiation and fixity, for the categories definition provides. And this is why the lesbian is particularly subject to definition, precisely because she is not readily assimilable in the binary system of sexual difference, yet she must be accounted for. As a point of stress, the definition of lesbian becomes necessary to feminist criticism, and definition itself becomes the basis for feminist categorical arguments such as Monique

Wittig's complex argument that "lesbians are not women" or Penelope Engelbrecht's attempt to bring the categories of lesbian and postmodern together.[43] Definition, knowledge, and the lesbian are critically bound together; as Bonnie Zimmerman observes, some "problems of definition" "may be inherent in lesbian studies" (207) and "the issues that face lesbian critics . . . are the interests of all feminist critics" (219).

Reminiscent of Cixous' splitting of the lesbian into phallic and feminine components, one reason for the need to define the lesbian within feminist communities is that the potentially lesbian configuration of female bonding inherent to feminism produces the need to define lesbianism in relation to feminism as a way of controlling the uncertainties of intimacy and female desire both within the feminist community and in the way the feminist community relates to dominant culture. In "Compulsory Heterosexuality and Lesbian Existence," Adrienne Rich's spectral definition of lesbian is an attempt to allay this anxiety about sexuality. Making homoeroticism into a figure for feminist political action and the primacy of all relations among women, sexual and nonsexual, broadening the definition of lesbian transmutes questions of sexual orientation into questions of political position. Turning a politically threatening term into a positive term, Rich undermines any definitional certainty about sexual orientation, making lesbianism a question of degree rather than an absolute category. She says:

> I have chosen to use the terms, *lesbian existence* and *lesbian continuum* because the word *lesbianism* has a clinical and limiting ring. *Lesbian existence* suggests both the fact of the historical presence of lesbians and our continuing creation of the meaning of that existence. I mean the term *lesbian continuum* to include a range—through each woman's life and throughout history—of woman-identified experience; not simply the fact that a woman has had or consciously desired genital sexual experience with another woman. If we expand it to embrace many more forms of primary intensity between and among women, including the sharing of a rich inner life, the bonding against male tyranny, the giving and receiving of practical and political support . . . —we begin to grasp breadths of female history and psychology that have lain out of reach as a consequence of limited, mostly clinical, definitions of "lesbianism." (192).

This definitional broadening is a renaming that disperses a binary difference—lesbian/heterosexual—into multiple shades of difference that make the category of sexual orientation somewhat theoretically meaningless within the feminist community. In relations between the feminist community and dominant culture, the potential split within feminism created by sexual orientation and exacerbated by what is seen as the derogatory association of feminism and lesbianism is returned to a totalized, lesbianized whole that defies attempts to discredit the movement on the basis of sexual orientation. Definition for Rich is a tool for distributing differences among women, making dissimilarities a question of degree rather than of essence. Theoretically, at least, the practice of renaming makes a place for the coexistence of differences at the place of the lesbian. These differences are also reflected in possible distinctions among the terms, *lesbian, lesbian sexuality,* and *lesbianism. Lesbian* (or *lesbian experience, lesbian continuum*) is a broader denomination that reflects the metaphor of female community to which it is associated. *Lesbian sexuality* is a much narrower term, applied to eroticized relations (real or imagined) among women. *Lesbianism*, a term Rich rejects, refers primarily to modes of existence associated with the real or imagined practice of lesbian sexuality.

Imported into the question of reading as a lesbian, Rich's definitional ploy is both critiqued and extended by Bonnie Zimmerman into a lesbian reading practice premised on the coexistence of multiple differences in perspective—on a lesbian "double vision." For Zimmerman in "What Has Never Been: An Overview of Lesbian Feminist Literary Criticism," "lesbian criticism continues to be plagued with the problem of definition," since "those who are developing lesbian criticism and theory . . . may need limited and precise definitions"[44] Echoing Flynn and Schweickart, Zimmerman sees a connection between definition and theory. For this reason, "Rich's "all-inclusive definitions of lesbianism" that "risk blurring the distinctions between lesbian relationships and nonlesbian female friendships, or between lesbian identity and female-centered identity" are not useful to the more precise needs of theory, which seems to depend upon such definitions as a starting point. Zimmerman proposes a lesbian critical practice premised on the dual perspectives experienced by minorities in mainstream culture between the "freedom and flexibility" of the "boundaries" and "imprisonment" in a culture other to oneself, between seeing as one included within cultural assumptions and as one to whom those assumptions are foreign (218).

These positions enable both the "unmasking" of heterosexist presumptions and the identification and celebration of more female-centered experience in texts, a kind of interesting combination of Fetterley and Rich translated into an overtly lesbian context. Zimmerman's "double vision," like Rich's "re-vision," is necessary for "survival" and is located in the realm of individual practice, not in a split or fragmented self, but in the individual's ability to manipulate more than one perspective, a conscious multiplicity that enlarges critical possibilities. Like Kennard's "polar" formula, Zimmerman's lesbian reading extends beyond the lesbian, becoming a model for minority practice itself that does not forget its double positioning. Definition engenders consciousness, not only of position but of one's theoretical practice, resulting in a consciousness of definition; as Jane Gallop points out: "Thanks to Zimmerman's 'double vision,' we can understand the need for such a strategy [definition], without relinquishing the sense that it is also finally limited, as definition and as theory" (117).

Zimmerman's practice is located at the point of an individual consciousness of the perspectives generated by one's cultural position. In *Feminist Dialogics*, Dale Bauer doubles these points of consciousness.[45] Bauer questions the inevitability of the reader-response path from multiplicity to monolithic theory and its reestablishment of a singular identity by postulating a coexistence of the two in what she calls a "dialogic community," which cannot exist "without the tension between the marginal and the central, the eccentric and the phallocentric" (xiii). Locating this gender-conscious Bakhtinian community in a place analogous to Fetterley's "critical dialogue" or Schweickart's "context of writings and the context of readings," Bauer redefines their points of mediation as "the point of contradiction between the alienated female voice and the interpretive community anxious to incorporate and domesticate that voice in order to silence its threat" (x). This place, the place of resolution for reader-response critics, becomes the place of solution in Bauer's Bakhtinian model—the place where the troublesome return to monolithic theory is perpetually avoided by the proposal of a space dedicated to ceaseless tension, conflict, subversion, and ideological turmoil created by the clash of gender and class (and no doubt differences in sexual orientation) with dominant discourse.

Bauer's model relies on the "double voice" of feminist critics instead of upon a "double vision" like that suggested by Zimmerman. The difference between voice and vision is the difference between Zimmerman's appeal to perspective and consciousness and Bauer's invocation of language as the agent that both constitutes prison house norms and conventions and "provides occasions for its own disruption and critique" (xiii). But while Bauer's language, curiously detached from any question of subjective consciousness, seems to operate on its own, like Zimmerman's double vision, it too is wielded by a consciousness that refers to an intact feminist subject underneath who already understands her alienation. This consciousness enables the subject "to read the contradictory moments of representation and sexual difference" by allowing her "own 'internally persuasive voice' (Bakhtin's term)—formulated in difference—to clash with the text" (xiv). While Bauer defers the constitution of an integrated subject one step further, suggesting by her "formulated in difference" that this subject must undergo some struggle to acquire this voice—some struggle beyond the mere consciousness of difference in Fetterley, Kennard, or Schweickart—still, at heart the feminist critic has the necessary subjectivity to avoid completely internalizing patriarchal culture. In response to questions about the possibility of internal self-contradiction and the impossibility of escaping the patriarchal culture that Jane Gallop characterizes as "always already there in each subject as subject," Bauer response with a hearty assertion of freedom, akin to "ourself behind ourself": "The answer is that nothing can be internalized totally and irrevocably; we always have internalized norms from various cultural contexts and contacts" (xii). Like language, which provides the means for its own subversion, so culture can where "each internalization of repression contains the possibility of rebellion" (xii). Bauer's reservation of the self within means that neither culture nor language is completely hegemonic; following Bakhtin and Marcelle Marini, Bauer posits that neither can ever "be completely totalizing" (xii).

Like the circularity between consciousness and identity basic to Fetterley and Rich, Bauer constructs a self-reflexive system that relies on the one hand on the power of language and culture to disrupt themselves and, on the other, on a core of female identity for whose benefit that disruption occurs. Her tendency to isolate individual will from mechanisms of language and culture—a kind of subjective dislocation—avoids any question of individual unconsciousness or split subjectivity by displacing those into mechanisms of representation such as language regarded as external. It also does not answer the difficult question of how feminist critics might make those disruptions work to their advantage. While Bauer's model relies upon and even celebrates the fertile coexistence of polylogue, multiplicity, and monolithic theory is a space similar to Cixous and Irigaray's feminine economies, it can only do so by relying upon a subject who is at the core both conscious and whole, reiterating the feminist appeal to a strong or strengthened subject in the context of this realm of indecision and uncertainty.

While Rich, Zimmerman, and Bauer all make use of the productive existence of some space of multiplicity and tension, Rich and Zimmerman within an overtly lesbian context, none actually enacts or plays with the possibility of a split, self-contradictory, desiring subject. The implications of Kamuf's analysis of "reading as a woman" are perhaps too easily dismissed. Part of the problem is that identity is defined as singular; its allure is certainty and knowledge. The originary but superficial connection between identity and lesbian sexuality in the figure of Emily Dickinson is lost in theoretical transitions to certainty. Desire and the erotic associated with lesbian sexuality are exorcised via the lure of identity and definition, which promise knowledge and control. Perhaps the work of Jane Gallop suggests another way readers might read productively, making use of textual and readerly splits, a consciousness of the workings of desire, and a flexibility of identity. While her interpretations of literary and critical texts are often authoritative, by remaining constantly aware of her own readerly subjectivity she also exposes and plays upon the role of desire and the unconscious in the reading process, retaining a flexibility of identity and interplay of multiples that suggests one way of simultaneously falling for the lure of identity and deferring the pleasure of mastery identity might endow.[46]

Both writing and reading depend upon the establishment of some certain space that reflects and enables a feminine reality that precedes what Broumas calls the "transliteration" of language and patriarchal culture. Within that space, both origins and identity are lures, decoys that promise power, knowledge, and a challenge to a patriarchal system or a way out altogether. At the origin of theories about writing and reading is a configuration of lesbian sexuality. Writing theories use lesbian sexuality as a metaphor for an originary feminine economy while denying the material lesbian. Reading theories are often catalyzed by the question of lesbian sexuality, which leads ultimately to more certain assertions of a singular feminist identity. In both cases, lesbian sexuality configures an enigma of multiplicity that must be excised or definitionally controlled. Configured as a specter of gender uncertainty, lesbian sexuality is split into heterosexual—masculine and feminine—components. In writing theories, the masculine is rejected, the feminine retained. In reading theories, this configuration of uncertainty is carried through figures of cross-dressing, permissible when the masculine is layered over the feminine (as in Dickinson, Fetterley, encodement theories, and Showalter's comments), reprehensible the other way around.

In both scenarios, lesbian sexuality is split to assure a more certain identity elsewhere—in a female space or in a feminist identity. The lure into both origins and identity, lesbian sexuality itself is reduced to a politically appropriate position: nominally disassociated from writing theories and representative of politically correct minority multiplicity in reading theories. While the differences in the fate of lesbian configurations are in part due to cultural and historical differences, their divergency around the subject of lesbian sexuality also reveals the way both writing and reading theories are essentially reliant upon a binary system of gender. If configurations of lesbian sexuality pose the question or provide the answer to the dilemma of patriarchal hegemony, the fact that the multiplicity or flexibility attributed to the lesbian isn't retained is an indication of the extent to which neither set of theories is able to understand and use plurality—the extent to which they inevitably return (and return the lesbian) to a singular, controlling position. In answer to Alice's question, while it might begin with L, it ends with I.

■ F O U R
Freud Reads Lesbians

IN THE year 1900, Freud saw a patient suffering from
hysteria. Giving her the fictional name Dora, (after his housemaid),
Freud listened to her story and her dreams and analyzed them according to the precepts of his developing psychoanalytical techniques.
These included not only his method of interpreting dreams, but also
his understanding of the mechanism of psychoanalytic transference
by which the patient transfers feelings of love and hate onto the
analyst. Dora felt that she was the pawn in a romantic triangle between her father, the wife of a friend, called Frau K., and Frau K.'s
husband, Herr K. She believed that she was being traded to Herr K.
by her father so that her father could continue his affair with Frau K.
After Dora recounted several incidents of sexual aggressiveness by
Herr K., Freud read her rejection of Herr K.'s advances as repressed
sexual desire for him, out of which arose her hysteria. Freud's treatment of Dora lasted less than six months; in the middle of the process
Dora announced to Freud that she was terminating her visits. Only
after she had ceased to be his patient did Freud see that his interpretation of her symptoms had probably been incorrect; instead of being
in love with Herr K., Dora was jealous of her father's relations with

Frau K.—not only because she was in love with her father, but because she was repressing desire for Frau K. His analysis a failure, Freud wrote up the case history and submitted it for publication in 1901, but he withdrew it soon after and did not publish it until 1905, when it appeared as *Fragment of an Analysis of a Case of Hysteria*, referred to by modern critics as "the Dora case"[1]

The case raises questions about the relation of desire, reading, knowledge, and interpretation manifested in the case's failures in knowledge, issues of timing, and the effects of Freud's identifications and assumptions as he reads Dora's history and motives. Perhaps the most difficult problem in Freud's narrative of the case is the question of knowledge, both Freud's knowledge of Dora and Dora's knowledge of sexual matters. In a suspiciously self-reflective way, the gaps in knowledge in the Dora case have to do with questions of knowing: What did Freud know and when? What did Dora know and how and when did Freud know she knew? Freud's repression of his knowledge of the typical relation between hysteria and homosexuality is part of the reason for his analytical failure; his spectacular resistance to this knowledge is largely responsible for the case's popularity as a critical topic in feminist criticism of the 1980s. His apparent blindness creates a kind of psychoanalytic dramatic irony, permitting us to see what Freud both did and didn't, engaging us with the idea that we can read both Dora and Freud where Freud couldn't and luring us with the promise of the knowledge that evaded Freud until it was too late. We become part of the critical circle; from the vantage of hindsight, we read Freud reading Dora from yet another frame outside, but in so doing, we reproduce again the tension of desire and knowledge that strains to master this text, just as Freud wished to master Dora.

While we might suspect that Freud's representational gambits are motivated by his own sexual investments, and no doubt to some extent they are, his stake is scarcely different from that of most critics, who accept, either unquestioningly or unconsciously, a dominant heterosexual premise. From the founding moment of Dora's analysis when Freud himself discovered and failed to appreciate this repressed and elusive nucleus, the Dora case has been an ever-widening circle of attempts to center first her eccentric lesbian desire, then Freud's desires and countertransferences, which ignore and supplant Dora's desire, then the political, critical, and identificatory investments of various critics and defenders of both Freud and Dora, which repeat and elaborate the balancing operations, corralling Dora and her lesbian desire in a reassuring ring of representational overcompensation.

A number of scholars commenting on the Dora case continue Freud's evasion of the issue of lesbian sexuality. Though such reader as Jane Gallop, Jacqueline Rose, Suzanne Gearhart, and Neil Hertz all discuss the significance of this missing lesbian "key," retrieving it from the "hole" in Freud's text, most commentators replicate Freud's repression of a lesbian sexuality in many of the same ways Freud does, ignoring Dora's lesbian desire, identifying with father figures, and emphasizing the question of Freud's own countertransference.[2] This is not to say, of course, that all critics of Freud need end up immersed in lesbian issues; it is to suggest that different perspectives or reading, especially when we are reading a "reading," either narcissistically reproduce their own positions or reiterate the position of reader constructed by the text. Much of this has to do with our acquiescence to the obvious paths of knowledge; in reading, our desire is to ascertain and master. As Freud admitted, he failed to "master" the transference in time, to know himself sufficiently. But as a result of that failure, he finally saw what he had missed: the relation between knowledge and desire located in the gap figured by the lesbian, a gap bound up with issues of knowledge and mis/reading. If, rather than retracing Freud's path, our desire is to locate a different knowledge, if we read from the position of the "knowledge" Freud evades, what kind of reading results?

Throughout his career, Freud's case histories of lesbian women seem to catalyze his work on theories of general sexuality. The Dora case occurs relatively early in Freud's career (1900–1905), but begins five years after the publication (with Joseph Breuer) of *Studies in Hysteria* (1893–1895).[3] The time from Freud's analysis of Dora to the first publication of the case history spans another five-year period, not only tying together his earlier works and linking his treatment of hysteria to his method of dream interpretation, but also joining his earlier work on hysteria to his 1905 "Three Essays on the Theory of Sexuality," which consider homosexuality as an aberration.[4] In addition, the five-year period of the Dora case encompasses the composition of two other works, *The Psychopathology of Everyday Life* and *Jokes and Their Relation to the Unconscious*, works that extend Freud's basic method of dream interpretation to more quotidian phenomena, seem-

ingly unrelated to questions of hysteria, but revealing a more univer-
salized theory of the pervasive causality of repressed sexuality. At the
center of this cluster or work that circles around questions of repressed
sexuality and extends from *Studies in Hysteria* to "Three Essays on the
Theory of Sexuality" and "My Views on the Part Played by Sexuality
in the Aetiology of Neuroses," the Dora case is the only fragmentary
report and notable failure, created by Freud's *repression* of his knowledge of sexuality.[5]

After an interval of twenty years, Freud describes another fragmentary and unsuccessful analysis of a lesbian in "Psychogenesis of a Case
of Homosexuality in a Woman" (1920).[6] Like the Dora case, this
second engagement with "deviant" female desire anchors another
decade of theorizing about female sexuality, work that appears in his
1922 essay, "Some Neurotic Mechanisms in Jealousy, Paranoia and
Homosexuality," in "Some Psychical Consequences of the Anatomical Distinction between the Sexes" (1925), and in "Female Sexuality"
in 1931.[7] Chronologically, "Dora" and "Psychogenesis" mirror one
another. Posed midway from either end of Freud's career, both fragments appear to instigate extended efforts to theorize about sexuality
in general. The fifteen years that separate the publication of the case
studies span the center of Freud's working years (1886–1939); just to
the side of the center, both cases represent clinical failures retrieved
and enveloped with flurries of theoretical activity that put the subject
of female sexuality back under Freud's control. And since in Freud's
cases of lesbians knowledge is precisely what is at issue, the two cases
of lesbian sexuality become eccentric gaps to be filled in with cascades
of overcompensatory knowing that bury lesbian sexuality under the
pressing but illuminating weight of sexual theory.

Between these two periods of sexual theorizing around failed analyses comes Freud's "successful" connection of homosexuality and
paranoia in "A Case of Paranoia Running Counter to the Psychoanalytic Theory of the Disease" (1915), linked both to the Schreber case
and to Freud's conceptions of the relation of homosexuality to narcissism.[8] An interesting gloss to the other two cases, where he failed in
some way, in this middle case Freud discovers an underlying lesbian
desire to prove his point, focusing upon the mechanisms—narcissism
and paranoia—that may well have induced his inability to read the
other two cases. That this case is also about knowledge and desire—
about who knew what when—but brings knowledge and desire to-

gether in good time resolves the dissatisfying temporal disjunctions of the Dora case while anticipating the problems of substance and visibility Freud encounters in "Psychogenesis."

Dora Always Already Again

THE CRISIS of knowledge in Dora's case history are almost always appended to the discovery that Dora's sexual desire is the source of her symptoms, something that Freud renders ambivalently: both Freud and Dora know and don't know it, can represent and are unable to represent it. The issue of Dora's potential lesbian desire is tentatively and tenuously reproduced by its treatment in the case study; both inside and outside, contemporary and afterthought, it is posed as a conscious intertextual problem of moral responsibility in relation to scientific truth and honest reporting or as an apologetic, corrective footnote in the postscript. The text of the Dora case is divided into five sections: "Prefatory Remarks," in which Freud describes his choices in recording the case history, "The Clinical Picture," a lengthy section where Freud sets out both his methodology and the narrative background of the case, two sections of analysis, "The First Dream" and "The Second Dream," and a short postscript where Freud discusses transference and his failure in the case.

Freud's most obvious problem with knowledge is timing. Beginning the configuration of delay and displacement that characterizes Freud's consistent marginalization of the issue of Dora's lesbian feelings, a long passage about Dora's homosexuality occurs at the end of the "Clinical Picture" section as a "further complication" (60), located at the center of the text. Separated graphically by a gap in the printing, this passage on the importance of lesbian sexuality appears as a kind of textual appendage or afterthought, while at the same time its reiteration of a key theme positions it as a completing coda, the displaced thematic center of the picture Freud has laboriously drawn in the first half of the case. This passage recognizes the existence of Dora's lesbian desire as an example of a general rule: "I have never yet gone through a single psychoanalysis of a man or a woman without having to take into account a very considerable current of homosexuality" (60); "these masculine, or more properly speaking, *gynaecophilic* currents of feeling are to be regarded as typical of the unconscious erotic life of hysterical girls" (63). "More properly speaking," we are to regard as "typical" these unconscious feelings; they are so typical that Freud forgets to regard them again until the postscript, a disregard that enables him to read Dora's dreams in a blindly heterosexual paradigm and permits him the unimpeded construction of the "fine poetic conflict" otherwise derailed by this gynaecophilic current.

While this "key" passage is central, but separated, in a footnote, the editor (James Strachey) attempts to connect it to the postscript at the end of the case where Freud finally recognizes his misreading. Thus cross-referenced in the margins, the two completely dissociated pieces about the importance of lesbian sexuality are linked, creating a direct line from the center of the case to the marginal footnote at the conclusion where Freud belatedly reasserts his earlier rule: "that her homosexual (gynaecophilic) love for Frau K. was the strongest unconscious current in her mental life" (120n). This strange inside/outside position of the passages on lesbian sexuality is characteristic of the ambivalent location of lesbian sexuality in Freud's work. Always in two places at once—in the center and on the outside, known and forgotten—it is outside by virtue of its centrality; it is central because of its eccentricity.

Freud's conceptual tardiness is more remarkable given the complex contradictions about when he knew what. Freud wrote the case "immediately" after the termination of the analysis, partly from notes on the dreams taken during the consultation. (see *SE* 7:10) The case history is by definition retrospective, a fact that brings into play the many questions about literary narrative raised by Freud in his prefatory remarks, as well as by Freudian critics such as Steven Marcus.[9] While Freud states that the case was composed "during the two weeks immediately following" (13) analysis, it is apparent from the text and footnotes that Freud must have added to the text at times increasingly distant from the analysis, yet before its 1905 publication. Freud's recognition of the importance of Dora's lesbian desire seems to come with time; as he acknowledges in the footnote near the end of the postscript: "The longer the interval of time that separates me from the end of this analysis, the more probable it seems to me that the fault in my technique lay in this omission" (120n), and he goes on to refer to his failure "to discover in time" Dora's love for Frau K. This footnote distances itself temporally from the analysis and from the drafting of the case history, pointing out what Freud characterizes as a mistake in timing during the analysis itself. But though the note is located at the end of the case, it refers back to a time during the analysis when Freud's knowledge came too late, locating itself not at the chronological end, but somewhere between analysis and the final version of the case history.

But Freud makes a second mistake in timing that reveals an even greater ambivalence in his representation of lesbian sexuality. In the middle of the case history, in his first attempt to broach the question of Dora's sexuality, Freud indicates that he "knew" or suspected the "homosexual current" *before* he undertook the case:

> "If this much can be established without difficulty of healthy persons, and if we take into account what has been already said [p. 50] about the fuller development in neurotics of the normal germs of perversion, we shall expect to find in these latter too a fairly strong homosexual predisposition. It must, indeed, be so; for I have never yet come through a single psycho-analysis of a man or a woman without having to take into account a very considerable current of homosexuality" (60).

He knew before; he has spared our feelings. But if he knew before, why doesn't he know "in time"? Was it simply the importance of this homosexual current that evaded him until it was too late? Was his mistake not in knowledge or timing, but in a repetition of that same de-centering, that same delay that characterizes his representation of lesbian sexuality in the case history? The passage above also refers back even further to an earlier, more general discussion in the case history of what he refers to as "perversion" in his formulation of another general rule: "When, therefore, any one has *become* a gross and manifest pervert, it would be more correct to say that he has *remained* one, for he exhibits a certain stage of *inhibited development*. All psycho-neurotics are persons with strongly marked perverse tendencies, which have been repressed in the course of their development and have become unconscious" (50). The rule is a rule of timing; lesbian sexuality is always already present, a remainder, a holdover rather than a change. But Freud is the one who disobeys his own formulation, disregarding what he already knows to be the role of lesbian sexuality, suspending the knowledge he demonstrates that he has until late in the analysis and late in the case history, where

Dora's lesbian desires are quite literally what remain appended in a footnote.

This, however, brings up yet another question in timing. Though Freud claims to have known about the importance of this "current of homosexuality" in work done *before* Dora's case, at no place in that previous work in there any indication of that discovery. In *Studies in Hysteria* Freud observes that his hysterical patients are unusual in the absence of sexual activity and lists that lack as a contributing factor but never explicitly mentions lesbian sexuality. At the end of the general passage on perversions in the Dora case, Freud indicates in a note that "these remarks upon the sexual perversions had been written some years before the appearance of Bloch's excellent book" and he refers to his own "Three Essays on the Theory of Sexuality," published the same year as Dora, "in which most of the points in the present paragraph are enlarged upon" (51n). Though his formulation of the relationship between sexual perversions and neurosis on page 50 precedes most of his case history of Dora, we don't really know when he arrived at that conclusion, since all of the case was written after Dora's analysis. If it was formulated in the context of his enlargement of it in "Three Essays," why then is he not more aware of its application in this case? If he formulated the generalization about the importance of homosexuality after the analysis but in the process of writing up the case, why does he not center that consideration in his discussion of the case? Or in the alternative, if he didn't formulate it until he later recognized its importance (footnote on 120), why does this formulation occur in the introductory material and not, as the other does, in a footnote? Perhaps Freud is a victim of the kind of unconsciously motivated forgetfulness he discusses in *The Psychopathology of Everyday Life*, where he describes his own unaccountable lapse of memory in forgetting that Wilhelm Fliess was the source of a notion of bisexuality Freud adopted in his own sexual theory: "I suspect that everyone who is willing to enquire into the motives behind his lapses of memory will be able to record a similar sample list of disagreeable subjects" (144). Now whether in Freud's case the disagreeable memory is his failed and vaguely homoerotic friendship with Fliess or the idea of lesbian sexuality, this forgetting is already bound up with the writing and publication of the Dora case, which he puts off publishing, as he informs Fliess, "because just a little earlier I had lost my last audience in you" (letter of March 11, 1902, 456).[10] Later in the correspondence, Freud and Fliess would argue vehemently over the issue of the origin of the theory of bisexuality, a battle that marked the bitter end rather than the original cause of their friendship's dissolution.[11] During the period from the analysis to publication of the Dora case, then, Freud's friendship with Fliess ends; Freud's ambivalent repression of lesbian sexuality could be partly related to his unconscious ambivalence toward this theory of bisexuality itself, whose ambiguous source and questioned ownership are associated with this former friend.

Or perhaps Freud's bad timing results from the repressive habits he accuses other medical writers of having: "The less repellent of the so-called sexual perversions are very widely diffused among the whole population, as every one knows except medical writers upon the subject. Or, I should rather say, they know it too; only they take care to forget it at the moment when they take up their pens to write about it" (51). This comment marks the transition from his more general discussion of sexual perversion to a specific discussion of fellatio. His description of the omission of material by medical writers actually enables Freud to "forget" material at the moment he "takes up his pen to write about it," repeating in his own text the scenario he describes. Shifting from general perversion to fellatio, Freud omits the lesbian possibility at the moment of its introduction by linking Dora on one side to male homosexual practices and on the other to heterosexual desire, reading the source of Dora's hysteria as her repression of a desire for fellatio and veering away from an application of his own rule about homosexuality. The shift toward fellatio suggests that the reason the discussion of perversion is included at all in the case is because it introduces fellatio and because it is about males, about "the sensual love of a man for a man" (50), something that makes the practice culturally central and historically precedented, if no longer socially acceptable, and perhaps unconsciously relevant to Freud in his relation to Fliess. If male homosexuality is, as he suggested in an 1899 letter to Fliess, "the primitive form of sexual longing for both men and women," perhaps Freud is confusing his own knowledge and desire with that of Dora, since he has already equate the same-sex feelings of males and females.[12] What he "knows," then forgets, in the course of the case history, in his own potential homosexuality as the case follows the course of his dying friendship with Fliess. Throughout his career Freud will make this symptomatic shift away from lesbian sexuality per se, enabled by this equation between lesbian sexuality and male homosexuality on the one hand and a connection between lesbian sexuality and female heterosexuality on the other.

When Freud finally gets around to the problem of Dora's attraction to Frau K., his narrative maneuvers parallel the temporal and textual ambiguities and delays played out in the construction of the case history. While Freud's art of narration may seem too exist partly in his ability to match form to content—to postpone and marginalize the inclusion of the lesbian sexuality he delays in discovering—this modern narrative gambit hardly represents anything more than a contrived and artful timing posed as a diarist's naive verisimilitude. The pretense of tardy understanding is contradicted by Freud's own comments at the beginning of the case as well as by his recognition of the pervasiveness of lesbian desire in relation to Dora as demonstrated by his earlier and contemporary letters to Fliess. In a letter to Fliess dated January 24, 1897 (226), written well before he saw Dora, he introduces the idea that hysteria is the negative of perversions, an idea he expands upon in other letters written around the same time.[13] Even if his curiously reluctant centering, then de-centering of this aspect of Dora's psychic life were an entirely narrative strategy (something like the purloined letter, unseen because it occupies the obvious place), the very confusion about its "proper" place in the narrative indicates that though Freud may be certain of the scientific writer's obligation to include it, he is still unsure of the place of lesbian sexuality in fiction, about how it fits into what he calls the "fine poetic conflict." In fact, his de-centering of it implies that he could not place it at all in the family romance he constructs, nor can he make it fit into the gendered oedipal patterns of either the family or psychoanalytic transference.

Even if Freud had consciously decided to approach the topic of lesbian sexuality directly in his narration of the case—if, in other words, he had decided to focus on Dora instead of upon his own analytic process in relation to her—Freud's rhetorical gentility on the subject of lesbian sexuality would serve as yet another rationale for delay and displacement. Characterizing the topic as one not discussed in polite society or even approached without rancor in medical circles, Freud casts his general discussion of "perversion" as part of the larger problem of discussing sexual instincts without being judgmental—as a problem of scientific objectivity. Hoping to ease into the topic, Freud argues that physicians have no "business to indulge in . . . passionate condemnation" (49) and exhorts doctors to a scientific objectivity while removing himself from any implied moral acceptance of deviant sexual behavior: "We are faced by a fact; and it is to be hoped that we shall grow accustomed to it, when we have put our own tastes on one side. We must learn to speak without indignation of what we call the sexual perversions—instances in which the sexual function has extended its limits in respect to the part of the body concerned or to the sexual object chosen" (50).

While the subject's sexual desires have extended the limits of the body, so Freud extends the limits of expressibility (and the narrative) in discussing these perversions, an extension necessary for the good of science and the discovery of truth. Lesbian sexuality is a "fact," a fact beyond, in excess of either good taste or moral acceptance and beyond even the limits (especially) of fiction, messing up what might have been good soap opera. Freud's representation of lesbian sexuality in its specific application to Dora's case requires yet another appeal to the exigencies of scientific discourse, this time in direct conflict with literary conventions. He begins: "I must now turn to consider a further complication to which I should certainly give no space if I were a man of letters engaged upon the creation of a mental state like this for a short story, instead of being a medical man engaged upon its dissection. The element to which I must now allude can only serve to obscure and efface the outlines of the fine poetic conflict which we have been able to ascribe to Dora" (59–60).

While his dramatically hesitant mention of this "further complication" is similar to his reluctant, but amply justified, use of sexual terminology, this self-conscious pause, like his delaying tactics, is analogous to the terms in which he finally does express and explain Dora's feelings toward Frau K. Using the metaphor of the "damned current" or the water that overflows its banks to represent the internal mechanics of lesbian sexuality, he figures it as excess, as clearly "beyond the limits." This running outside is echoed by his repetition of the terms "supervalent" and "overdetermined" in relation to Dora's desire and is complemented by images of annihilation and effacement present in his use of terms like "obscure" and "efface," "give no space" and "dissect." The excessiveness of the descriptive terminology—the position of lesbian sexuality as narrative excess—triggers the destructive discourse signified by the second set of terms, reflecting verbally the repressive delays and de-centerings that occur structurally and temporally in Freud's case history.

In his first explanation of the mechanics of lesbian desire, Freud depicts it as a current that "in favorable circumstances" "often runs completely dry" (60). However, he adds, "if a girl is not happy in her love for a man, the current is often set flowing again by the libido in later years and is increased up to a greater or lesser degree of intensity" (60). This metaphor of the current repeats Freud's earlier, more general explanation of "perversions": "A stream of water which meets with an obstacle in the river-bed is dammed up and flows back into old channels which had formerly seemed fated to run dry. The motive forces leading to the formation of hysterical symptoms draw their strength not only from repressed *normal* sexuality but also from unconscious perverse activities" (51). In excess of normal, perversions are occasioned by an obstacle. The paths of perversion are always already present; perversions are really diverted circles that return to a previous place and time. Like his own text that acknowledges that he already knows what he subsequently forgets, perversions—lesbian sexuality—refer back to a place one has already been; they are always already there, but abandoned until excess forces the libidinous or textual current back in their direction.

But what is the obstructive block that forces the deviation? In the above account Freud suggests that an unhappy heterosexual affair may form an obstacle, that if the straight stream is blocked, the water returns to older "channels." In Freud's attempts to narrate, however, the obstacle is Dora's lesbian desire itself; as he confesses at the end of the case history: "Before I had learnt the importance of the homosexual current of feeling in psychoneurotics, I was often brought to a standstill in the treatment of my cases or found myself in complete perplexity" (120). The connection between the libidinous current and the current of the narrative is made explicitly by Freud at the beginning of his presentation when he uses the same metaphor to describe narrative that he uses to characterize perversions: "This first account may be compared to an unnavigable river whose stream is at one moment choked by masses of rock and at another divided and lost among the shallows and sandbanks" (16). The homosexual obstacle brings the heterosexist analysis and narrative to a stop, and perhaps,

like the old channels, the dam itself is always already there, both
creator and repressor of desire. Lesbian desire is both the primordial
stream and the dam that diverts the flow of the libido and of the
narrative, forcing both back into the extraordinary currents of expression that were already there.

Both heterosexual misfortune and lesbian desire, the character of
the narrative/libidinous barrier shifts, is here suggestively male in its
masses of rock (rocks? testicles?), the escape then evocatively female
in its scattered and indefinite sandbanks. At the same time masculine,
an instance of heterosexual unhappiness and lesbian, the "rocks" that
constitute the barrier to the libidinal flow make the means of the cure
—the narrative dissection of this diverted course—more reciprocally
painful. In his introduction to the subject, quoted above, Freud states
that he would "give" the topic "no space" except for its "dissection."
A rough paraphrase, but precisely what Freud is about to try to do in
the space of the text that would otherwise not be there. He adds a
consideration of lesbian sexuality only to dissect it: he cuts it up
instead of out. As the excess, lesbian sexuality should be cut out:
"This element would rightly fall a sacrifice to the censorship of a
writer, for he, after all, simplifies and abstracts when he appears in
the character of a psychologist" (60). And to effect the cure, lesbian
sexuality must be cut up—dissected—instead, since its inclusion is
due to Freud's role as a "medical man bent on its dissection" (60).
Cut out or cut up: one cures the text, the other the patient.

However, the need to either cut out or dissect the lesbian is a
projected reversal of a castration of the writer/analyst. Like the quaint
mechanism of "reversal of affect" that Freud applies to Dora's nau-
seated rejection of Herr K.'s advances (28), the cutting Freud wishes
to execute as either author or analyst is the reverse of an introjected
fear that something in him might be cut—a fear of castration. And he
has reason to fear lesbian sexuality: the writer is castrated by its
inclusion, the analyst castrated—paralyzed—by its exclusion. The
analyst/writer has no place to turn except to forget or repress the
knowledge altogether, to lose the lesbian "key," so it is both there
and not, to sacrifice—to suspend—temporarily this central "fact" to
retain both the integrity of the text and the analysis. While lesbian
sexuality should "fall sacrifice to the censorship of the writer," especially in "the character of a psychologist" (60), its introduction into
the text actually makes Freud's mastery fall sacrifice in the symbolic

dissection enacted by the analysis. The dissection is as much Freud's as it is Dora's; As Freud explicates Dora's lesbian desire (finally), he reveals his own weakness and failure. Freud's confessed inadequacy in knowledge and analytic effectiveness is a figurative castration, constituting a wound that must be covered over by the ensuing surplus of theoretical work on female sexuality that follows both of his lesbian cases. Representing lesbian desire becomes a castration; failing to represent it is an equal castration.

While the analyst is paralyzed when the scientific obligation to represent lesbian sexuality is countered by a threat of castration, the resulting representation take the form of compensatory but displaced excess. Though "forgotten," Dora's lesbian feelings are abundantly and redundantly characterized, occurring three times in an uncannily similar phraseology, twice within two pages. Both concealed and overdetermined, her feelings for Frau K. are narratively related to other kinds of excess, to the hyperbolic melodrama of jealousy and betrayal outside the bounds of the regular romance. In parallel passages at the end of the "Clinical Picture" where Freud first introduces the factor of Dora's feelings for Frau K., behind the mask of her "supervalent" concern "with her father's relations with Frau K." (60), lies the "jealousy" associated with Dora's lesbian "affection." Just as Freud must preface his introduction of the subject of lesbian sexuality with protestations about the propriety of both fictional and scientific writing, so even Dora's feelings for Frau K. must lie behind a mask of propriety—behind her feelings for her father, which conceal behind their supervalence the excessive possessiveness that shifts "the fine poetic conflict" from the realm of the oedipal to something else, to something unaccounted for by either myth or the primacy of the father. Only in his position as mask does the father figure in this romance, and while he is the "front man," the rule is that jealousy reigns in same-sex affairs of the heart, a fact emphasized through the unnecessary doubling of the passages that present this "drama." Note the repetition of terminology in the following extended passages that occur within the two pages of one another in the text:

For behind Dora's supervalent train of thought which was concerned with her father's relations with Frau K. there lay concealed a feeling of jealousy which had that lady as its object—a feeling, that is, which could only be based upon an affection on Dora's part for one of her own sex. It has long been known and often been pointed out that at the age of puberty boys and girls show clear signs, even in normal cases, of the existence of an affection for people of their own sex. A romantic and sentimental friendship with one of her schoolfriends, accompanied by vows, kisses, promises of eternal correspondence, *and all the sensibility of jealousy, is the common precursor of a girl's first serious passion for a man.* (my emphases) (60)

Two paragraphs later, Freud restates this account:

I believe, therefore, that I am not mistaken in supposing that Dora's supervalent train of thought, which was concerned with her father's relations with Frau K., was designed not only for the purpose of suppressing her love for Herr K., which had once been conscious, but also to conceal her love for Frau K., which was in a deeper sense unconscious. The supervalent train of thought was directly contrary to the latter current of feeling. She told herself incessantly that her father had sacrificed her to this woman, and made noisy demonstrations to show that she grudged her the possession of her father; and in this way she concealed from herself the contrary fact, which was that she grudged her father Frau K.'s love, and had not forgiven the woman she loved for the disillusionment she had been caused by her betrayal. *The jealous emotions of a woman were linked in the unconscious with a jealousy such as might have been felt by a man.* (my emphases) (62–63)

The drama of jealousy, betrayal, and sacrifice couched in one large reversal of affect or what Hamlet's mother, Gertrude, might call protesting "too much" finally serves as the link between the "jealous emotions of a woman" and those of a man. Via this emotive bridge the masculine is reintroduced, again a mask for what is, "properly" speaking, something else, something requiring the invention of a new term.

Just as the narrative cannot embrace a lesbian motive, so neither can language. The end of the second passage above connects and corrects Freud's attribution of masculinity to lesbian sexuality: "The masculine or, more properly speaking, *gynaecophilic* currents of feeling are to be regarded as typical of the unconscious erotic life of hysterical girls" (120). Etymologically meaning a tendency toward or abnormal attraction to women/females, gynaecophilia substitutes for the masculine without entirely replacing it. Not properly masculine, "gynaecophilic" occupies an underside, flip side; like the damming barrier, it is potentially both masculine and feminine, referring to the gender of the attractive object rather than to the gender of the person attracted. By displacing the overt masculinity with which Freud initially modifies lesbian feelings and concealing it under an overtly feminized word that refers to object, Freud avoids the connection between lesbian sexuality and masculinity while maintaining it, concealed behind the more proper appellation, gynaecophilic. Making this shift, Freud avoids any direct disruption of traditional gender roles (masculine loves feminine, someone is attracted to women) and diverts the direct sexual association· of woman and woman. "Gynaecophilic" "feelings" are "typical" of the erotic life of hysterical girls." Delayed by the intervention of "typical" and "hysteria," the fact that girls might have gynaecophilic feelings is rendered as indirectly as possible, tainted already by Freud's introductory gloss of masculinity, relegated to the realms of the erotics of the hysterical. Dora's feelings are hidden behind this "supervalent" mask of concern for her father; Freud conceals Dora's feelings behind the "gynaecophilic" version of the masculine mask that when overturned reveals a gender ambiguity.

In the final parallel passage of the delayed footnote quoted below, Freud again slides lesbian sexuality in behind the masculine. In this concluding specimen "homosexual" introduces the term "gynaecophilic," which has been relegated to parentheses, a modifier/synonym rather than a more "proper" term. Already itself a mask, gynaecophilic lies this time under an ambiguously masculine term; "homo" meaning same, "homo" referring as well to *Homo sapiens*, to the *man*, and presumptively masculine unless modified: *female* homosexuals, "homosexual (gynaecophilic)." The general term by default "male," lesbian sexuality against shifts, as it did earlier, toward fellatio, toward an obscuring inclusion in a masculine class defined structurally by its failure to embrace difference.

The "supervalent" masculine mask that conceals Dora's feelings and Freud's expression of them also conceals both sexual knowledge and self-knowledge. In his last footnote Freud overtly links the question of Dora's desire to the question of her source of knowledge about sexuality, completing the circuit of desire and knowledge in the case, while still masking this process behind a gloss of masculinity. Freud reviews his error in knowledge:

> The longer the interval of time that separates me from the end of this analysis, the more probable it seems to me that the fault in my

technique lay in this omission: I failed to discover in time and to inform the patient that her homosexual (gynaecophilic) love for Frau K. was the strongest unconscious current in her mental life. I ought to have guessed that the main source of her knowledge of sexual matters could have been no one but Frau K.—the very person who later on charged her with being interested in those same subjects. Her knowing all about such things and, at the same time, her always pretending not to know where her knowledge came from was really too remarkable. [cf. p. 31] (120)

"Brought to a standstill," Freud has repressed "key" knowledge, knowledge that slides down a metonymic chain of knowledge and desire that serially displace one another. Knowledge of the source of Dora's sexual knowledge becomes the knowledge Dora represses along with her desire for Frau K., which becomes at long last Freud's knowledge of Dora's desire, retrieved from his own repression to become the "key" to the case. The "riddle" Freud discovers that he should have attacked was the connection between lesbian desire and knowledge, but the real riddle for Freud was why he had repressed that link when he had clearly made the connection among lesbian sexuality, hysteria, and knowledge from the beginning of his case history. In the Dora case lesbian sexuality *is* knowledge, stands in the same place as does knowledge, though the knowledge it represents is now knowledge about lesbian sexuality. Instead, lesbian sexuality as the apparent "answer" to the riddle is finally a decoy, something *like* knowledge, but in the wrong place, leading both away from and toward another knowledge that is like it but different in that this other, even more elusive knowledge is "real," genuine in relation to the kind of inauthenticity (or incomprehensibility) of lesbian desire.

The relation between knowledge and desire as the answer to Dora's lesbian "riddle" is metonymically transformed into Freud's new riddle concerned with is own motive for repressing both Dora's mystery and its answer, which lie in the same place—in the substance Freud attributes (or misattributes, since his own fantasy may govern its content) to Frau K.'s sexual knowledge of fellatio. Freud's forgetting, his repressive inability to link the source of Dora's knowledge and desire, while imparting *his* desire not to know and to forget what he already knows, also conceals a repressed desire to know this secret knowledge, this fellatio, this gift that returns from his own unconscious finally to solve the case too late for the patient, on time for Freud to finish up the history.[14] Like Dora, who conceals her contrary feelings under a veneer of oedipal jealousy, Freud conceals his desire to know under a polite drama of lost and found where the glasses he seeks have always been on his nose. Freud's insistent shift from lesbian sexuality to male homosexuality and his positioning of lesbian sexuality as a mask for the masculine trace the trajectory of his own desire. While Freud characterizes lesbian sexuality as primeval, archaic, erotic, primal, and immature, under the bisexual aegis that authorizes and accepts it, he constantly displaces it in favor of something else, something both more primal and more mature, something more central—the "key" rule that male homosexuality is "the primitive form of sexual longing for both men and women." His insistent return to the masculine form, not heterosexuality, but specifically male homosexuality, suggests that what is repressed under the guise of lesbian sexuality is knowledge of male homosexual desire.[15] It also suggests that Freud can only read lesbian sexuality from the parallel perspective of male homosexuality, a parallel he continues through his theoretical work on inversion, even though he suspects that the symmetry between male homosexuality and lesbian sexuality cannot be maintained.

The centrality of the masculine—of the homosexual—also accounts for the representation of lesbian sexuality as displaced and decentered. Dora and her desires are not central to his case; lesbian sexuality is excessive in the context of male homosexuality. Lesbian sexuality is knowledge, stands in for knowledge, is the pretext for knowledge, but is finally marginal, unnecessary, eccentric to a male homosexual center. A tantalizing decoy that inspires the hunt, lesbian sexuality is a counterfeit masculinity that doesn't exist in itself, for it is a transitive position that configures the slide from heterosexual to homosexual, as well as the shield that covers it all up. Always already there, it is only a mask for the masculinity that masks it, obscured by the phallus it stands in for, still an empty place, a psychoanalytic glitch Freud must obsessively efface/plug in his ensuing theories of sexuality.

Freud retrieves his "failure" in the Dora case with a resounding return of theoretical mastery in "Three Essays on the Theory of Sexuality." Freud regarded the Dora case as a stepping-stone between *The Interpretation of Dreams* and "Three Essays" or, perhaps more accurately, saw the case as a fertility rite for the marriage of his ideas with those of Fliess. While in 1899 he comments to Fliess that "[a] theory of sexuality may be the immediate successor to the dream book" (October 11, 1899, 379), he uses the five-year era of the Dora case as a period of gestation for this theory, born of this Fliess-Freud cross-fertilization centered around a notion of inherent bisexuality. Commenting in November 1899, Freud holds off a rather monstrous premature birth: "With regard to the sexual theory, I still want to wait. An unborn piece remains attached to what has already been born" (November 19, 1899, 387). Part of what has been born is the Dora case, referred to by Freud as "Dreams and Hysteria," important because it combines his dream work and his work on hysterics, but also because it provides "glimpses of the sexual-organic foundation of the whole" (January 25, 1901, 433). For Freud, then, the case is an introduction to something else, preparing the ground for further theoretical seeding:

> There are only glimpses of the organic [elements], that is, the erotogenic zones and bisexuality. But bisexuality is mentioned and specifically recognized once and for all, and the ground is prepared for detailed treatment of it on another occasion. It is a hysteria with tussis nervosa and aphonia, which can be traced back to the character of the child's sucking, and the principle issue in the conflicting thought processes is the contrast between an inclination toward men and an inclination toward women. (January 30, 1901, 434)

However, as Freud and Fliess undergo a kind of divorce, Freud delays the birth of the child, waiting four years to publish "Dora," but also trying to avoid the notion of bisexuality in "Three Essays." In a letter to Fliess on July 23, 1904, he writes: "At present I am finishing 'Three Essays on the Theory of Sexuality,' in which I avoid the topic of bisexuality as far as possible. At two places I cannot do so: in the explanation of sexual inversion . . . ; furthermore I mention the homosexual current in neurotics. There I plan to add a note that I had been prepared for the necessity of this finding by certain remarks of *yours*" (464). The founding idea—bisexuality—that Freud unconsciously represses in *Psychopathology* he deliberately suppresses in "Three Essays," a partial abortion of the long-awaited birth. But this truncation of bisexuality, this excision of Fliess, still masks the repression of the same lesbian glitch repressed in Dora. It is another

kind of failure—the failure of friendship—marked by an over-
whelming return in the form of theoretical mastery, a mastery that is
able to minimize (put in its place) Fliess' theory of bisexuality and
with it lesbian desire as the evasive mask for male homosexuality.

Freud's "Three Essays on the Theory of Sexuality" are theory
unmediated by the narrative of a case history. In shifting from an
interpretive narrative, with its authorial entanglements and problems
of subjectivity, to a theoretical narrative, with its posture of authority
and objectivity, Freud eliminates the frank interference of personali-
ties—his own and his patient's—that generates the revelatory circuits
of desire and knowledge in Dora. In "Three Essays" Freud has
arrived at a compromise combination—knowledge *about* desire—in
response to his desire for knowledge. He takes control of what Frau
K. knows by regularizing and schematizing it, centering homosexuality in the eccentric realm of "sexual aberrations" related to infantile
sexuality, the "cornerstone" of his sexual theory. But this "objective"
control actually masks another narrative, the narrative of the etiology
of inversion, which is also the inverted narrative of Dora, where Freud
also puts in its place this lesbian "key," relegating it to an unmistak-
ably minor position in his theoretical formulations, hidden by and
subordinate to male homosexuality.

Characterized by this masculine myopia, Freud's project in "Three
Essays" is control by categorization. While a consideration of the
sexual aberrations constitutes the first essay, the second two essays
are divided developmentally and chronologically, treating first infantile sexuality in Essay Two and the transformations of puberty in
Essay Three. Splitting his consideration of inversion into categories
of "object choice" and "sexual aim," Freud parses subject and predi-
cate in a way that dismantles the connection between "invert" and
deed. Classifying types on the basis of the exclusivity of their behavior, Freud first salvages inversion from medical accusations of degeneracy and innateness, arriving at a theory of inherent bisexuality that
positions inverted behavior somewhere between the innate and the
acquired. Next, he saves inversion from theories of physical hermaphroditism or a "mixture of sexual characters" (146n). His entire
consideration, however, is of male homosexuality, not merely by
default, but in overt description. Even his reformulation of the rule
about perversions in neurotics has taken a decidedly male turn: "The
unconscious life of all neurotics (without exception) shows inverted

impulses, fixation of their libido upon persons of their own sex . . . I can only insist that an unconscious tendency to inversion is never absent and is of particular value in throwing light upon hysteria in men" (166). This rule would have been "of particular value in throwing light upon" Dora's hysteria, but Freud's footnote appended to this line possibly throws even more light upon the repressed male homosexual desire at work in Freud's narration of Dora's case history: "Psychoneuroses are also very often associated with *manifest* inversion. In such cases the heterosexual current of feeling has undergone complete suppression. It is only fair to say that my attention was first drawn to the necessary universality of the tendency to inversion in psychoneurotics by Wilhelm Fliess of Berlin, after I had discussed its presence in individual cases" (166n). His discovery of Dora's "key" is due to conversations with Fliess where he discovers a "necessary universality" that both reveals and camouflages inverted desire. From Dora to Fliess, from female to male, "it is only fair to say" that Fliess is responsible here for both insight and repression. The politics of Freud's sexual theorizing—his shift from lesbian to male homosexual —are motivated by Freud's sense of debt to Fliess or Freud's attempts to disentangle himself from Fliess by setting forth a "fair" account of the importance of bisexuality, an account that divides its discovery up between the two men in an amicable settlement that gives Freud primacy and Fliess universality.

Within this categorization, Freud still subscribes to a libido theory likened to a current of water or stream that, "blocked by repression," results in a "collateral filling of subsidiary channels" (232). But this stream has become unquestionably masculine:

> So far as the auto-erotic and masturbatory manifestations of sexuality are concerned, we might lay it down that the sexuality of little girls is of a wholly masculine character. Indeed, if we were able to give a more definite connotation to the concepts of "masculine" and "feminine," it would even be possible to maintain that libido is invariably and necessarily of a masculine nature, whether it occurs in men or in women and irrespectively of whether its object is a man or a woman. (219)

Another "necessity" following the first "necessary universality" of bisexuality, now "necessarily" a libido of a masculine "nature," this inverted story fills out and around the lesbian sexuality that remains as a sore point in the Dora case. Appearing specifically only in two brief mentions in the middle of the essay on aberrations, Freud returns the lesbian to the masculine category, sewing up the disturbance created by the apparently nonmasculine lesbian sexuality of Dora. Following a discussion of inversion conducted entirely in male terms, Freud appends to the theory a brief consideration of the female: "The position in the case of women is less ambiguous; for among them the active inverts exhibit masculine characteristics, both physical and mental, with peculiar frequency and look for femininity in their sexual objects—though here again a closer knowledge of the facts might reveal greater variety" (145). A closer knowledge of the facts has already revealed a greater variety in the Dora case, but this variety is still dependent, in excess, beyond the scrutiny of the investigation, which has declared lesbians "less ambiguous" in the "peculiar frequency" of their masculinity. Their case, at least, is clear. The lesbian is recuperated for the masculine, is now identified as masculine and recognized by her masculinity.

The story is nearly complete except for the necessary turning of the narrative circle from adult inversion to the archaic sexuality of childhood, that period during which the "collateral" streams of inversion are already there. While finding one's way to the opposite sex "is not accomplished without a certain amount of fumbling" (229), deliverance to the opposite sex occurs for both boys and girls through a competitive relation with a parent of the same sex, through the same jealousy and betrayal that has characterized Dora's lesbian desire. In the final stage of a family romance, "girls, whose sexual activity is particularly subject to the watchful guardianship of their mother, . . . thus, acquire a hostile relation to their own sex which influences their object-choice decisively in what is regarded as a normal direction" (229–230). The failure of the mother's attention or watching, in combination with the blocking repression of "the instinctual stream" (232), forces the girl's libido to flow back into those collateral streams already characterized as masculine, since for Freud all childhood sexuality is masculine. Thus the lesbian cannot avoid being categorically masculine in this account, recycled as she is, into an archaic world defined as masculine, a masculinity that also avoids mother-daughter homosexuality. Freud appears to have resolved his failure to identify lesbian desire by immuring lesbian sexuality in an inevitable cycle of masculinity where the homosexual relations among women are denied by means of a masculine categorical imperative and the strategic separation of instinct and object.

But there is still a curious lapse related to the repression that blocks the flow of the girl's libido, since it is still not clear what is being repressed "when the main current of the instinctual stream has been blocked by 'repression' " (232). The story fails again at this gap, which is in the same place occupied by Dora's desire for Frau K., the point of a repression of knowledge or a knowledge of repression. It would seem in 1905 when "Three Essays" were first published that what is repressed is ambiguous; homosexuality has been defined as both an archaic drive and that which blocks the libido. If, as described in the Dora case, the heterosexual impulse itself is blocked, what motivates the repression of this heterosexual impulse but another, more dominant impulse—in this case, an archaic drive toward the mother, which in a same-sex logic would define the female as always already lesbian, if this archaic period is sexualized at all. But this archaic drive has just been included in the masculine labeling of the infantile libido, which means that the infant female lives out not a lesbian desire but what is redefined as an oedipal heterosexual scenario between a feminine mother and a daughter with a masculine libido. While homosexuality would seem to have priority, threatening to repress a secondary heterosexuality at any moment same-sex parental hostility failed, this danger of primal homosexuality has been nullified by a simple act of recategorizing: libido becomes masculine, avoiding the threat of a founding lesbian scenario, a recategorization that removes the originary moments, the primitive streambed to which lesbian adolescents are supposed to have returned. Or the preoedipal is desexualized altogether. Both definitions eliminate any origin at all outside of a kind of primeval, asexual heterosexuality or a disappearance into the indistinguishibility of preoedipal lack of differentiation.

Freud attempts to plug this hole in his 1915 notes added to the case, where he augments his theory of this first mechanism of repression, which occurs in "negative tendencies of perversion," with an account of the regressive effects of this repressive block in "positive" perversions. Repression has become regression, a return. The blockage now clearly becomes a regressive return to archaic homosexual feelings, which in the case of the female are not quite homosexual, but rather speciously heterosexual. In another note also added in 1915, just after the publication of his work "On Narcissism" (1914),

Freud recasts this blockage in terms of narcissism, perhaps the perfect evasive completion of the cycle: "In inverted types, a predominance of archaic constitutions and primitive psychical mechanisms is regularly to be found. Their most essential characteristics seem to be coming into operation of narcissistic object-choice and a retention of the erotic significance of the anal zone" (146n). This note is actually part of a lengthy appendage to his mention of bisexuality, an evasion of Fliess, but it locks inversion into a closed cycle of primitive feelings and behaviors that govern alternatively when the subject becomes fixed on self. What this becomes, then, is a battle between an oedipal heterosexuality and a regressive narcissism that constitutes those former currents now defined as love of the same, love of self, fixation on the anal zones.

The Turning Point

Having devised his first round of sexual theories, in 1915 Freud sees another patient, in whom this time he hopes to *discover* a strong homosexual disposition. The change from almost missing it in the Dora case to wanting to find it fifteen years later reflects the connection between Freud's elaboration of theories of narcissism and infantile sexuality and his formulation of a theory of the blocking that effects the libidinal shift from infantile narcissism to heterosexuality. In "Three Essays" he also suspects the narcissistic character of object choice in homosexuality, but he is still unable to clearly characterize the libidinal nature of the blockage. In the 1911 Schreber case he observes a connection between homosexuality and paranoia, and in 1914 he continues to elaborate his theories of narcissism and homosexuality in "On Narcissism."[16] Bringing together these three elements —homosexuality, narcissism, and blockage—in "A Case of Paranoia Running Counter to the Psychoanalytic Theory of the Disease," Freud hopes to define the relation between narcissism and paranoia as it operates to arrest the libido in a regressive, narcissistic homosexual stage. Associating narcissism and paranoia in homosexuals appears to resolve the difficulty he has in determining the orientation of the libidinal block; only when he characterizes the barrier as a regressive return to archaic libidinal paths and specifically defines both these paths and their barriers as homosexual is he able to eliminate any ambiguity about the block and about the process by which the female infant turns from maternal, clitoral love to heterosexual vaginal sexuality. In this case, the patients' clitoris serves as the turning point.

"A Case of Paranoia" is also connected to issues of psychoanalytic technique and knowledge, serving, as the editor comments, as "an object-lesson to practitioners on the danger of basing a hasty opinion of a case on a superficial knowledge of the facts" (262). Here superficial knowledge—stopping too quickly—can act as a block, just as narcissistic investments can block the normal direction of the libido. Knowledge and technique are again, as they were in the Dora case, overtly connected to the discovery of a lesbian sexuality. In this case, finding a homosexual disposition enables completion, mastery, proof of a theory, and a prognosis of eventual libidinal advancement for the patient. She can be cured.

Like Dora, this patient complains of being molested by a man. She is brought to Freud by her lawyer, who recognizes the "pathological" nature of her accusations that the man used alleged photographs of their lovemaking to blackmail her into continuing the affair. Like the patient of "Psychogenesis," the woman is "most attractive and handsome," "of a distinctly feminine type," and like her, she "resented the interference of a doctor" (263). The girl's story is that a coworker who was attracted to her convinced her to meet him at his apartment where, while they were caressing, she heard a click. Alarmed by this noise, the girl left the apartment only to encounter two men with a box on the stairs, a box she decided was a camera. At work the next day, the girl believed that the man and a favored coworker whom the girl linked to her mother were discussing the assignation, and the girl, angered, accused the man of betraying her with the older woman.

Freud sees the accusations she makes against her erstwhile lover as paranoid. The apparent heterosexual direction of this paranoia is a problem for Freud, who wants to connect homosexuality, narcissism, and paranoia. Since what is missing is the narcissism and without narcissism he cannot find her homosexuality, the facts would seem to disprove the point he wishes to illustrate, that "the case had a special interest for me other than a merely diagnostic one. The view had already been put forward in psycho-analytic literature that patients suffering from paranoia are struggling against an intensification of their homosexual trends—a fact pointing back to a narcissistic object-choice" (265). Heeding the lesson he learned in Dora, Freud looks again for her evasive homosexual attachment, unwilling to choose between proof of his law of delusion and the possibility of "actual experience": "The theory must be given up, or . . . we must side with the lawyer and assume that this was no paranoic combination but an actual experience which had been correctly interpreted" (266). He sees the patient a second time: "I recollected how often wrong views have been taken about people who are ill psychically, simply because the physician has not studied them thoroughly enough and has not learned enough about them" (266).

With a theory on the line, Freud gets beyond the barrier of the obvious, scrutinizing this patient again and finally discovering her narcissistic object choice in the person of the office coworker who reminds the patient of her beloved mother. Finding this homosexual path, Freud is free to elaborate the mechanism of the paranoia, seeing it as the effect of a blockage of the libido caused by the strength of the patient's narcissistic, homosexual attachment to her mother. Understanding that the paranoia must also be produced by a conflict, Freud must also determine what it is that this homosexual attachment blocks. He therefore looks to the moment of the blocking, to the agent of the "click" the patient described, uncovering finally what he thinks is a link between the audial click the patient thought she heard and her sexual response, or "pulse" of her clitoris.

Freud's discovery of this clitoral click is what puts all in its place, saving his theory and the patient from an exclusively homosexual doom. At the same time, this click reopens the ambiguity surrounding the basic nature of the libido at issue in "Three Essays." Unraveling the condensed signifiers represented by this sound, Freud sees the click as an external projection of a sexual response. The displacement of her genital feelings and ensuing paranoia are triggered by her homosexual disposition, but Freud locates the origin of the audible click as a sexual response—a clitoral click—created by the sexual stimulation of her male lover. The clitoris thus comes to stand simultaneously for the homosexual, narcissistic barrier against a "normal" libido and the functioning of a heterosexual libido.

So what is blocking what? Comparing sexual development to a road along which one must progress, Freud posits that the patient's homosexual feelings function to "arrest" her "first step along the new road to normal sexual satisfaction" (267). But if she responds genitally to stimulations by a man and then is interrupted by her homosexual disposition, doesn't this indicate that her heterosexual capabilities are already in place and are only interfered with by a homosexual block also represented by clitoral response? The fact that Freud discovers a thriving heterosexual response under this complex of homosexuality, narcissism, and paranoia suspiciously equates his successful uncovering of homosexuality, his "solution" to the case, the mastery of knowledge this solution represents, and a heterosexual foundation. It also resolves the other case, the lawsuit against the young man whom Freud finds sympathetic. The "truth" that underlies everything here is the "fact" that the male lover is guilty only of arousing the patient.

Looking for a lesbian, Freud finds a healthy heterosexual click. She has a homosexual object choice, but her response and her paranoia against the man prove that she has already "advanced" along the road of satisfaction. The patient's narcissism and homosexuality come close in this case to constituting a pathological condition that only normal heterosexuality can cure. This pathology also proves the theory, but paradoxically, this proof can only come with Freud's discovery of a heterosexual rather than a homosexual response. As in the Dora case, lesbian sexuality serves as a decoy that leads to another, more authentic knowledge. While Freud thinks he's looking for homosexuality, he's really looking for heterosexuality, proof that homosexuality acts as an inhibitor that ultimately creates paranoia—the result of blocked roads. And homosexuality can inhibit only a pre- or coexisting heterosexual capability. Equating homosexuality with narcissism does make this case (and the clitoris) a stopping point that contains homosexuality within a perpetual, narcissistic self-reflective cycle, unless, as happens for this patient, the blockage that prevents escape from the cycle is somehow overcome. And this case, too, though it is overtly concerned with female homosexuality, has in a kind of narcissistic economy equated male and female homosexuality —love of same is same and can only be cured by the discovery of difference. Though the subject here is a female patient, the case is posed to prove the truth of the proposition discovered in the case of a male homosexual.

Perhaps Freud looks too hard this time and finds what may not be there, using the case not only to prove a point, but also to establish the primacy of advanced heterosexual responses over regressive, archaic homosexual fixations. As the case was attached to a lawsuit, finding the cause was the same as locating guilt or proximate cause and imprisoning it in a narcissistic cycle. Though Freud is satisfied that justice has been done, as in the Dora case Freud's theory wins at the price of the possible truth of his patient's allegations.

Legislating Lesbians

LESBIAN SEXUALITY serves a fifteen-year sentence before its case is reconsidered in Freud's 1920 essay, "Psychogenesis of a Case of Homosexuality in a Woman." Beginning the case history with the observation that "homosexuality in women, which is certainly not less common than in men, although much less glaring, has not only been ignored by the law, but has also been neglected by psychoanalytic research" (147), Freud emphasizes the chronic legal and psychoanalytic disregard of lesbian sexuality. "Not less common" but "much less glaring" accounts for its remarkable invisibility and hence its neglect. Or perhaps its lack of glare (or fetishized glint?) accounts for a kind of wariness rather than neglect, recalled by Freud's first disappointing encounter with lesbian sexuality in the Dora case. While psychoanalytic inattention might be characterized not as neglect per se, but rather as a defensive deflection of the topic into the more glaring and compelling principles governing male homosexuality, neglectful psychoanalysis is the law that has ignored—evaded—what has become a gap in the account of human development, since lesbian sexuality is "not less common," only unaccounted for. Freud's discovery in 1920 of a "single case" "not too pronounced in type" (not too glaring) where he could "trace its origin and development in the mind with *complete certainty and almost without a gap*" promises to fill in what the law and psychoanalysis have left out.

While Freud admits that the patient is not neurotic and that she doesn't see herself as in need of psychoanalytic help, the case has distinct, if not uncanny, parallels to the Dora case, providing what promises to be a nonhysterical history ("almost without a gap") by which this issue might be narratively inscribed and thus controlled. Central to the two cases is the question of suicide, threatened by Dora and attempted by the unnamed "beautiful and clever girl" of "Psychogenesis." And while Dora is hysterical and her lesbian desire repressed, the "clever girl" of "Psychogenesis" undergoes treatment because the fact of her lesbian desire is known from the beginning and thus cannot evade discovery as Dora's desire did. Beginning with the "fact" of lesbian sexuality makes "Psychogenesis" a reverse narrative of Dora and "A Case of Paranoia," where Freud "knew" theoretically what he only found after looking twice. Leaving aside his 1915 equation of homosexuality and narcissism, Freud traces back through the melodrama of father love, jealousy, betrayal, and revenge that reiterate the oedipal drama into which he cast Dora and reinvokes the differences between male homosexual and lesbian that had disappeared when narcissism was the prime consideration. Overt where Dora has been covert, "Psychogenesis" conspicuously ends up back with the question of male homosexuality, tracing more clearly the errant male homosexual trajectory of the Dora case and again subordinating the lesbian pretext to the more insistent question of the male.

Freud depicts two lesbians in this case. The patient of this case, the "beautiful and clever girl of eighteen," defies the normal "rule" that in women "bodily traits and mental traits belonging to the opposite sex are apt to coincide" (154). From the outset, her example disenables any superficial equation between lesbian and masculine, a correlation Freud disclaims as a fixed rule, but mainly as it applies to male homosexuals. Freud notes that though his patient is beautiful, her acuteness of comprehension and her lucid objectivity" might be attributed to some "conventional" notion of masculinity, and further, behaviorally, she has adopted what Freud characterizes as a "masculine" attitude toward a "feminine" love object. Superficially feminine, emotionally masculine, she possesses the independence of bodily and psychical hermaphroditism Freud attributes specifically, though not exclusively, to male homosexuals. As Freud formulates: "In both sexes *the degree of physical hermaphroditism is to a great extent independent of psychical hermaphroditism*. In modification of these statements it must be added that this independence is more evident in men than in women, where bodily and mental traits belonging to the opposite sex are still apt to coincide" (154). The rule then is that male homosexuals manifest a disjunction between the physical and the psychical not usually shared by lesbians. Unfortunately, in this case the lesbian patient belies the rule. The other lesbian depicted by Freud is the girl's love object, a "cocotte" who "carried on promiscuous affairs with a number of men" but who lived in an amorous relationship with a woman. Like Frau K., the object is older and licentious, stereotypical of the image of the lesbian as a sexually loose woman, in fact, a bisexual object whose sexual relations are governed by economics rather than by any recognized psycho-sexual mechanism.

The underlying psychical structure of the beautiful and clever girl is fixed on the males in her family; like Dora, her lesbian sexuality is defined as a male derivative, a product of and alternative to failed incestuous desire for the father. Noting the girl's attraction to young mothers, Freud locates the genesis of her lesbian object choice at the point where the girl's mother conceived a belated child at "the revival of her [the daughter's] infant Oedipal complex." That her mother, "her hated rival," bore the father's child forced the girl, "furiously resentful and embittered," to turn "away from her father and from men altogether," and she "forswore her womanhood and sought another goal for her libido" (157). Excessive rivalry and jealousy with the mother and disappointment and desire for revenge on the father "revive her earlier love for her mother" (158), which takes the form of both a love for young mothers and a love for women resembling, oddly enough, her brother. Her shift in object choice from male to female is accompanied by her assumption of a masculine attitude toward the object. In both cases her object choices clearly stand in for inaccessible males, presenting a lesbian gloss for an underlying heterosexual desire.

But is it finally really heterosexual? Freud declares that what happened to her "was the most extreme case. She changed into a man and took her mother in place of her father as the object of her love" (158). This seems to suggest that she made a simultaneous and correlated shift: she became a man and her object choice became a woman, a trade-off that avoids any of the homosexuality implicit in the oedipal drama. But dutifully retiring again in favor of the father, she falls in love with a woman who looks like her brother, enacting another solution that Freud sees as typical of the behavior of male homosexuals: "Her latest choice corresponded therefore, not only to her feminine but also to her masculine ideal; it combined satisfaction of the homosexual tendency with that of the heterosexual one. It is well known that analysis of male homosexuals has in numerous cases revealed the same combination, which should warn us not to form too simple a conception of the nature and genesis of inversion . . ." (156–157).

Rather than being too simple, this artful configuration actually enacts a double reversal. She becomes a man who loves a woman, but that shift from a woman who loves a man to a man who loves a woman masks the underlying economy: that she becomes a man in order to love her father better. This situates Freud's analysis of lesbian sexuality as an enactment of male homosexuality, as a normative response to an entirely male-defined and male-centered desire—the love of a son for the father. Even the girl's love for her mother is seen in relation to the love of male homosexuals for their mothers. As Freud observes in his concluding remarks, any correlation between physical traits and the gender of object choice "blocks the way to a deeper insight into all that is uniformly designated as homosexuality, by rejecting two fundamental facts which have been revealed by psychoanalytic investigation. The first of these is that homosexual men have experienced a specially strong fixation on their mother" (171).

Though the problem is that she is a lesbian, her homosexuality is somehow inauthentic. Freud characterizes her sexuality as a disingenuous show, a melodramatic display of disobedience and attempted suicide that stands in for a more deeply hidden heterosexual and male homosexual desire for the father. But despite Freud's confidant grasp of the "fact" of this analysand's lesbian behavior, this analysis is a failure as well. While the case is "almost without a gap," the "gap" is what normally provides psychanalysis with a place to begin, and in this case Freud has to go to the birth of the patient's brother even to find an opening. The lesbian patient fails to enact a transference to her physician; she provides him with "lying dreams" designed to deceive Freud "as she habitually deceived her father" (165). Armored by three primarily theoretical sections (1, 3, 4), Freud prepares his reader for the failure to come, rationalizing it as a combination of a lack of neuroses to fix, as an unwillingness on the part of the patient, and as the general unfixability of homosexuality. For Freud, the pieces—sexual love for mother, rivalry with father—though there, can never be assembled into the neat oedipal symmetry he can create around male homosexuals. Gender makes all the difference here, since a habitual neglect of female development and the phallocentrism of both method and culture make it difficult to conceive of anything that might exceed male terms.

He covers over his analytic failure with more rules, more laws about homosexuality, and, despite his protests, relegating the patient to the realm of the masculine ("she was in fact a feminist" with a "strongly marked 'masculinity complex' " [169]). She even has penis envy—a kind of correlative evidence that Freud does not yet specifically link to her lesbian inclinations. He completes the case with a discussion of "cases of male homosexuality" and "physical 'hermaphroditism' " (171–172), but notes that "any analogous treatment of female homosexuality is at present quite obscure" (172). Returning her, then, to the obscurity that he had first attributed to lesbian sexuality in the Dora case, Freud ends the narrative with considerations of male homosexuality. And as he did after the Dora case, Freud launches into more theoretical work on sexuality in the ensuing ten years: "Some Neurotic Mechanisms in Jealousy, Paranoia and Homosexuality" (1922), "Some Psychical Consequences of the Anatomical Distinction between the Sexes" (1925), "Female Sexuality" (1931), and *New Introductory Lectures on Psychoanalysis*, lecture 33 (1933).[17] The first of these treats male homosexuality exclusively, as if the lesbian sexuality didn't exist.

The second, "Some Psychical Consequences of the Anatomical Distinction between the Sexes," superficially promises to treat both genders but actually marks his discovery of the difference between male homosexuality and lesbianism that Freud has consistently seen as an unaccountable mystery. The difference he finds is physical, based on two anatomical versions of the same: the visible masculine genitalia that set the standard for comparison and the inadequate female versions of these that force girls into both compensatory psychic gymnastics and veiled adoration of the protruding abundance that must become their object. In a biological trope this anatomical differentiation returns to the question of personal prehistory and infantile sexuality, founding subsequent libidinal shifts on the tangible, visible effect of anatomical admiration. The ambiguous blockage over which Freud had struggled, which was located in the clitoris in "A Case of Paranoia," is now displaced to the penis. The phallic foundation finally unambiguously accounts for the psychic difference in sexual development between the genders. This schematic reduction also overtly ignores but covertly captures the problem of lesbian sexuality, which becomes an irrational response to displays of anatomical superiority, a kind of prolonged, delusive wishful thinking, finally comprehensible as a brand of "penis envy": "Here what has been named the

masculinity complex of women branches off. It may put great difficulties in the way of their regular development towards femininity, if it
cannot be gotten over soon enough" (253).

While Freud doesn't relate this "masculinity complex" to lesbian
sexuality until "Female Sexuality" six years later, he sees this "flash"
of penis envy as a point of branching, of a block that forces a diversion
to an invisible lesbian result, an issue he doesn't take up here, in
"The Dissolution of the Oedipus Complex" (178), or in "A Child Is
Being Beaten" (191), other places where he mentions this complex.[18]
In these texts lesbian sexuality is supplanted by a "masculinity complex" in which lesbian sexuality is created by an error in timing. If
the female doesn't accept her castration in time, she'll either disavow
her lack, "which in an adult would mean the beginning of a psychosis" (253), or she'll harden herself in the conviction that she *does*
possess a penis, and may be subsequently compelled to behave as
though she were a man" (253). Envy obliging a masculine masquerade, the lesbian will "harden" in this role and seek to wield the
phallus rather than merely have access to it on the body of another.
The archaic, narcissistic currents of infantile sexuality have been
transformed into a visible economy of possession. The fluid preoedipal boundaries of the libidinal current in Freud's earlier work, always
of ambiguous gender and orientation and only gradually appropriated
for the masculine, have been hardened into an anatomically based
duality and stiffened into a genital reduction of difference centered
on the penis, which was also always already there until the "disappointed" girl realizes that it isn't. Never directly referred to, but
nonetheless demystified, the lesbian is the woman who thinks she has
a penis.

Fortunately, Freud doesn't stop at this rigid penisification, but
returns to the still mystical "Minoan-Mycenean civilization behind
the civilization of Greece" in "Female Sexuality." While in the Dora
case Freud had already characterized male homosexuality as part of
the realm of Greece, here he finds as a "surprise" a female preoedipal
stage behind this Greece. The problem he addresses in this short
theoretical excursion into prehistory is the question of how the girl
gets from her attachment to her mother and her "masculine" genital
zone, the clitoris, to her father and her new "feminine" zone, the
vagina. The answer to this question fills in the gap left by his three
previous analyses of lesbians, cases that were either left in the obscu-

rity of an oedipally oriented male homosexual melodrama or resolved by a responsive pulse in the clitoris. To answer the question Freud poses three alternatives for female sexual development: 1) the girl gives up her sexuality altogether out of a sense of complete dissatisfaction with her clitoris in relation to the penis; 2) the girl defiantly clings to her masculinity (clitoris) in hopes of someday gaining a penis; and 3) by a "very circuitous" path the girl takes her father as her object in rivalry with her mother. Of these the third is the most impossible and most normal: it leads to "normal" heterosexuality. The second "can also result in a manifest homosexual choice of object" (230). The first explains frigidity.

The "defiant over-emphasis of her masculinity" (232) reduces lesbian sexuality to a manifestation of the anatomical gender oppositions Freud develops in "Some Psychical Consequences." But the reduction here occurs within the more complex dynamic of the girl's relation to the mother, something Freud admits is difficult. He observes that "we have found the same libidinal forces at work in it [female sexuality] as in the male child and we have been able to convince ourselves that for a period of time these forces follow the same course and have the same outcome in each" (240). Beyond his earlier solution of self-cycling narcissism, he finds it more difficult to explain the girl's libidinal investment in the mother. Amazed as he always is in the face of the preoedipal libidinal character of females, Freud notes the "very surprising sexual activity of little girls in relation to their mother" "manifested chronologically in oral, sadistic, and finally in phallic trends directed towards her" (237). But these sexual activities are hard to find, since they are later transferred to the father (as in "Psychogenesis"), "where they do not belong and where they seriously interfere with our understanding of the situation" (237). Such activities culminate in "clitoridal masturbation . . . probably accompanied by ideas of the mother, but whether the child attaches a sexual aim to the idea, and what that aim is, I have not been able to discover from my observations" (239).

The preoedipal girl's "active" sexual impulses enacted through her "masculine" organ are directed at the mother in a heterosexual scenario that obscures behind a thin veil of terminology the lesbian sexuality located in these archaic and primitive libidinal streambeds. Freud perceives the threateningly homosexual mother-daughter pair as a mother-son couple. The girl isn't a girl (and is masculine) until she graduates from clitoris to a healthy vaginal fixation on her father and hostile rivalry with her mother. Freud doesn't mention homosexuality in this context; he relegates it only to the second "masculine" alternative in his sexual tryptic. What he suggests in this account of female development is that all women desire the mother at some time, that all girls have sexual feelings for women that are repressed by the turn toward their fathers. This shift is accomplished by a maternal interdict against the girl's masturbation, a case of the phantasmal object denying the fantasy, as well as by a "castration" of the girl's libido as she graduates from the pathetic penile pretender, the clitoris, to the necessary "feminine" passivity of the vagina.

This seems to reverse the paradigm of homosexual narcissistic libidinal blockage Freud formulated and proved in "A Case of Paranoia" and to return to a theory of competitive oedipal disappointed love as that which steers the child's sexual development. Now normative heterosexuality blocks the more originary homosexual structure, and the mother, agent of this heterosexuality, denies the child's narcissistically homosexual investments, becoming the block that forces the daughter's detour to father and vagina. The melodrama of both Dora and the patient of "Psychogenesis" is an adolescent repetition of this oedipal moment: the girl jilted by her mother seeks another object in another gender. If she clings to the mother, she becomes a rival son to the father, casting outside of the family for another female to take her mother's place in her sexual affections. But Freud can never relate this as a woman-woman love, making the daughter a son when she loves the mother, making the daughter's love for the mother a love for the father, making the masculine daughter love the father in a re-creation of a male homosexual attraction. While lesbian sexuality functions as the mask for male homosexual feelings—for father love—Freud can never penetrate that to find the love for the mother behind this "Greek" love masked by love for the father and male homosexuality. For Freud, the pieces—sexual love for mother, rivalry with father—though there, can never be assembled. Lesbian sexuality flounders at its point of origin in the constantly displaced Greece of an undifferentiated preoedipal, never really constituted except through an adolescent return to these older currents and remaining a gap, masculine and not, heterosexual and not, there and not, on the occasions he specifically examines it. A fertile gap, though, in inverse relation to the theoretical activity that returns on the heels of failure.

In the course of his work, from the Dora case to "Female Sexuality," Freud makes a symmetrical, heterosexually informed reversal. At the time of the Dora case, Dora's lesbian desire for the woman is masked by her desire for her father. Male homosexuals desire the father through the mother. In other words, heterosexuality masks homosexuality. In "A Case of Paranoia" Freud reaches a mediate compromise: heterosexuality masks homosexuality, which masks heterosexuality. By the end of his investigations in the 1930s, Freud has shifted to the complementary ideas that male homosexuals have a fixation on their mother that is masked by their supervalent desire for males and female homosexuals have a fixation on their father masked by their supervalent desire for females. Now homosexuality masks heterosexuality. What seems a simple reversal represents, however, a more complex rearticulation centered around the mother. The lesbian equation actually requires another step going from mother to father to mother. While the male's relation to the mother is already heterosexual, the female's is already homosexual. To return to even a masking love for females, the girl must make a heterosexual detour, reiterate the male homosexual trajectory of loving the father in place of the mother, then go one step further to return to what becomes the pretense of loving women. This paternal detour adjusts the symmetry of gender in a way that reconciles lesbian sexuality to a reverse version of the male homosexual model. Freud's insistent repetition of the male homosexual model is important, for it is only via this masculine trajectory that one gets to the mother in some essential heterosexism that continues to deny any same-sex commerce.

Throughout his career, Freud's readings of lesbians tend to reiterate the same configurations. The most obvious is its connection to knowledge. In all three of the lesbian cases, Freud seeks a knowledge that is bound up with female homosexuality. In the Dora case, lesbian sexuality is the knowledge he symptomatically misses; in "A Case of Paranoia," it is the fact he pursues. In "Psychogenesis," lesbian sexuality is what he thinks he knows, but even so the knowledge does not contribute to a successful analysis. Though in the Dora case knowledge of a lesbian attraction would seem to be the answer to a mystery and though in "A Case of Paranoia" it would seem to be the

factor that proves Freud's theory, in both cases the lesbian answer is
a decoy. As a decoy or lure, lesbian sexuality has the appearance of
knowledge, but as soon as Freud thinks he knows, especially in the
latter two cases, it evaporates in favor of something else. In the Dora
case, the exploration of Dora's feelings provides a pretext for a consideration of heterosexual and male homosexual economies. In "A Case
of Paranoia" it serves as the symptom for a developing heterosexuality, and in "Psychogenesis" it becomes the mask for the patient's
latent love for her father characterized as heterosexual and male homosexual.

The connection between knowledge and lesbian sexuality reveals
several ways lesbian sexuality seems to operate in Freud's texts and
in his schemes explaining human sexual development. As a decoy, it
never exists in itself, but always retires in favor of something more
authentic. Its function as decoy parallels and in fact may be an exter-
nalization of the fact that Freud, while appearing to look for lesbian
sexuality, actually avoids it. Its appearance always facilitates the discussion of something else. Never the subject, it is a point of transition; never the essence, it is always the mask or the blockage or that
which obscures or prevents normal development, either of analyses or
of female psycho-sexual development. In Freud's texts, lesbian sexuality is thus essentially metonymic and transitive.

A point of transfer, lesbian sexuality is instrumental to Freud's
connections between preoedipal and oedipal, infancy and adulthood,
heterosexuality and male homosexuality, masculine and feminine. As
metonymic, lesbian sexuality is also intermediate, coming between
opposing terms and providing a kind of fleeting middle state between
them. This lesbian intercession is both positive and negative: positive
when it eases the transition, negative when it blocks it. In accounts of
infantile sexual development, female homosexuality is a natural stage,
existing before the mother's interdict. But intermediate and passing,
it barely exists at all, except to mark the stage where the infant
daughter is still a son; no female to female sexuality per se ever exists.
This fixation on the mother can reappear in adolescents according to
Freud, the result of blocked libido or disappointed hopes. Here too it
is a fall-back position, a regression to the fleeting infantile attachment
to the mother and a mask for the more authentic heterosexual feelings
that have been forbidden temporarily. In both scenarios, lesbian sex-

uality is cast as immature, adolescent, penultimate, as leading to a more permanent state.

Though later in his career Freud declares that the libidos of infant daughters are directed toward their mothers and that those libidos are masculine in character, Freud cannot decide whether or not lesbian women are necessarily masculine. In fact, all of his cases are exceptions to any necessary connection between masculinity and lesbian sexuality. Nonetheless, he still tends to want to characterize the lesbian as masculine and must catch and correct himself when he does it. Seeing the lesbian as masculine solves the problem of lesbian sexuality by rendering it as essentially heterosexual—as a relation between a woman who thinks she's a man and another woman. The problem, of course, is the other woman, who must stay feminine in order for the formula to remain heterosexual. As Freud later ossifies his perceptions of development and formulates the concept of penis envy, he masculinizes lesbian sexuality indirectly. But even this later formula is of mixed gender: the lesbian is the *woman* who thinks she has a penis.

Freud's ambivalent and indirect masculinization of lesbian sexuality, however, aids him in making the transition from heterosexuality to male homosexuality always at the foundation of his discussions of female homosexuality. Though Freud both accepts and denies any essential parallelism between male and female homosexuality, his discussion of lesbians always reverts to a discussion of male homosexuality, and his configurations of lesbian attraction always veil an underlying male homosexual economy. That the daughter in "Psychogenesis" goes from being a daughter who loves her father to girl who loves a woman to a son who loves her mother to a son who loves his father configures the slide from female homosexual to male homosexual.

While the lesbian configures this transitivity and immaturity, she also functions as blockage, as that which gets in the way of human development, of case histories, of knowledge itself. If the girl's feelings for her mother stay too long, they impede her development, as Freud hypothesizes in "A Case of Paranoia." Though Freud characterizes this patient's clitoral response as both a blockage and a symptom of incipient heterosexuality, he later relegates the clitoris to the realm of the masculine. If she clings to her clitoris, a girl cannot advance to normal heterosexual function. Retaining an infantile maternal object choice is an expression of an imprisoning narcissism that impedes further progress. It is the dam that blocks the current of normal heterosexuality; it is the attractive older current to which disappointed girls regress and which impedes their progress down the correct stream. Not finding lesbian sexuality brings Freud to a standstill in the Dora case and in "A Case of Paranoia"; finding it brings him to an equal impasse in "Psychogenesis." Only in his more theoretical treatises on sexuality is he able to manage female homosexuality, detaching it from real cases and relegating it to more simple formulas that are belied in experience.

Lesbian sexuality is in Freud multiple as well as metonymic, embodying in those moments of transition the conditions that both precede and follow it as well as something beyond either. Though usually transitory, it is an ambivalent stage where oppositions, inevitable developments, and confining gender roles are broken open, allowing for multiple coexisting possibilities. This suggests that representations of lesbian sexuality in Freud's work do disturb the gendered dualities of sexual difference by breaking open the closure of oppositions, enacting a model—a time—for the perpetual interplay of knowledge and desire. Adolescent and premature, the figure of the lesbian represents a subversive operation created by increasing possibilities rather than by delaying an inevitable trajectory. This breaking open at the point of transition is characterized by a multiplication of metonymies analogous to both the representation of lesbian sexuality as a narcissistic recycling and its representation as excess. This is different from seeing lesbian sexuality as that which merely delays and complicates the route to an inevitable heterosexual end by doubling the terms of difference. The first is a model of potential, the second a model of recuperation; both models operate, but the position of the lesbian is finally a question of timing and of which moment—deferral or delay—we can be at and how long we can stay. Poised at the penultimate moment, lesbian sexuality is a perpetual becoming rather than a being, which on the one hand consistently infantilizes lesbians, on the other suggests the infinite potential of failing to end.[19]

This is not to say that this is what lesbian women are; Freud's accounts of the etiology of lesbian sexuality tend to fail because they always evade the lesbian and surpass the penultimate to become ultimate, definitive, and entrenched in the binary oppositions of sexual difference he tries to avoid. Beginning with the unsolved mystery of Dora, he ends with penis envy. To his credit, Freud visibly tries to resist this reduction, endeavoring instead to retain the complexity of the moment, something he is able to do (barely) until anatomy finally becomes destiny. Though he is insistent on his own objectivity, his considerations of lesbian sexuality also reveal the narcissism of his own reading. From his unrecognized countertransference in Dora to his increased emphasis on the importance of anatomical envy, Freud reads lesbians in ways that promise their conversion to heterosexual objects or make them the pretext for a more compelling consideration of male homosexuality—positions that can include and reflect Freud's own desire. This desire and Freud's desire for knowledge cycle around the figure of the lesbian, unable to fix there, using the lesbian as a means to another end: the bringing together of desire and knowledge in analyses of human sexuality.

Freud offers several possible psychogeneses for lesbian sexuality but, more crucially, enacts its sliding and evasive configuration again and again. While we may see Freud as hopelessly patriarchal and sometimes obsolete, this same scenario replays itself in contemporary culture. Sliding, as Freud does, from the heterosexual to the male homosexual, current cultural manifestations of lesbian sexuality certainly configure it as "much less glaring," a condition that catalyzes certain cultural confusions and inconsistencies that tend to displace or erase the figure of the lesbian. For example, in one state male homosexuality constitutes grounds for adultery in a fault divorce while a proven lesbian affair can be nothing more than extreme cruelty.[20] In a recent issue of the respectable *South Atlantic Quarterly,* titled *Displacing Homophobia,* of the thirteen articles only one, Eve Sedgwick's "Across Gender, Across Sexuality: Willa Cather and Others," even purports to treat lesbian sexuality, and it rather spectacularly takes the same male homosexual route as Freud.[21] The rest of the articles are written by men, mainly about men. Somehow in displacing homophobia the editors have also displaced lesbians, manifesting a kind of sapphophobia. And the lesbian is still a special case in feminist criticism, included in special chapters, in special issues, on special panels, a laudatory practice until we see that the very fact that lesbian sexuality is set off tends to enable the lesbian to disappear from surrounding texts in anthologies, for example, which no longer have to treat any question of lesbian sexuality at all.[22]

In the combined press of sexuality and gender the female homo-sexual is elided and comes to stand for the unresolved—and hence ignored—enigma of multiple unincorporated terms. In politics, in culture, and specifically in academe this makes a difference; the enigma is most often settled by merging the lesbian position with whatever is politically stressed: with gay men in matters of sexually transmitted diseases and preventive measures, with the large range of feminist critics, the majority of whom are somewhat heterosexist, in criticism of women's literature and feminist theory. The result is a continued lack of visibility—and hence political and critical consid-eration—for the lesbian. Insofar as the lesbian configures the inter-section of gender and sexuality, the constant displacement of the lesbian represents a persistent inability to recognize and incorporate multiple differences in our thought and methodology. This is not to say that making the lesbian visible will change all of that or do anything other than reproduce the same merging tendency but from a different perspective. What Freud's analyses might show, however, is the regressively sexist mechanism by which the very act of taking account avoids much of an account at all and instead enacts the displacement that pretends consideration while effecting an erasure.

Retrospective

WHEN I first looked at Sigmund Freud's descriptions of lesbian sexuality, I was, like many feminist critics, appalled by what seemed the blindness and bias in his exercise of an institutional phallic privilege. In fact, I was already heavily influenced by Kate Millett's schematic indictment of Freud's sexism and by a strange essay called "The Myth of the Vaginal Orgasm."[23] Seeing Freud as an oppressive political enemy and assuming the heinous practical effects of his theories, I read his project not as a search, but as an erring attempt to define the truth about human sexuality. I thought that by demonstrating his bias I could reveal his error; what was at stake was control over the definitions that governed our lives. Reading and discrediting Freud (which mere demonstration of sexism could do) might emancipate women from the effects of a masculine culture that had the power to define categories and assign reprehensible etiologies. I superficially assumed that Freud would see lesbian sexuality as masculine (everyone else did) and that seeing it as masculine was incorrect and only revealed the inescapable binarism of representation itself. Paradoxically, in analyzing Freud I placed myself in opposition to what I saw as his embodiment of masculinity, ensuring for myself the feminine place, the politically correct place. My desire for knowledge was equally narcissistic: I looked for the crimes and limitations, the misunderstandings and errors.

But removing the oppositional dynamics of sexual difference that informed my own reading and appeared to make lesbian sexuality so disturbing raised new questions. There seemed to be a certain political stake in controlling origins, in defining them so that the feminine is subversive—a kind of philosophical-analytical analogy to praxis. It has been crucial to a feminist political ideology to see ourselves as both unaccounted for and accounted for incorrectly, alternatives that provide the illusory potential for change through a kind of defiant self-engenderment, a taking over of origins that would lead, in this psychosomatic fantasy, to a shift throughout the body of oppressive representation. As Freud's enactment of the interrelation of knowledge and desire illustrates, the reading may be more important than the source; the imbrication of desire in reading tends to find what desire is looking for.

FIVE

All Analogies Are Faulty: The Fear of Intimacy in Feminist Criticism

FOR FEMINIST criticism, the decade of the 1980s has been occupied with the attempt to recognize and comprehend the multiple differences that exist among women and to work these different perspectives into a feminist methodology that can allow and theorize multiplicity while remaining politically and intellectually effective. Stimulated by the publication of writing by women of color as well as by confrontations and deliberations occurring at such national conferences as those hosted by the National Women's Studies Association, one symptom of this change is that around 1983 editors of mainstream, primarily white, academic feminist anthologies attempted to include different perspectives in the range of critical material.[1] Despite our best efforts, however, feminist critics have only really begun to formulate strategies by which questions of multiple differences among women can be integrated into feminist theory and criticism. Though we are working toward more inclusive and inventive epistemological tactics, we still need to be aware of the habits and practices that resist the comprehension of diversity and reduce differences to dualistic positions in binary oppositions.

As I read collections of feminist literary criticism from this decade I notice a peculiar habit: in 1985's proliferation of feminist literary critical anthologies, the myriad differences among women are often reduced to the formula "black and lesbian." Though this does not always happen, it occurs enough to make me suspicious. This "black and lesbian" contingent represents female diversity in anthologies that otherwise represent a white, heterosexual, academic feminist discourse. I suspect that this editorial and critical reliance upon black and lesbian is symptomatic of some underlying critical difficulty with multiplicity and that an analysis of the placement, characterization, and roles of black and lesbian essays in mideighties anthologies will reveal something about the kinds of fears and perceptions of differences that shape the way feminist critics consider diversity.

My starting point is to examine feminist anthologies of literary criticism published in 1985, a bumper year for a crop of feminist collections edited by established scholars and published by prestigious presses that all laudably attempted in some way to include the work of cultural "minorities" as a regular part of mainstream academic feminist criticism. It is the year of Elaine Showalter's *The New Feminist Criticism: Essays on Women, Literature, Theory*, Judith Newton and Deborah Rosenfelt's *Feminist Criticism and Social Change: Sex, Class, and Race in Literature and Culture*, and Gayle Greene and Coppélia Kahn's *Making a Difference: Feminist Literary Criticism*.[2] These are not the first anthologies to incorporate different voices, nor are they anthologies devoted to the work of specific "other" perspectives such as Marjoric Pryse and Hortense Spillers' *Conjuring: Black Women, Fiction, and Literary Tradition*, also published in 1985. They all do, however, demonstrate an awareness of the omission of such work and what that says about mainstream feminist criticism.

In 1985, all of the primarily white feminist collections instate diversity by inserting representative essays by black women on black feminist criticism, essays by lesbian critics on lesbian criticism, or, in the case of Barbara Smith, both. A black lesbian feminist essay by Barbara Smith and a lesbian feminist essay by Bonnie Zimmerman are each reprinted twice in these three anthologies; though 1985 offers diversity, it does so in a very limited fashion. Two collections, Showalter's and Newton and Rosenfelt's, reprint Barbara Smith's excellent seventies black lesbian feminist essay "Toward a Black Feminist Criticism." Smith's essay should be particularly useful as a model matrix for the interplay of black and lesbian criticism, but it is treated as a kind of token that simply represents these two varieties of difference.

Both anthologies extend Smith's association of black and lesbian and include, in addition to Smith's essay, another representative essay from each position—one black and one lesbian. But the differences imported with these essays do not merely compensate for formerly unrepresented perspectives, since others still remain absent, or enact any kind of random diversity or variety for variety's sake, but provide a specific diversity with an express evidentiary role in another arena —as the differences combatting egalitarian sameness in the controversy generated by Annette Kolodny's 1980 essay, "Dancing Through the Minefield."[3] Signals of an expanding consciousness, the essays function as the spoils in an underlying structuring battle between Showalter and Kolodny.

In the Showalter anthology, the three essays—Smith's, Deborah E. McDowell's "New Directions for Black Feminist Criticism," and Bonnie Zimmerman's "What Has Never Been: An Overview of Lesbian Feminist Criticism"—are placed in a block in the middle section of the book titled "Feminist Criticisms and Women's Cultures," following Elaine Showalter's reprinted essay "Toward a Feminist Poetics" and the reprinted version of Annette Kolodny's "Dancing Through the Minefield." In light of Showalter's introductory remarks on these essays, it is evident that they are not only included out of a sincere expansive impulse, but also, given their position following Showalter's and Kolodny's essays, inserted as support for Showalter's gynocriticism and as evidence against Kolodny's pluralism. As Jane Gallop points out in her reading of this anthology, the essays in *The New Feminist Criticism* are "new" in the sense that they represent "a criticism which has emerged in the second half of the 1970s" (111).[4] They are not, however, "new" or current in the year 1985, since only one was originally published after 1981. The 1980s "new"ness of the anthology may reside in Showalter's arrangement of the essays, since that seems as much a response to the changing scene of feminist criticism in the early to mideighties as it is a cogent attempt to organize the material.

Part of this response is overtly focused on the debate surrounding Kolodny's 1981 proposal of a "playful pluralism." In the introduction to the anthology, Showalter, who usually proceeds through paragraph summaries of the contributions in the order of their arrangement in the book, comments that Kolodny's essay "touched off sparks in some sectors of the feminist critical community," including specifically sparks from a community of three critics—Judith Kegan Gardiner, Elly Bulkin, and Rena Grasso Patterson—who, in a series of three responses appearing in a 1982 issue of *Feminist Studies*, criticize Kolodny's "conciliatory" equation of all differences and her exclusionary politics in general and, in particular, chastise her pluralism for being classist, racist, and heterosexist.[5] But in the introductory summary, Showalter alters the distribution of perspectives in the complaints made about Kolodny: as it appears in *Feminist Studies*, the critique of Kolodny contains three separate critiques and a response: Gardiner's distinctions between the political differences in feminist critical approaches, Bulkin's critique of Kolodny's racism, ethnocentrism, and heterosexism and her "checklists" for identifying them, and Patterson's charge of classism. Dropping Gardiner's arguments completely, Showalter fuses the plaints of Bulkin and Patterson in the penultimate sentence of the Kolodny paragraph: "Bulkin and Patterson criticized the absence of black and lesbian feminist criticism from a discussion purporting to be comprehensive" (13). The two critics, Bulkin and Patterson, now stand for black and lesbian, for what had been mainly Bulkin's critique (and not even all of that, since Bulkin includes an argument about ethnocentrism), while Showalter summarily dismisses Patterson's specific class critique of Kolodny in her final recapitulation: "They also pointed out the heterosexism, ethnocentrism, and class bias of much feminist critical writing of the 1970s" (13). The phrase "black and lesbian" makes its appearance, prepared for by the conflation of Bulkin and Patterson, but while lesbianism/heterosexism is doubled, a repeated concern both about Kolodny's pluralism and about all feminist critical writing of the seventies, problems of racism are restricted to Kolodny and classism and ethnocentrism are dispersed among the range of seventies criticism.

The effect of this gratuitous redistribution is to provide a place and specific function for the three essays that follow Kolodny's in the anthology, creating the critical space in which black and lesbian can be both included and contained. The essays are substitutes for the rules formulated by Bulkin, upping the ante by actually including work by black and/or lesbian feminist critics omitted by Kolodny. While class drops out as a consideration, Bulkin's white lesbian comments about racism and heterosexism are supplanted by Smith's black lesbian criticism, McDowell's black feminist criticism, and Bonnie Zimmerman's lesbian criticism. Curiously, this also stands in for half of Kolodny's own proposed but never written second installment of "Dancing Through the Minefield," which was to have argued "that black and Third World American feminist literary critics stand as a group apart from the whites, united by their more probing analyses of the institutions which give rise to current literary tastes and their angrier indictment of current critical practice and theory" (see note 3). While Kolodny planned only to treat a racial perspective, her rhetoric anticipates mideighties strategies for the inclusion of these perspectives—they remain "a group apart," a status Jane Marcus echoes in her essay in the 1984/85 volume of *Tulsa Studies in Women's Literature.*[6]

Showalter begins her paragraph on Smith's essay with the statement: "These vital questions of differences between women in terms of race and sexual orientation were also being vigorously raised by black and lesbian feminist critics" (13), echoing Kolodny's notion of a critical separatism. Separating out black and lesbian critics differentiates between Bulkin and Patterson's comments about the need to consider questions of differences and the black and lesbian criticism represented by the essays included in Showalter's volume. Showalter's expression of the simultaneity of Bulkin and Patterson's critique and Smith's own production of these positions only wishfully simulates a significant authorizing parallelism in the intellectual timing of white, black, and lesbian criticisms, since, in fact, Smith's article precedes Kolodny's essay by three years and the Gardiner/Bulkin/ Patterson critique of Kolodny by five years. Showalter's use of the term "also" seems to indicate that Bulkin and Patterson are neither black nor lesbian feminist critics and that the raising of these questions by black and lesbian critics happened independently from this mainstream feminist debate, though McDowell and Zimmerman's essays were originally published in the same or the following year as Kolodny and Zimmerman's in the same journal, *Feminist Studies.*

Posed, then, as auxiliary to the Kolodny debate, but usefully corollary to its moment (certainly the founding moment of this section of the anthology, if not of the integrative impulse of other mideighties anthologies), Smith's essay is characterized by Showalter as a "protest" against "the neglect of a black women's literary tradition by male critics of African-American literature, and by white feminist critics of women's literature" (13), a neglect now healed by Showalter's inclusion of the essay, plus two more. In her descriptions of Smith, Showalter is careful to keep both black and lesbian in play, appearing to do so even as she moves to McDowell's black, nonlesbian essay, stating that McDowell takes up only the "race" half of the question, continuing the development of a black feminist criticism, and Zimmerman considers the lesbian other half. While the four terms *race, class, ethnic origin,* and *sexual orientation* are initially reduced to two—*Bulkin and Patterson, black and lesbian*—after Smith, the categories black and lesbian come apart in what would appear to be a recognition of their differing perspectives. As Showalter discloses in her introduction to Zimmerman's essay, "the problems are again different" (13). But what might be real difference is really only different flavors of the recovery project of gynocriticism, the project introduced at the very beginning of this section in Showalter's essay "Toward a Feminist Poetics." Posed against Kolodny, in the place of Bulkin and Patterson, the "black and lesbian" perspectives are also mustered *for* Showalter as exempli of the gynocritical technique. Smith, McDowell, and Zimmerman are not really different at all; Showalter depicts both Smith and Zimmerman as "defining a tradition," Smith "angry," Zimmerman making "a strong case," each concluding with a vision of "the powerful bonds between women as a significant aspect of all women's writing" (14), Smith in *Sula,* Zimmerman as a tradition. Black and lesbian are gynocritics, not different at all, but just the same, different from white and straight.

Though the scapegoat Kolodny would seem to have disappeared from Newton and Rosenfelt's *Feminist Criticism and Social Change,* in fact, the entire collection is defined both as a move toward a "committed materialist practice" that sees itself as "an act of political intervention, a mode of shaping the cultural use to which men's and women's writing will be put" (xv) and as a practice against a kind of panoramic blend of American academic feminist practice, at the heart of which again appears, in numerous footnotes, Annette Kolodny. Cited more than any other critic except, perhaps, Terry Eagleton, in the massive footnotes to the editors' brief introduction (ten pages of footnotes for fourteen pages of introductory text), notes to Kolodny's work are less mere references and more discursive than notes devoted to any other single source. The notes approve of Kolodny when she anticipates or practices a materialist analysis, but when her criticism

—here again specifically "Dancing Through the Minefield"—fails to "live up to its own potential," it receives another resounding critique, this time from critic June Howard.[7]

In *Feminist Criticism and Social Change*, Kolodny is no longer the specific pretense for the inclusion of "minority" perspectives. Instead, Showalter's antipluralist analogy is reinscribed in broader terms, becoming the clash between a materialist critical practice that can absorb differences and an Anglo-American practice that can't. So-called minority perspectives are now evidence of the diverse potentials of materialism. The real enemy here is the arch-foe "essentialism," pervasive in American feminist criticism from Gilbert and Gubar to Kolodny, combatted by the materialist practice of "elucidating the complex web of relations—social, economic, linguistic—of which literature is a part" (xvi) in a "fluid" criticism that is "committed out of its concern for gender relations and . . . out of its concern with the economic" (xviii). This committed practice also has the virtue of being more flexibly able to "work on the power relations implied by gender and simultaneously on those implied by class, race, and sexual identification" (xix). Class is undoubtedly a primary concern, coming first, followed by race and sexual "identification," a curious misnomer for lesbian sexuality.

As in *The New Feminist Criticism*, race and sexual orientation take a supportive role, a role that proves the open-mindedness of the materialist methodology, but again race and sexual orientation coalesce under the rubric "black and lesbian." In the introduction, following an explanation of the feminist/materialist commitment to both gender relations and the political/economic sphere, the editors observe that "many materialist-feminist critics, in fact, have a triple or quadruple commitment by virtue of being racial and/or lesbian liberationists as well" (xix). With the introduction of these additional categories, something shifts. While the materialist commitment to gender and the economic is a commitment to an "analysis," a racial or lesbian commitment is defined differently, as anachronistically political— "liberationists"—as activism instead of analysis. Why for this moment are gender and class cerebral and race and sexual orientation experiential? This is perhaps a reflection of what Jacqueline Rose identifies as Terry Eagleton's reduction of feminist criticism to political activism, simply another version of the analogy that relegates political minorities to the oppressed "activist" position in a gendered oppressor/oppressed paradigm.[8] While the editors reabsorb this experiential black lesbian drift into their critical "double work shift," black and lesbian still consistently follow class and gender as lesser terms.

In this anthology the premiere quadruply committed feminist is again Barbara Smith, whose reprinted "Toward a Black Feminist Criticism" is the first essay of the book. And her quadruple commitment is reflected by the four essays on race/lesbianism included in the collection. Newton and Rosenfelt follow Smith's essay with Paul Lauter's article "Race and Gender in the Shaping of the American Literary Canon: A Case Study From the Twenties" in the "Theory" section, and Sonya Ruehl's essay on Radclyffe Hall and Barbara Christian's essay, "Shadows Uplifted," which appear together in the "Applied Criticism" section. Among these four essays, Smith's sets the tone for the collection, though the editors describe it rather meagerly as asking us "to consider how 'our thoughts connect to the reality of black women's writing and their lives' " (xi–xii). Its appearance in two of the anthologies, both published eight years later than its initial publication, makes it seem like a displaced cast regular, as "a consistent, if minor, mainstay among the stock" (189) essays of white late feminist anthologies in the same terms used by Barbara Christian to describe the role of the Mammy. Smith's essay is the Mammy of the volume, reliable, visible, and beloved. Though the contributors to the anthology are in general conscious of questions of gender/race/ class/sexual orientations, in relation to the primacy of gender and class issues, race and sexual orientation are still relegated together to slim communal chunks of the book, proof of materialist/feminist grip on diversity.

In *Making a Difference* Greene and Kahn also implicitly attempt to correct the omissions of both Kolodny and Showalter, aligning themselves with trends in materialist/ideological criticism, placing both Showalter and Kolodny in a remedial stage for "redressing the imbalances of a male-dominated tradition" (24). But that now-familiar couple, black and lesbian, shows up again in this revisionist, gynocritical context as the differences that correct feminist homogeneity. In the introduction, the editors augment Kolodny's "revisionary rereading" from "A Map for Rereading" with a tradition-altering recognition of both black and lesbian contributions. But they limit the radical potential of black and lesbian first by characterizing them as "traditions" in a gynocritical project and finally by graphically substituting both categories in the place of woman in an analogy of gender oppression, the place of difference where white academic feminism perceives itself to be. "Making a difference" means making an analogy, an equation in which the work of black women and lesbians (and only black women and lesbians) is the "same" as white, straight women's literature. As Greene and Kahn express it: "Moreover, the existence of a black women's tradition and a lesbian tradition raises questions analogous to those that women's literature raises in relation to the male-dominated tradition: how will women's literature be altered when the work of lesbian and black women writers is not merely added to but really incorporated into it?" (23). Black and lesbian are to white straight women as white straight women are to men. They are "moreover"; they are the excess that disrupts the disrupters, but they also take their place in the paradigm, are made the same, are kept separate but equal.

Greene and Kahn provide an overt example of what has been going on in Showalter's anti-Kolodny deployment of black and lesbian and in Newton and Rosenfelt's use of black and lesbian to prove the diversity of feminist materialist criticism against the dangers of feminist essentialism. In all three anthologies, *black* and *lesbian* are included as terms in analogies central to mainstream feminist literary criticism. Anthologies traditionally demand some logical coherence; in these, radicality of difference is sacrificed for an arrangement that makes differences fit into the underlying feminist paradigm of the collection. That paradigm has to do with competing claims to academic power: Showalter vs. Kolodny, materialism vs. essentialism, mainstream feminist vs. mainstream male critics. Greene and Kahn reveal what is at stake here; whoever can muster the support of the oppressed is the more politically correct practice.

While providing a place for difference, this use of analogies prevents any real recognition of the radically other perspective introduced by women who appear to be different. Requiring a reduction or stereotyping of differences to be included in an analogical comparison, analogies abstract, separate, and distance terms from their original, perhaps fearsome, referents. Thus in mainstream feminist criticism, though many differences such as class, ethnicity, or racial groups other than black are routinely included in lists of differences among women, these differences, when diversity per se is called for, are insistently reduced in 1985 to the combination "black and lesbian," which then functions as a synecdoche for the range of differences among women. This kind of shorthand is useful for analogies, which then create another layer of distance by requiring the separation and insertion of discrete categories of difference into slots in a generalized paradigm of oppressor (male literary and critical tradition)/oppressed (feminist criticism), one at a time. Occupying the same position in the analogy (though not simultaneously) establishes an identification between culturally diverse women and white, heterosexual academic women; they are both groups oppressed by gender or an oppressive relation analogous to gender (race, class, ethnic origin, sexual orientation) that is seen as operating within the same paradigm. The insertion of the formula "black and lesbian" in the female position in a male/female, oppressor/oppressed analogy of sexual difference creates an illusion of assimilation and acceptance. But different categories of women don't occupy the same analogical position at the same time. Intimacy is defended against.

While analogies may be a convenient way of including different perspectives, it is useful to ask why any such structure is necessary at all. On the one hand, it consolidates visible differences in a politically effective way. On the other, the use of analogy is a symptom of a mixed message. Feminist mainstream critics intend to include difference, but something prevents them from really integrating such perspectives—from exchanging with and changing in relation to these perspectives—something that could be anything from ignorance to fear, but which is probably more like fear. The fact that black and lesbian are included in analogies that prove the efficacy of one or another mainstream critical philosophy could be construed as a fear that black and lesbian might upset that philosophy. All the more reason to sew them into the system. The programmatic placement of black and lesbian as players in what in 1985 are white, straight feminist arguments prevents the recognition of the radical implications of these differing paradigms or any acceptance of their contributions as theoretical in themselves rather than as augmentative diversity, as supplements to Kolodny, Showalter, or materialist feminism—as backup for a more overarching and all-encompassing feminist theory.

Greene and Kahn, for example, repeat Showalter's analogy of a same difference, of black and lesbian attesting to the virtues of gynocriticism, but from a more pluralistic perspective. As in the previous two anthologies, black and lesbian are represented by specific essays dedicated to those perspectives. Bonnie Zimmerman's central essay on lesbian criticism, "What Has Never Been," which has already "been" at least twice, is reprinted along with Susan Willis' feminist essay on black women writers. The two essays are relegated almost to the end of the volume, together again, apparently as a kind of burgeoning challenge to the oppression of dominant white heterosexual feminist criticism. Their function in the volume is best characterized by Sydney Janet Kaplan's depiction of black and lesbian parts of a gynocritical project, described as the "search for lost women writers" "outside the mainstream" (42). For Kaplan the recovery of black and lesbian literature functions as "a much-needed revision of earlier work that tended to assume a homogeneity of race, class, ethnicity and sexual orientation in writing by women" (43). Together, black and lesbian stand for this potential range of gynocritical diversity. Envisioned as a future project, the integration of black and lesbian perspectives in this anthology is projective, and apart from a chorus of inclusive gestures like Kaplan's, lesbian and black criticisms are put off, still critically segregated in separate by equal chapters. To return to Greene and Kahn's own analogy, mainstream "playful pluralism" —this anthology—takes the place of the male-dominated tradition, opposed by the Showalterian lesbian and black feminist criticism that attempts to retrieve oppressed women's voices. Diversity can play only in the paradigm of gender oppression and is contained by it.[9]

As the anthologies demonstrate, the need for a single front disallows the play of difference; the valorization of theory as a monolithic and all-subsuming paradigm denies difference except as it can be supportive, aligned with the pattern—with Showalter or against Kolodny or against men or against essentialism or with all difference accounted for and contained. Perhaps the most extreme example of this kind of theoretical blindness occurs in Toril Moi's declaration: *"in so far as textual theory is concerned* there is no discernable difference between" Anglo-American feminist criticism, black feminist criticism, and lesbian feminist criticism.[10] In her 1985 "introduction to feminist criticism," *Sexual/Textual Politics,* Moi is fooled perhaps by Anglo-American anthology practice and blinded by the italic turgidity of her fixation on a rather narrow conception of theory. Difference is erased as difference and made the same in the name of theory. Moi can no longer see or admit difference except between theory (French or Marxist-materialist) and nontheory (those things Anglo-American), and because theory is such a monolithic thing, Moi misses the purely theoretical formulation of Zimmerman's lesbian "double vision" and the intriguing theoretical potential of Smith's enactment of a multiple reading of *Sula* as they are hidden beneath the double-whammy of Kolodny and Showalter, with whom Moi argues in her introduction. In fact, Moi's polemical single-mindedness enables her to trample past American feminists' tentative flirtation with differences, as she carelessly achieves a complete denial of difference when she declares: "So far, lesbian and/or black feminist criticism have presented exactly the same *methodological* and *theoretical* problems as the rest of Anglo-American feminist criticism" (86) (emphases Moi's). True if our notion of theory is already bound in a white, heterosexist paradigm and true if we ignore the shifts in 1985 feminist critical practice already inspired by the publication in the early eighties of anthologies of black feminist criticism. While this monolithic concept of theory is a problem, part of the fear incited by multiple differences is that feminist theory won't cohere—that it won't qualify as "theory" at all.

This analogy is repeated again by Jane Marcus in her essay "Still Practice A/Wrested Alphabet," included in *Feminist Issues in Literary Scholarship* (1987), edited by Shari Benstock. Marcus makes two telling comments about the relation of white academic feminist criticism to the theory/criticism of other, variously categorized groups. At one point, she declares a kind of critical segregation, explaining that "women of color and lesbians are working on their own theories of feminist criticism" (87). Later she identifies a critical anxiety: "The white, heterosexual critic often fears such an intimacy with black, Chicana, or lesbian writers, and class can constitute a serious obstacle" (91). She defines the relation between white heterosexual critics and other groups of women as a "fear of intimacy." But what kind of intimacy can criticism represent? What kind of intimacy is it that "white, heterosexual critics" fear? Perceiving class as only an "obstacle," a thing, Marcus locates this fear of intimacy in relations among different kinds of people, in relations between "writers." But does this intimacy threaten guilt by association, a kind of fear of contagion, or does it present the threat of having to be too close, of having, in the face of these other writers, to confront one's own minority, powerlessness, and lack of privilege reflected in the close encounter with the work of women who are, in terms of patriarchal culture, only too obviously dispossessed?

Benstock's anthology provides another clue about the defensive use of analogies in connection with this fear of intimacy aroused by the perceived critical need to include diverse perspectives. The volume embodies the mideighties trend toward greater inclusion of diverse perspectives, as it is a 1987 anthology built around a core of essays initially published in *Tulsa Studies in Women's Literature* in 1984–85. In 1984 many of the contributors of the *Tulsa Studies* volume are sensitive to the need to integrate work from different perspectives, though most essays still focus on mainstream concerns. While contributors such as Jane Marcus reveal an awareness that diverse perspectives exist, racial questions are still in the background. Considerations of sexual orientation and class are represented by Benstock's attempt to see a relation between Gertrude Stein's lesbianism and her writing and Lillian Robinson's and Judith Newton's considerations of the impact of class.[11]

The primary difference between 1984/85 and the 1987 *Feminist Issues in Literary Scholarship* is the addition of three essays treating questions of race that are appended onto the end of the complete, original collection.[12] Though neither their sudden inclusion nor their supplementary position at the end of the volume is accounted for in Catherine Stimpson's introduction to the 1987 anthology, the added essays play an important—maybe all too central—role, even while their supplemental position in the volume is quite marginal. In the introduction to the anthology, Stimpson sees Elizabeth Fox-Genovese's essay on African-American women's autobiography as a safeguard "against both the totalizing tendency of theory and against powerful theories within feminist criticism itself" that Nina Baym cautions us about in her essay in the anthology (4). Located between her discussion of Baym and a synopsis of Roland Barthes generated by Fox-Genovese's essay, Stimpson produces another analogy: "More obliquely, Elizabeth Fox-Genovese asks why white, Western, male critics are moping about the death of the 'subject' and of the 'author' when feminist critics, 'like critics of Afro-American and third world literature,' are valorising new subjects, different authors" (4). Here Stimpson makes two important changes in Greene and Kahn's analogy of "minority is to feminist as feminist is to masculine academic tradition." The main shape of Stimpson's analogy is death and life, death associated with high theory and life with the work of feminist critics and critics of "Afro-American and third world literatures," rather than the progressive subversion/challenge model of Greene and Kahn. Stimpson's analogy is less fluid, more polar, a rhetorical statement about the potential and attitudes of different critical postures practiced on different literary traditions, one (white, male, theoretical) that delivers death and stagnation, the others promising life and change.

The association of feminist critics with critics of African-American and third world literatures puts feminist criticism in the arena of political change and challenge, making it a useful practice that produces and discovers difference, rather than enacting the death-dealing totalization of theory Baym warns about. But while feminist critics and critics of African-American and third world literatures are aligned on the same side of Stimpson's oppositional analogy—an arrangement that might enable critical intimacy—they are separated by another analogy: they are "like" one another in the criticism they produce, like one another in their opposition to high theory. But they are not together, not intimate. The likeness they share is via their critical product; they are separated by Stimpson's asymmetrical insertion of literatures on the side of the project of African-American and third world criticism. Their projects and results are the same, but the practitioners and subject matters are different, echoing Showalter's critical separatism and Marcus' observation that "women of color and lesbians are working on their own." In focusing the analogy on the product rather than on the actors, Stimpson avoids the simplistic assumption that all critics of African-American and third world literatures are racial and ethnic minorities, but she also avoids bringing feminist critics and critics of African-American and third world literatures together, the situation that would create what Marcus has described as intimacy between white academic critics and diverse other "writers." The critics of these two literary traditions are parallel instead of together. This is just another version of the power analogy; feminist critics battle male theory and have again enlisted diversity on their side.

The analogical patterns employed in feminist anthologies, though varied, recreate the same oppositional battle scenario, and all, through the insistent use of binary analogies, result in the same separation of white from other voices. African-American and third world criticism either proves the validity of white feminist theory as it does in Showalter, Newton and Rosenfelt, and Greene and Kahn or works alongside white feminist criticism, proving the same points but operating separately. Greene and Kahn's analogy of a progressive challenge offers one clue to feminist criticism's fear of intimacy. If, as Greene and Kahn suggest, third world and African-American is to feminist as feminist is male tradition, then in the same way that feminist criticism challenges the total centered vision of male tradition, cultural diversity challenges the total centered vision of white academic feminist criticism. Intimacy in all of its connotations and implications: sharing, exposing weaknesses, giving, listening, compromising, changing in relation to an other, de-centering self, means potentially relinquishing the certitude, centrality, consistency, identity, and power of theory and position. And though feminist critics see clearly the dangers of monolithism and (phallo)centrism, intimacy with African-American and third world critics threatens to take them out of their own center, sense of identity, and habits of academic practice. The response to this fear of intimacy is to cover over the threat with even greater control, a conciliatory takeover of the other (whatever or whoever she is) in a generous and open-minded gesture, then making her work for the total project of feminist criticism rather than allowing her influence to shift substantively that project or, more crucially, its practitioners. Despite theoretical commitment, we resist change.

But Benstock's anthology represents a slight shift in emphasis of feminist criticism, a shift already implicit in feminist theory. Feminist literary criticism in this anthology has become repoliticized in the advent of a new combo, race and class, and in a de-emphasizing of lesbian sexuality that has become, in an eighties echo of Kristeva's earlier characterization, an apolitical category in the face of a diversity that has become increasingly perceived as racial and ethnic.[13] Though Stimpson declares in her introduction that "fortunately, some of the most intelligent writing" in the book "is about differences among women" (3), the essays she lists at that point are essays that treat only race and class. Missing from this list are Benstock's and Susan Stanford Friedman's essays, which do attempt to understand the effects of sexual orientation and interracial relations upon the writing of specific women—essays that specifically treat lesbian or bisexual writers. The lesbian has a curious habit of disappearing in this introduction; the appeal to the political makes the lesbian bow to questions of class and race.

Recognizing the importance of the political, arguably stimulated by the influence of the work of diverse American and third world critics as well as Marxist and materialist criticism, returns us to the basic analogy: the analogy of oppressor/oppressed. This analogy, a more polar version of Greene and Kahn's analogy, shifts categories away from their attachment to gender, suggesting that all people are oppressed by "structures of dominance and submission" beyond gender (4). This distributes differences within two large political categories, bringing diversity together in common categories and/or making it disappear. But Stimpson brings both gender and lesbian sexuality back into the argument at the end of her introduction when she calls for a diversity of action in feminist criticism. Citing questions of subjectivity, truth, and recommending a feminist "political commitment to writing history" (5) as well as a continued feminist critique of culture and ideology, Stimpson evokes Gertrude Stein's exhortation to "act so that there is no use in a center" (5). Though Stimpson's concluding overture to a kind of critical multiplicity exists apart from her consideration of different perspectives except that of Gertrude Stein, her path from diversity to the political to a critical diversity that is still politically committed appears to outstrip the containing analogies that have subordinated or separated differences from the feminist mainstream. But don't be fooled—while feminist theory appears to become multiple, the differences that might have stimulated a multiplication of critical questions and approaches are no longer evoked. They have been digested. What seems like a critical shift is finally more a rearrangement of the terms into a more politically self-conscious version of the same old analogy. Diversity, now aligned with white, mainstream feminist criticism is the oppressed, politically correct position of the face of the oppressive hegemony of white male theory.

Proving the insight of Stimpson's use of the political oppressor/oppressed analogy, Peter Shaw, reporting "from the Academy" in *American Scholar,* reverses the analogy to depict a far more fearsome portrait of intimacy, revealing, in a perverse way, the relation between oppression and intimacy.[14] While some post-1985 anthologies such as Teresa de Lauretis' *Feminist Studies/Critical Studies* (1986) and Bella Brodski and Celeste Schenck's *Life/Lines* (1988)[15] are inspired to try to overcome tokenism, Shaw paints the relation between white, mainstream feminist practice and cultural difference as a criminal intimacy between mainstream balance and the challenge of "extremists," now perceived as the unlikely alliance of French theorists, Marxists, and lesbians (both white and black):

> It has to be said that when it comes to French structuralist biologism, to Marxism, white and black lesbianism, and other radical forms of expression, mainstream liberal feminist criticism has allowed itself to be taken intellectually hostage. By subordinating literary critical values to considerations of political solidarity and a desire not to insult political radicals, it has made itself complicit in radical feminism's most damaging tendencies. (512)

Shaw's analogy is a political analogy: the potentially fecund differences introduced by the experiences and perspectives of culturally diverse women are depicted by Shaw as "political" positions. He aligns all threatening differences on the "radical" side of a political split; in a reversal of the analogy, they become the oppressors. Thus "French feminists," Marxists, and white and black lesbians are in the same power-wielding, intellectually extorting space. Sexual orientation, reduced to nearly apolitical invisibility in Benstock's anthology, becomes the archradical force, nurtured by gangs of what Shaw sees as Marxist, lesbian French feminist theorists.

Shaw's notion of what a feminist fear of intimacy should be is a fear of those categories that threaten an American, capitalist patriarchy; fear of intimacy is a fear of revolution, of an excessive terrorism he imagines differences import. In a tidy reflection of Reagan's (and now Bush's) foreign policy, the only possible relation between white and other for Shaw is a "hostage" situation, a violent bondage premised on the political power gained by the misled guilt of mainstream liberals who prefer solidarity over divisiveness or who practice a foolish and excessive politeness stimulated by a liberal desire "not to insult." Ironically, the "damaging tendencies" he sees in feminism's attempts to accommodate diverse perspectives—what he argues are feminism's "fatal tendency to denigrate rather than elevate women" and "the extremes of critical self-contradiction" (512)—are precisely the strengths of a feminist criticism that has begun to listen to differing perspectives and challenge mainstream patriarchal hegemony in a refusal to play by the same rules. What is damaging, of course, is feminism's stalwart failure to reproduce a white, capitalistic, patriarchal model of a consistent, detached literary criticism where the interests of feminism are represented by an "elevation" of woman akin to promotional advertising. In the face of Shaw's "Academy," which has apparently returned to red-baiting as intellectual practice, feminism's struggle with intimacy looks like a love feast so threatening that it has to be characterized as treason or felony kidnapping. Or maybe Shaw projects his own fears onto feminist critical practice, recreating once again Greene and Kahn's analogy: minorities are to white women as women are to men. If minorities hold white women hostage, feminist critics hold white male mainstream literary critics hostage.

Since 1985, mainstream feminist criticism has begun to perceive itself as the home of diversity. One thing we may have discovered is that really permitting differences to coexist requires both increased political awareness and the forging of a different critical practice, one that avoids the insulating reductiveness of analogies that make all differences the same, make them safe and consumable, or, as in Shaw's case, cast them out again as terrorists who threaten the body politic. If Benstock's anthology is typical, then there is an increased awareness of the relation between political action and literary criticism. Mainstream feminist criticism would like to see itself as coalesced with the range of diverse perspectives in a solidarity that rids feminism of both divisions and collective guilt and which also provides a challenging body of support against oppression.

How do we avoid analogies, since shifting from one seems to land us in another and prevents an intimacy that might enable change. The difficulty with the analogies employed in literary criticism is that they all rely on a rather fixed notion of subject placed in an analogy defined by a polar notion of sexual difference. While Stimpson wants to multiply the projects and modes of feminist criticism (a suggestion remotely reminiscent of Annette Kolodny's original pluralism), because the underlying paradigm of critical practice still relies upon an oppressed/oppressor analogy of sexual difference as well as upon a fixed subject, diverse perspectives can still really only coexist as discrete positions on the side of the oppressed. The analogy itself suppresses combinations of difference—intimacy—because of either its fixed subject of its reductive polarity. As Biddy Martin and Chandra Mohanty in their essay in *Feminist Studies/Critical Studies* comment, "The reproduction of . . . polarities (i.e., West/East, white/nonwhite) only serves to concede 'feminism' to the 'West' all over again" (193).

All analogies rely upon and create categories that artificially separate scholarly endeavor. These categories are analogically pitted against one another, especially in the oppressor/oppressed analogy, where the most oppressed occupies the privileged position of being the most political and where political becomes the basis upon which differences can be hierarchized and finally leveled. Do we analogize to prevent intimacy and change, or do the analogies prevent an intimacy we strongly desire? Is the fault in our fear and insecurity or in limitations in the way we think? Or are the two so inextricably interwound that resolving one could resolve the other? Even if analogies are somehow intrinsic to Western thought, we might subvert them momentarily by being constantly aware of their terms and structure, by deliberately keeping them in constant flux, and by constantly shifting, redefining, or denying the categories.

Another way to solve the problems posed by the oppressor/oppressed analogy is to break apart its operative assumptions. In *Feminist Studies/Critical Studies*, which bills itself as feminist studies rather than literary criticism, editor Teresa de Lauretis optimistically sees "a shift" in relation to questions of differences among women, which she locates in feminist understandings of subjectivity. Consciousness of differences in addition to other feminist notions of subjectivity "all together define *the female subject of feminism* in its very specificity, its inherent and at least for now irreconcilable contradiction" (14–15). This female subject, now constituted by difference, can no longer be "collapsed into a fixed identity, the sameness of all women as Woman, or a representation of Feminism as a coherent and available image" (15). The unfixity of the female subject collapses the oppressor/oppressed analogy by preventing any clear alignment of sides, any fixed point around which the totalized discourse implicit to polarities can operate. But even if the subject is de-centered, several questions remain. By locating the effects of diversity in consciousness and subjectivity, do we merely displace the operation of analogies from an inter- to an intrapersonal plane? Does lack of theoretical fixity for the female subject allow an interpenetration of boundaries, an intimacy among female subjects that might sustain their unfixity not only in theory but diachronically and dynamically, or does lack of fixity simply fix the female subject somewhere else, in a fixed notion of unfixity? And how does a shift in feminist notions of subjectivity affect a feminist literary practice, make it face its fear of intimacy?

De Lauretis' emphasis on subjectivity and consciousness is interesting in relation to feminist psychoanalytic criticism, another brand of mainly white feminist literary criticism widely practiced in the eighties. But the psychoanalytic interest in the structure of subjectivity and its lack of fixity and unity leads to anthologies with even less consciousness of questions of differences among women. Up to this point, in its attention to mainly Freudian and Lacanian psychoanalytic concepts of the subject, feminist psychoanalytic literary critical anthologies don't even begin to broach questions of multiple differences among women except as those questions are already contained in psychoanalytic discourse (sexuality), or insofar as such differences are comprehended within a notion of the "other," or as theories of the subject can be seen to work on all subjects despite cultural and ethnic differences. Of three feminist psychoanalytic literary anthologies published in the eighties—*The (M)Other Tongue: Essays in Feminist Psychoanalytic Interpretation, Discontented Discourses: Feminism, Textual Intervention, Psychoanalysis,* and *Feminism and Psychoanalysis*—though they all contain some consideration of lesbian sexuality, questions of race, class, ethnocentrism, or other categories of difference are minor or nonexistent.[16] The point is not to chastise (including myself), but to ask whether considerations of a disunified subjectivity are sufficient without an additional consciousness that even structures of subjectivity may vary between cultures, genders, classes—without a broader critique of the cultural assumptions of psychoanalysis. De Lauretis' location of the shift in feminist criticism at the point of subjectivity, though formulated in ways that are roughly similar to a Lacanian model, is both broader and more politicized, more a challenge to any theory of one size (subjectivity) (theory) fits all.

As Moi perhaps unwittingly illustrates, really accepting divergent viewpoints and recognizing the unfixed and contradictory nature of the subject threatens the traditional notion of theory itself and the very way we seek to unify, universalize, and control through theory —the theory that stands up against the male-dominated tradition, "the tool from our master's house."[17] Intimacy with difference disallows a monolithic perspective, even about subjectivity, suggesting theor*ies* instead of theor*y*, actions instead of action, multiple and changing consciousnesses instead of a fixed subject, shifting the emphasis of any feminist endeavor from a singular political position that represents all women to the intersections of the differences that emphasize that there is no such category as *all* women or even all black women or all lesbians or all Chicanas or all poor women. Allowing the play of differences, allowing flux, dismantles categories and analogies and enables us to see instead the potentially increased understanding that exists in those places "between the lines," which might ultimately erase the rigid categories represented by those lines. As Gloria Anzaldua suggests in *Borderlands*, these edges "are physically present wherever two or more cultures edge each other, where people of different races occupy the same territory, where under, lower, middle and upper classes touch, where the space between two individuals shrinks with intimacy."[18] But as it is, analogies depend upon maintaining the space between the lines, the categories of difference, the notions of consistency, the theoretical profile of singularity, purity, and detachment that guarantees the acceptance of any critical practice by the kind of narrow-minded academe represented by the likes of Peter Shaw. But Shaw should not be taken lightly, for the paranoia of his fears, McCartheyesque parody that it is, may reflect an entrenched white, middle-class paranoia that dances even on the edges of a well-meaning feminist consciousness caught between the conservatism of the academy and the formulation of new ways of seeing.

SIX

Polymorphous Diversity

TENNIS PROSE

From the *Wilmington News Journal,* July 13, 1990:

Former tennis great *Margaret Court* says nine-time Wimbledon champion *Martina Navratilova* is a poor role model for young players because she is a lesbian. Court, who won 25 Grand Slam events, said Wednesday in newspaper and radio interviews that Navratilova's homosexuality is a bad example. "She is a great player, but I'd like to see somebody at the top to whom the younger players can look up to [sic]," said Court, 47, a born-again Christian who lives in Perth, Australia. "It is very sad for children to be exposed to it." Court, who said some players had been led into lesbianism by veteran players, added, "If I had a daughter on the circuit, I'd want to be there. There are now some players who don't even go to the tournament changing rooms because of the problem. Martina is a nice person. Her life has gone astray."

OF COURSE, Martina Navratilova is a poor role model if she is a lesbian, because the idea of a role model is the hallmark of a heterosexual system, the epitome of gender ideals centered around and propping up the phallocracy. Reflecting the ideology of "career woman," Court's grievance is not that Martina plays tennis poorly, manages her money poorly, or—to be superficial—presents an unattractive appearance when she plays. What Martina does poorly in Court's terms is play the part of a talented and accomplished woman still devoted to men, which is, after all, what being a career woman is all about.

Given Court's rancor, one might diagnose the malady of her complaint as a severe case of *logica homophobia* brought on by stress and manifested by symptoms of self-righteous self-contradiction. Simply, at a time of a challenge to her own centrality (Navratilova had just broken Court's all-time Wimbledon win record), Court not only evokes Navratilova's sexuality, but also mouths a flurry of common misconceptions about it: it's a contagious disease; lesbians endlessly proselyte; lesbians, like some men, are likely to lunge at women *en déshabille*. Popular renditions of the configurations of lesbian sexuality operating in more "theoretical" discourses, Court's assumptions reveal the illogical absurdity of attempts to depict lesbian sexuality in terms of a "hommosexual" system, attempts that inevitably result in contradiction or in a polymorphously diverse view of the lesbian as powerful, sirenlike, and/or enigmatically alluring. Despite her earnestness, Court's comments fail to contain either Navratilova or lesbian sexuality: both go "astray" from the rigid limits of phallocentrically defined sexualities and the dismissive tenor of her complaint.

That this item appeared in the newspaper at all illustrates the ambivalent tangle around lesbian sexuality.[1] Customarily ignored, euphsmized, or only hinted at, especially by befuddled sports broadcasters who delicately tiptoe around the nature of Navratilova's relationship to Judy Nelson, "a Texas Housewife," Navratilova's sexuality is made momentarily visible in the "People" column of the Gannett chain of newspapers. Navratilova's sexuality is certainly not news in 1990; the timing of the piece undermines her Wimbledon triumph, bringing to the fore the latest of a series of condemnations from jealous competitors. The item, under the byline of Al Mascitti, can be read as either straight reporting or snide undercutting of Court's narrow-mindedness. In either case, it manages to disseminate Court's (and a general public) condemnation of lesbian sexuality while providing enough information about Court's perspective—she's a "born-again Christian"—to enable readers to discredit (or agree more heartily with) her opinion. The question is, What is going on in Western culture in July 1990 that makes this silly condemnation necessary? What threat to phallocratic supremacy (Glastnost? Economic recession? The S & L scandal?) spurs the appearance of such pathetic sensationalism?

The main assumption of Court's diatribe is that lesbian sexuality is a disease. Children shouldn't be "exposed" to it; players are afraid to go into the locker room. The disease model evoked by Court appeared in the wake of nineteenth-century psychoanalytic examinations of sexuality joining the earlier sin model and adding the possibility of a genetic predisposition to a stubborn belief in the homosexual's voluntary choice.[2] Rather than replacing the sin model, the disease model added an element of predisposition akin to religious doctrines of predestination. Together, disease and sin rendered lesbian sexuality an unfortunate condition that had to be controlled by the virtuous woman ill-fated enough to have been dealt that lot. Those who didn't succeed in virtue were seen as moral and psychic degenerates, like prostitutes.

Situating lesbian sexuality as both choice and unavoidable predisposition, the disease model is internally inconsistent. Late nineteenth-century psychoanalysts and psychiatrists such as Freud, Krafft-Ebing, and Havelock Ellis believed that homosexual behavior had a biological base, though they disagreed on other factors in its shape and etiology. Despite the fact that biology or heredity created a lesbian disposition, an aberration that was certainly not contagious, women might still later "catch" the lesbian disease: "Causes for it in women being the segregation of the sexes, extreme sensuality, masturbation, fear of disease, fear of pregnancy, abhorrence of men."[3] Not spread by a germ, the contagion of lesbian sexuality is environmental, proliferating through the expression of "excessive" forms of female sexual behavior that occur exclusive of men. Krafft-Ebing's causal list becomes a circle: lesbian sexuality is is created by elements correlating closely to configurations of lesbian sexuality operative in Western culture. Caused by itself, lesbian sexuality is its own germ, a self-contained source of disease and agent of contagion. If that is the case, then Court is right to fear it and it is no surprise that the way to prevent it is to promote an atmosphere of preventive patriarchy, something Court, whose statement reiterates the disease model's contradictions, is anxious to do.

The contradictions of the disease model reflect the logical impasse of projected homophobia in the 1990s. Why should something be seen as innate, contagious, and self-generating at the same time unless that something is unusually threatening, ubiquitous, or mysterious? As Sander Gilman notes in his analysis of the anxiety that underlies such pathological models of otherness: "The magic of any over-arching explanatory model such as degeneracy disguises, but does not eliminate, the potential loss of power. The only buffer 'science' could provide against the anxiety that remained because of this inherent flaw, the fear of oneself eventually being labeled as degenerate, was to create categories that were absolutely self contained."[4] These self-contained categories such as lesbian "disease" not only prevent the "spread" of a contagious degeneracy, they also enclose their threat in a way that is symptomatic of the nature of the danger they pose.

The danger posed by lesbian sexuality is precisely the danger of contagion: that tennis players will be attracted to it and that through a more metaphorical contagion "straight" players will be mistaken for lesbians. The symptomatic nature of the contagion logic of Court's statement is located in her categorizing reference to lesbian sexuality as a "problem" like drug abuse or alcoholism, problems "scientifically" understood today as both innate and voluntary. Addictions are the modern degeneracy; seen as the response of weak natures to societal pressures, they underlie the current disease model of lesbian sexuality. Court's evocation of an addiction model situates lesbian sexuality as an alluring abused substance, a forbidden thrill that, like drugs or alcohol, enables the user to escape the pressures of a patriarchal existence. If we follow the analogy, this means that lesbian sexuality provides a "high," intense pleasure, and perhaps an escape from oppression. In the addiction model, this escape is momentary, but the addiction and the problems it causes are long-lasting. Like addictions, then, lesbian sexuality provides only the illusion of an answer to the woman who should make herself sexually available to men. And addictions inevitably make lives "go astray," ruining otherwise "nice" people like Martina.

Lesbian sexuality, however, provides an allure and transgression different from that of drug or alcohol addictions. Addictions in general defy capitalism by incapacitating workers (users) or bypassing the work ethic (pushers). In a similar way, lesbian sexuality defies heterosexual patriarchy, as Luce Irigaray suggests, by removing women from the commodity exchange.[5] This defiance is in both cases translated as excess, but while drug and alcohol addictions are seen as offering oblivion, crime, and death, lesbian sexuality is feared to offer more—the knowledge of something other: the degenerate otherness that might also be located in self. The addiction model merely tries to contain the "other" lesbian knowledge by restricting its allure and effects to a temporary degenerative delusion.

The mysteriousness of lesbian sexuality—its out-of-sight, locker-room dissemination, the secret initiation of younger players by older players (prevented by the presence of mothers)—is also evidence of the allure of its supposed clandestine knowledge of something beyond the heterosexual. Martina's "sin" in Court's eyes is making this secret identity public; like Avon, who in the Rita Mae Brown era threatened to stop funding its women's tennis tournament if Martina Navratilova publicly admitted any lesbian attachment, Court perceives the dangers to patriarchy this open flaunting might have. Stated in terms of "damaging the tour," suspicions of lesbian sexuality among professional women athletes are always made public by other women professionals. While this might reflect some real threat, it also both serves the patriarchy and immunizes the speaker against the practices she condemns (lest we be confused). The problem is not so much Navratilova's sexuality, but rather the fact that she does not deny or hide it openly challenges the precepts of the heterosexual patriarchy Court religiously defends.

Court's statement contains additional symptomatic traces of configurations of lesbian sexuality as both excess and knowledge. Her desire to go into the locker room to protect her hypothetical daughter from lesbian attack is as much curiosity as it is wrongheaded gallantry; what is to prevent Court herself from catching the disease? Apparently the sheer quantity—an excessive number—of lesbians makes it dangerous. And this excess is exacerbated by Navratilova's openness in a way that refers to another question of knowledge. Navratilova's public image—a combination of strength and feminine style—creates the mystery of contradictory gender signals that bring her sexuality into question. The titillating possibility of the sexual question is the lure: we like to think we know without having been told what a celebrity's sexuality is. Unannounced, the answer to the Navratilova enigma allows the imagining of a lesbian sexuality against the backdrop of the mundane probability of heterosexuality. Navratilova's openness disallows the tantalizing pleasure of the imagination, eliminating the safety of uncertainty. The possibility of her lesbian sexuality is no longer the lure of knowledge, but rather the certainty of an excess reflected in increased numbers of seduced young players.

The connection of media representations of Martina Navratilova to configurations of lesbian sexuality found in more theoretical discourses suggests that what are perceived as "theoretical" discourses and the discourses and representations of mass culture are parts of the same cultural imaginary. The similarities indicate that instead of theory imposing sets of strictures upon culture or instead of theory only deriving its theses deductively from culture, theory is a part of culture and affected by this cultural imaginary in the same way as other parts of culture. Configurations of lesbian sexuality are thus distributed and reflected through the range of discourses from theory to street language, not in any vastly different form, but rather in forms that reflect the same underlying heterosexual, phallocentric, binary structure by which lesbian sexuality is comprehended.

If, in a cultural imaginary shaped by a two-gender, heterosexual system where all difference is defined in reference to the phallus, sexuality is impossible without the phallus and women have no phallus, then lesbian sexuality is impossible.[6] This apparently simplistic logic actually gives rise to most lesbian configurations and also explains their centrality. The paradox of a sexuality without phallus exists in a phallocentric imaginary as the system's own self-defiant space, defined by and within a phallocentric logic, but as the point where such logic is undone—where something is inaccessible. Represented by configurations of excess, immaturity, impossibility, and the idea of lesbian sexuality as standing in the place of knowledge, not of the woman, but of the phallocentric self who seeks knowledge of her, lesbian sexuality is the point of failure—the symptom of a lack of knowledge. Simultaneously, it is the point of a return to a binary logic whereby the system recuperates itself, "knows itself," cramming lesbian sexuality into the only logical slots in a limited system, seeing it as masculine, immature, heterosexual, and/or a fetish. Incorporating failure and the exposed marks of recuperation in its complex configurations, lesbian sexuality marks stress and ambivalence while seeming to lead toward knowledge. Thus configurations of lesbian sexuality appear at points where the cultural imaginary seems to fail—origins, female sexuality, the preoedipal, narrative uncertainty, identity, psychoanalytic inadequacy—and where it recuperates its binary gender fix in a confident surge of certainty and knowing. Condemnations of Navratilova's sexuality, then, are attempts at recuperative displays of knowledge symptomatically made public at the moment primacy is lost.

The space of the lesbian is the space of ultimate cultural recuperation, central because it is that space—the space of no phallus—that reassures the whole of its phallocentricity. But the instability of an asymmetrical gender system still resides in and is contained at least in one place, by lesbian configurations that embody contradictory instability. For example, threats to phallocentrism spark complaints about a feminism perceived as male exclusive, and such feminism is nearly always characterized as lesbian, not because feminists necessarily are lesbian, but because the space that threatens to de-center the phallus is configured as lesbian. Attacking the lesbian becomes a way of discrediting feminist projects and simultaneously recentering the phallocentric. That's why lesbian sexuality shows up so much—in pornography, in horror films, in complaints about feminism made by disgruntled lovers and academics. Berating the lesbian has become almost a trope in the grievances of some male academics, not because lesbian activity occupies a significant portion of the Western literary imagination, as do heterosexuality and male homosexuality, but because it occupies the space of the inaccessible menace to phallic primacy. One prominent male faculty member rails against lesbians in the classroom, blaming lesbians for instigating what are to him unpalatable changes in the literary canon that essentially de-center the white, male literary tradition. Though lesbians might like to take the credit for progressive changes, this professor's grumbling is merely aimed at the object of greatest threat to any phallocentric primacy, be that literary or sociocultural. Like Peter Shaw or Walter Jackson Bate, who bring up the lesbian as the extreme example of whatever threatens them the most, phallocentric culture, including women, tends to associate the lesbian with marginalized excess: prostitutes, criminals, terrorists, and movie stars.[7] Even as I write this, a tabloid accuses Marilyn Monroe simultaneously of being a murderer and having "gay lovers" and reports excessive Madonna's "relationship" with excessive comic Sandra Bernhard.

Girls Will Be Boys

CONFIGURATIONS OF lesbian sexuality operating in theoretical discourses seem distant from everyday experience and from the lives of women who define themselves as lesbian, especially if such theoretical discourses can be dismissed as erroneous or inapplicable because of their obvious display of homophobia. Preserving the distinction between theory and life, however, perpetuates a split between the historical individual and the forces that shape that individual, a division that prevents a perception of how individuals exist in the complex interplay of representations, material forces, political considerations, and psychic processes. Instead, such a theory/reality split romanticizes the individual (or the category), imagining it as an alienated but pure and innocent space with an originary consciousness. Configurations of lesbian sexuality, existing throughout the range of cultural discourses, illustrate how the same structures proliferate through the range of an imaginary constructed within binary parameters. This is, of course, not to argue for the "truth" of those structures as necessarily descriptive of individual experience, but rather to expose the mechanisms of their working and the possibilities for the existence of something else.

The relation of this cultural imaginary to individual women is complex, as women internalize imaginary configurations while at the same time producing images that confirm the configurations. Configurations help define the lesbian and help the woman identify herself as a lesbian, though like other kinds of stereotype, they never quite succeed in thoroughly containing her. Depending on cultural variables such as class, education, age, race, ethnic group, geographical location, historical context, and even accidents such as whom they know when, women internalize or accept aspects of these configurations. Which comes first, the configuration or the lesbian model for such configuration—the idea, for example, of the Butch as a position adopted by a woman who perceives herself as a lesbian or the "masculine" behavior on the part of the lesbian that creates the idea of the Butch—may be impossible to determine. In any case, configurations of lesbian sexuality as they play through various kinds of discourse already encapsulate a self-contradictory, polymorphous diversity not symptomatic of lesbian sexuality per se, but rather indicative of the configurations' functions in the systems by which they were produced and which they reflect. This does not mean either that configurations have nothing to do with lesbians or that they successfully define lesbian sexuality. What it does mean is that the relation of lesbian sexuality to cultural configurations of lesbian sexuality is as complex, contradictory, and diverse as the configurations are.

The configuration of Butch/Femme, for example, like a configurations of lesbian sexuality, contains both evidence of a failure of the cultural imaginary and its most symptomatic recuperation. The practice of Butch/Femme consists of the two women of a lesbian couple assuming respectively "masculine" and "feminine" roles. The idea of assuming these roles may result from the introjection of cultural paradigms of sexuality as heterosexual or of lesbian as masculine, a conscious political declaration, a performance of gender or heterosexuality, a parody of gender, heterosexuality, misconceptions about lesbian sexuality, or a mixture of all of these. On the surface Butch/Femme seems to be a resolution of the "inconceivability" of lesbian sexuality in a phallocentric system, recuperating that inconceivability by superimposing a male/female model on lesbian relations. Linked to several different configurations of lesbian sexuality, Butch/Femme reflects the layering of gender operative in feminist theories of writing and reading and particularly in encodement theories, the masculinization of the lesbian in Freudian accounts, and lesbian sexuality as excess and as impossibility or inconceivability.

Butch/Femme, however, is internally self-contradictory from the beginning: inconceivability is nonetheless conceivable; a woman is nonetheless a man. What is important in the case of Butch/Femme is that the two processes—inconceivability and recuperation—and their internal contradictions coexist in a tension that never quite resolves itself, producing a systemic challenge to the necessary connection between gender and sexuality while appearing to reaffirm heterosexuality and forcing a consciousness of the artificiality and constructedness of gender positions. Neither completely regressive nor completely subversive, Butch/Femme is diverse in itself, encompassing a range of possibilities that all operate very differently in relation to a phallocentric system.

One version of Butch/Femme exists in the internalization of gender roles as a way of understanding lesbian desire. The prevalence of cultural ideologies of sexuality as necessarily phallic and heterosexual makes it difficult to conceive of sexuality outside of those terms.

Lesbian women thus sometimes conceive of their own sexuality within heterosexual parameters. Using the language of the culture to describe something outside of that culture creates what Broumas calls a "transliteration," the expression of a desire or experience in terms not its own. If lesbian sexuality is "inconceivable" in a phallocentric imaginary, then the best expression of lesbian sexuality that can be achieved is an approximation whose significance lies in the ways in which representation fails to account for it. This transliterative process is partly at issue in Cherrie Moraga's play *Giving Up the Ghost,* which traces the splits and disjunctions between past and present, gender and desire, woman and herself in Corky/Marisa's love for the older, more heterosexual Amalia. Marisa can only comprehend her feelings for Amalia in terms of a binary gendered system:

> It's odd being queer.
> It's not that you don't want a man,
> you just don't want a man in a man.
> You want a man in a woman.[8]

Her attempts to approximate play on the quality of eroticism evoked by the transgression or layering of gender. Transliteration produces not a bad approximation, but an excess signified by the fact that the whole exceeds the sum of its parts, refers elsewhere, to the otherness of the scene being transliterated. To want "a man in a woman" is to want a being who exceeds normative gender, who is more than either woman or man, and who doubles gender back on itself. This is not to say that lesbian sexuality simply plays with gender or seeks perverse forms of it, but rather that interlayering genders shifts their meanings. A man in a woman is different from a man: the layering transgresses and extends both. In this sense Moraga's characters have escaped gender binaries, though as the play traces Corky/Marisa's development, we see also that in some ways, she is, as Teresa de Lauretis describes, "split . . . by her internalization of a notion of hommosexuality which Marisa now lives as a wound, an infinite distance between her female body and her desire for women."[9]

When Butch/Femme is external, the visible portion is the "masculinized" woman, not only because of the phallocentrism of culture, but also because the Butch is the more obvious play on gender. Seeming to depict lesbian sexuality as masculine, the Butch appears to accept and embody not only the terms of a phallocentric system, but also the projected threat of phallic usurpation that images lesbians as male pretenders. But there are really two different problems of masculinity at issue here. One is the actual acceptance of a "masculine" position by a lesbian woman, an act that changes form and significance depending upon its historical context. A woman such as Radclyffe Hall cross-dressing as a male in the early twentieth century is far more radical than a woman cross-dressing in the 1990s. Radclyffe Hall, as Jane Rule describes her, "was known to everyone as John. She wore men's jackets and ties, had a short haircut, and in all manners was gallantly masculine. When she was criticized for calling such attention to herself, she explained that dress was simply an expression of nature, which she could not change, one of the honest ways she faced her inversion" (52). Radclyffe Hall's Butch appearance was a political choice that reflected her belief in Havelock Ellis' formulation of homosexuality as inversion. Seeing homosexuality as simply the internalization of a gender reversal, Havelock Ellis reiterated already prevalent understandings of the necessary relation between gender and sexuality in its imperatively heterosexual form. Materially displaying a literal version of inversion, Radclyffe Hall's challenge, like Navratilova's, is in her openness, her defiant display of a masculine over female persona radical at the time. In the 1990s such cross-dressing has lost its radical meaning: in the age of wing tips for women, we are now accustomed to both mainstream performative drag and a commercialized habit of cross-dressing. Wearing signifiers of masculinity has become a conventional quasi-erotic practice, domesticated into a commercial realm that dresses women in men's underwear not to signify their lesbianism, but rather to provide another fetish prop for phallocracy. The only circumstances in which butchiness like Radclyffe Hall's might approximate her strategy is when a "mannish" woman wears clearly male attire or when a woman wears masculine clothing in contexts not conducive to camp.

Another way of understanding Radclyffe Hall's choice is to see it as an expression of her eccentricity—her inability to fit into traditional women's roles. Similar to Emily Dickinson's adoption of masculine pronouns or Judith Fetterley's notions of "immasculated" women readers, masculinity becomes a sign of both female oppression and female threat. No longer signifying male, this masculinity concerns the mechanism by which women who do not adhere to traditional role expectations are masculinized as a way of attempting to control and restrain behavior that threatens in some way the primacy of masculinity and/or the centrality of the phallus. Freud, for example, fixed on the element of inversion, puzzled over the "masculinity" of the young woman patient in "A Psychogenesis of a Case of Homosexuality in a Woman," looking for some vestige of masculinity where none was clearly perceivable.[10] Finally resorting to a definition of masculine as "active," he is able to define the way the young woman deviates from normal gender expectations.

This second meaning of masculine, however, both depends upon and reveals a weakness in a binary gendered system. One way of looking at this is categorically or definitionally, the logic adopted by Monique Wittig in her argument that "lesbians are not women."[11] Being a woman, according to Wittig, means occupying a certain set place in a rigid heterosexual gender system. If one does not occupy that place, one is not a woman. Lesbians are, therefore, not women because they do not, like women, give in to a heterosexual imperative. The category lesbian thus does not have to do with women loving women, but rather with a position that challenges the necessary relation between gender and sexuality created by and essential to heterosexuality. Denaturalizing the relation between gender and sexuality in "The Straight Mind" and "One Is Not Born a Woman," Wittig sees that rejecting gender categories is a fundamental political requirement and situates the lesbian as a political position.[12] But by bringing the natural status of binary gender into question, Wittig also reveals the gender logic by which women who do not act as women are represented as men.

In a binary system of gender, to call a woman a man is an insult intended to control her behavior. But that a woman who doesn't act as a woman should or can act as a man brings the correlation between gender and biological sex into question, undermining as well the correlation between gender and sexuality. Admitting the possibility that a woman can be a man, that the traits attributed to masculinity are not exclusively masculine, and perceiving lesbians as masculine reveals the threat to masculine supremacy and to a heterosexual system lesbians potentially pose. The representation of the lesbian as masculine is thus two-edged: a put-down, it also encapsulates the very instability of gender prerogatives that undermines heterosexuality. For this reason, attributions of masculinity to lesbians are often expression of anger and anxiety about a de-centering of phallic privilege. For example, in *Lady Chatterley's Lover* Mellors is symptomatically outraged when a woman seeks to sexually pleasure herself:

> — Then there's the hard sort, that are the devil to bring off at all, and bring themselves off, like my wife. They want to be the active party.
> —. . . Then there's the sort that puts you out before you really "come," and go on writhing their loins till they bring themselves off against your thighs. But they're mostly the Lesbian sort. It's astonishing how Lesbian women really are, consciously or unconsciously. Seems to be they're nearly all lesbian.
> "And do you mind?" asked Connie.
> "I could kill them. When I'm with a woman who's really Lesbian, I fairly howl in my soul, wanting to kill her." [13]

Masculine, active, lesbian, the women Mellors hates are women who can please themselves, who don't need him. A challenge to literal phallic power, it is but a short hop from bitch to Butch.

It is also possible to perform rather than simply accept a masculine persona. The performance of gender or drag involves a conscious challenge to gender ideologies, though it too also relies upon and reaffirms them. The potential erotics of the performance of masculinity within lesbian settings works on the principle of a layering of gender suggested by *Giving Up the Ghost*. The woman performing the masculine in the context of other lesbians becomes erotic for some lesbians because of internalizations of heterosexuality, but also because of the powerful excess created by the transgression, assumption, and parody of gender. Carnivalesque in a Bakhtinian sense, the performance of masculinity suspends the restrictive operation of gender and opens up a polymorphous space where the layering of genders explodes heterosexual presumptions by denying the correlation between biology, gender, and sexuality.[14] Connected to the performance of masculinity, Butch/Femme as a cultural practice relies upon the carnival space of lesbian subcultures, and like the carnivalesque, such practices are enabled by a particular suspension of rules within a specific community. Not all lesbian subcultures accept Butch/Femme as an appropriate expression of lesbian sexuality, though even the most "politically correct" community will perform it on special occasions. The fear, of course, is of reiterating the heterosexuality from which lesbians hope to have escaped.

Butch/Femme is inherently diverse, occupying more than one subject position, one gender, at a time. The potential subversive qualities of the oft-ignored Femme side, as the womanish woman who falls in love with a woman, involve the most powerful challenge to the hegemony of heterosexuality. While the mannish woman's attraction to women can be explained in heterosexual terms, the feminine woman's attraction cannot; she remains the impossible space, in and out of gender, unaccountable.[15] The fact that the womanish lesbian tends to be ignored reiterates, even here, the phallocentrism of culture. Or perhaps the relative visibility of the Butch lures us away from the more enigmatic power wielded by the womanish woman whose lesbian desire evades heterosexual logic. While the Butch always conveys at least two levels of signification at once: the woman transgressing gender and the woman caught in gender, the Femme brings into question the necessary heterosexual orientation of the feminine woman, a challenge that potentially explodes any possible function of the woman as stabilizing and reassuring mirror for the man. While both Butches and Femmes incite anger on the part of excluded males, the anger is generated by different threats: the Butch by her seeming usurpation of phallic prerogative, the Femme by failing to reassure masculinity. Together, Butch/Femme create a complex rereading and performance of gender and sexuality in Western culture that reveals the heterosexual stake in gender, the lesbian's stake in heterosexuality, and the artificial nature of it all. This artificiality residing in camp performances of Butch/Femme creates what Sue-Ellen Case argues is "excess, an exaltation of the 'I' through costume, performance, *mise-en-scène*, irony, and utter manipulation of appearance."[16]

What the multiplicity of the Butch/Femme configuration illustrates is the vast polymorphous diversity within the category lesbian, a denomination split within itself by multiple desires, diverse races, classes, ages, educational levels, sexual backgrounds and practices, political consciousnesses, and physical appearances. A category by virtue of a binary gender system, lesbian sexuality exists as a coherent group only in contrast to heterosexuality and male homosexuality. The prominence of sexuality as a mode of dividing is itself an expression of a phallocentrism that classifies all in relation to the operative importance of the literal phallus. Even claiming the lesbian as out of the system is an expression of the function of the category lesbian within the system. As Wittig argues, without gender categories of sexuality are meaningless.

This is not to deny the material existence and desire of lesbian women, nor to suggest that the category is not meaningful. It is to propose a more careful cognizance of diversity within groups and, as de Lauretis observes, within individual women.[17] A sexuality, though important, does not constitute an identity, nor can something as diverse as lesbian sexuality form a place from which one can necessarily "know," bond, or even completely identify. Problems in groups of lesbian women are often created by the presumption that lesbian sexuality forms a sufficient basis for collective action. While notions of Gay pride and lesbian folk culture identifications with lesbian celebrities sometimes constitute points of identification, they do not suffice as complete positions. Expecting lesbian sexuality to carry the burden of political or epistemological positions is like asking a specter to support the weight of critical challenges to ideology. While women who identify as lesbian may easily see the heterosexism of culture and while Wittig may be correct in that the lesbian intrinsically brings the sex/gender system into question, lesbian sexuality is already too completely intertwined with cultural constructions and configurations to comprise more than a partial perspective in any politics premised on identity.

And lesbian does not constitute a monolithic category. Lesbian sexuality exists more at the interstices of multiple differences rather than necessarily constituting a core identity strong enough to completely fix an individual. Such an essential identity tends to come from outside—from a phallocentric culture, for whom the category lesbian is sufficient. Most lesbians know quite well that lesbians are a widely divergent group, organized only loosely in their exclusion from the privileges of heterosexuality. A lesbian student easily listed for me one day the different categories of lesbians on the campus complete with their ideological positions: "style queens," "nature crunchies," "jocks," "new age," and "politicos." These categories, which have more to do with "life-style," coexist with other already evident differences such as race, class, age, physical appearance, sexual preference (bisexual, s/m, into sexual devices, no sexual devices), whose relative importance may shift depending upon the community or subgroup. And as Audre Lorde points out in *Zami*, lesbians are certainly not exempt from racism. The appearance of racism and other intolerances among lesbians indicates the diversity of a group some members of which want to see as singular.[18] Made even more visible by such texts as *This Bridge Called My Back*, *Borderlands*, and the work of Audre Lorde, Barbara Smith, Cherrie Moraga, and other women of color, lesbian diversity reveals more variety than similarity.[19]

While lesbian may not constitute an identity sufficient to carry an identity politics, its inherent variety, along with a consciousness of the operation of configurations of lesbian sexuality, may provide a way to construct a varied critique premised on a flexible and diverse awareness of the processes by which a phallocratic singularity recuperates that which evades it. This is not to suggest merely a counterposition, but rather the delicate juggling of an identity constructed as inherently multiple in the context of multiple cultural systems and contexts that each have their own ways of understanding, configuring, and controlling those elements that elude them. The diversity that exists within the lesbian category is troublesome to the political and theoretical functioning of the position if political and theoretical function are seen as necessarily emanating from a singular identity. In this context not only is the category lesbian seen as monolithic from without, it tends to be seen that way as well from within, even though common sense would indicate otherwise. For there to be any concerted lesbian politics, criticism, or theory, the fact and features of diversity as well as the lack of a monolithic group must be considered; otherwise, we risk merely reiterating centrism or performing cultural expectations.

While lesbians know this diversity, they also tend to forget, deny, or condemn it, often in the name of politics, but also probably from the same fear of difference that motivates many people. The belief is that political and doctrinarian strength comes from ideological unanimity and uniformity, disallowing divergent expressions as traitorous, politically incorrect, or ideologically inconsistent, Lesbian feminists, for example, often decry Butch/Femme behavior as politically incorrect either as a performance of oppressive heterosexuality or in a confusion of Butch/Femme with sadomasochism. And lesbian sadomasochism within lesbian communities becomes the deviant to "straight" lesbian sexuality, reiterating, for whatever reason, an oppressive relationship premised on sexual practices. Seen as advocating violence, lesbian s/m becomes conflated with the most brutal aspects of gender oppression. Violence becomes the point of stress that exposes the very diversity of the category lesbian, a diversity that nonetheless must be kept in check. Reporting on the opposition to s/m at the Michigan Women's Music Festival, *On Our Backs,* a lesbian s/m magazine, pointed out the violence and intolerance of the women who opposed the presence of an s/m contingent: "The *vanilla militia* [those opposed to s/m] did get their licks in, though—complaining to the management, screaming insults at women going up the trail to s/m events, and plastering the porta-jeans with anti-s/m flyers. Ironically, the festival was accused of being pro-s/m for tearing down these flyers, which they considered to be 'violent.' "[20] Circling around the issue of violence, the lesbian community reiterates itself, splits apart. Whether or not one approves of s/m or Butch/Femme, they are evidences of a diverse presence within the category lesbian and are the point where the category is likely to make itself visibly and ideologically diverse.

PROLEGOMENON

Understanding the configurations within which lesbian sexuality is represented while retaining a cognizance of the diversity of the category suggests the necessary coexistence of several approaches to a lesbian criticism or theory. It should be clear, however, that any such theory is not claimed for all lesbians, nor does it enact a special privileged view held by lesbians by virtue of their sexuality. The relative impossibility of a singular lesbian worldview suggests that a lesbian theory might take instead from understandings of the multiple cultural configurations of sexuality, race, and gender to play usefully on the excess, the penultimateness, the multiplicity, the necessity for transliteration gleaned from readings of culture. Wittig, for example, forwards the idea of a rejection of gender categories, based in part upon the impossibility of the lesbian within them. Elaine Marks argues for the strategic deployment of excess, and Sue-Ellen Case sees Butch/Femme camp as an excess that subverts "dominant ideology" from a joint subject position.[21] Jane Gallop's work, though not explicitly lesbian, plays upon the perpetuation of desire and flexible identity that construct a practice of penultimateness—of deferring knowledge and mastery in recognition of the virtue of continuing to desire to know.[22] Olga Broumas' politics of transliteration suggest the continual lack of correlation between experience and systems of dominant discourse, wrenching the discourses from their illusion of stable meaning by making them stand for something other, just as the Butch stands for more than the man.[23] Rather than enacting what might appear to be pure postmodernism or a playful plurality, the use of these strategies depends upon an accurate reading of context, its configurations, and purpose. The polymorphous diversity of lesbian sexuality exhorts that all be deployed, together, separately, gaining in the never complete whole, more than the sum of the parts.

Configurations of lesbian sexuality contain the clue to the threat conveyed by the lesbian. By discovering the nature of those threats, we might also be able to see how to turn threats into theory and go beyond the limiting, self-cycling pattern of failure and return. Adopting a desire for desire instead of a desire for identity or stability may enable a lesbian theory and criticism that really do exceed the singular, the patriarchal, the category lesbian, deploying the lure of knowledge beyond certainty, identity, and mastery.

Notes

INTRODUCTIONS

1. Anaïs Nin, *Henry and June: From the Unexpurgated Diary of Anaïs Nin,* 71.

2. Anaïs Nin, *The Diary of Anaïs Nin: 1931–1934* (volume 1), 58–60.

3. Anaïs Nin, *The Delta of Venus: Erotica,* 168–172.

4. Anaïs Nin and Henry Miller, *A Literate Passion: Letters of Anaïs Nin and Henry Miller, 1932–1953,* 35.

5. As this book is in press, the Rue Blondel scene emerges again, this time as the center of a battle over film ratings. Director Philip Kaufman's film *Henry and June,* based on the "unexpurgated" diary, was threatened with an X rating from the Motion Picture Association of America's movie-ratings board because of its explicit sexual content, including the Rue Blondel scene. According to *The Advocate,* "the crux of the MPAA's objections have to do with the film's depiction of lesbian sexuality" (#561, October 9, 1990, 76). While the film boasts three scenes of lesbian sexuality, the Rue Blondel scene and two between Anaïs and June, the collected material of *Henry and June* upon which the film is based offers no lesbian scene between Anaïs and June. The only such scene published appears in the journal *Anaïs* and takes place November 1932, after the period covered by the *Henry and June* collection. The film essentially augments and exploits the vaguely lesbian reputation of the incident. The result of the latest additional layer to the Rue Blondel configuration is the new rating of NC-17.

6. There are many of these, including Jeannette Foster's *Sex Variant Women in Literature* and Jane Rule's *Lesbian Images.*

7. Sander Gilman's *Difference and Pathology: Stereotypes of Sexuality, Race, and Madness* explores the representational configurations of blacks in nineteenth-century European culture. *The Female Body in Western Culture: Contemporary Perspectives*, edited by Susan Rubin Suleiman, explores various rhetorical uses of the female body.

8. While Jardine's book is a suggestive example for me, its task is very different, treating a subject that is both more broadly dispersed and more narrowly focused.

9. Denis Diderot, *Memoirs of a Nun. The Pure and the Impure*, is a translation of *Ces Plaisirs* . . . .

10. The two omissions I found marked with ellipses both quite literally omit material from Diderot's descriptions as soon as they venture below the waist. On pages 156 and 157, Birrell omits two passages that are located in Denis Diderot, *Oeuvres romanesques*, 343. The use of ellipses disguises the omissions.

11. In English: These pleasures that we call, casually, physical . . . (my translation).

12. Sigmund Freud, "Psychogenesis of a Case of Homosexuality in a Woman," 18:142–172.

1. VIEW TO A THRILL

1. *Emmanuelle* (1968), directed by Just Jaeckin, starring Sylvia Kristel. *Melody in Love* (1978), directed by Hubert Frank, starring Melody O'Bryan. Both films follow the general adventure pattern of John Cleland's *Memoirs of a Woman of Pleasure* (*Fanny Hill*).

2. This follows generally Roland Barthes' ideas of narrative pleasure in *The Pleasure of Text* and the observations of Teresa de Lauretis in *Alice Doesn't: Feminism, Semiotics, Cinema*.

3. The question of the interplay of race and colonial status here is worth another essay. Privilege, here defined primarily as sexual, is mainly accorded along gender lines. Hence both native and colonial males end up with access to white women, though the "right" of the natives is always endowed by the white men. Issues of power tend to be imbricated in the heterosexual economy in these films; discussing them has the effect of erasing lesbian sexuality, which appears in primitive and/or private settings, almost exclusively between white women. Lesbian sexuality is positioned as an evasion of all differences: sexual, racial, and cultural.

4. The parallel of the native girl is an entirely heterosexual subplot, apparently included to prove the superior masculinity of the white Octavio. Her sexual exploits include following a native teacher who turns out to be a male homosexual and being molested by an impotent and klutzy white private detective from whom she flees. While her connection at the beginning of the film to the nature gods of sexuality might indicate that she "naturalizes" the three-way, in fact, it is the libertinism of Rachel and Octavio that initiates her. She is sexually colonized.

5. Annette Kuhn, *The Power of the Image: Essays on Representation and Sexuality*, 32. Kuhn also suggests that the portrayal of lesbian scenes bridges the gap

between soft- and hard-core porn, but that assumes that the lesbian scenes contain real sexual activity in soft-core porn—that is, the real lesbian activity can be portrayed without "penetration."

6. I would have preferred here to use stills from the film to illustrate this discussion. Even though stills would not convey camera movement or the feeling of the whole sequence, they might have clarified the shots' composition and feeling of disorientation. Of course, stills of these exact moments are unavailable and I was unable to get permission to use photographs of the scenes. The reasons for the denial of permission ranged from "it's too costly for us to check it out so we never give permission" to "photos are not in the actresses' contracts." In any case the rights accorded the owners of film images conflict with the interests of scholarship, making the analysis and discussion of commercial film more difficult. While this is not the place for a legal argument, I do question the ideology that privileges, even within the exceptions provided by the doctrine of "Fair Use," property rights over scholarly debate. I would add, however, that the absence of images of lesbian sexual behavior in this book is in keeping with the notion of lesbian sexuality configuring a point of failure. I am also not entirely unhappy that those images are not available for random consumption outside of their context.

7. Andrea Dworkin, *Pornography: Men Possessing Women*.

8. E. Ann Kaplan, *Women and Film: Both Sides of the Camera*, 23–25.

9. Monique Wittig, in "The Straight Mind," says that the discourse of pornography "is the most symptomatic and the most demonstrative of the violence which is done to us through discourses as well as by the society at large" (106).

10. Laura Mulvey, "Visual Pleasure and Narrative Cinema," 6–18. Judith Mayne, "The Woman at the Keyhole: Women's Cinema and Feminist Criticism," 56.

11. Jacques Lacan, "The Mirror Stage As Formative of the Function of the I As Revealed in Psychoanalytic Experience," 1–7. Jane Gallop's useful reading of the mirror stage upon which I rely appears in her book *Reading Lacan*.

12. Jean-Louis Baudry, "The Ideological Effects of the Basic Cinematographic Apparatus," 33–34.

13. Christian Metz, *The Imaginary Signifier: Psychoanalysis and the Cinema*, 49.

14. Sigmund Freud, "On Fetishism," 21:152–157.

15. Laura Mulvey, "Afterthoughts on 'Visual Pleasure and Narrative Cinema' Inspired by *Duel in the Sun* (King Vidor, 1946)," 12.

16. Stephen Heath, "Difference," 104.

17. Kaplan's reliance on the example of the lesbian as one who defies gender assignments unwittingly reproduces the configuration of lesbian as unfixed and roving. Kaplan, however, seems not particularly conscious of the assumption she makes and is anxious instead to move from the lesbian to all women.

18. Kaplan's use of the word "gaze" here is somewhat confusing. I suspect what she means is the act of looking at something rather than the Lacanian usage of the word as meaning, roughly, the sense of being looked at.

19. Teresa de Lauretis, "Oedipus Interruptus," 36.

20. Mary Ann Doane, "Film and Masquerade: Theorising the Female Spectator," 74–88.

21. Mary Ann Doane, *The Desire to Desire: The Woman's Film of the 1940s*.

22. Teresa de Lauretis, *Alice Doesn't: Feminism, Semiotics, Cinema* and *Technologies of Gender: Essays on Theory, Film, and Fiction*.

23. de Lauretis, *Technologies*, 16.

24. *Lianna*, directed by John Sayles, starring Linda Griffiths and Jane Hallaren, 1983.

25. *Desert Hearts*, directed by Donna Deitch, starring Helen Shaver and Patricia Charbonneau, 1985.

26. Lucy Fischer, *Shot/Countershot: Film Tradition and Women's Cinema*. Fischer discusses how *Lianna* "idealizes" lesbian sexuality.

27. Mulvey, "Visual Pleasure and Narrative Cinema," 14. Metz, *The Imaginary Signifier*, 69–78.

28. Doane, *The Desire to Desire*, 32.

29. Kaja Silverman, "Lost Objects and Mistaken Subjects," 14–29.

30. Kuhn, *The Power of the Image*, 4.

31. See Heath's exhaustive discussion of the problem of sexual difference in "Difference."

32. See Doane, *The Desire to Desire*, 13–14, where she explains why the fetish implies a male viewer.

33. See Lucy Fischer's discussion in *Shot/Countershot* of the way this scene repeats "avant-garde" film practices while also appearing to avoid providing another opportunity for scopophilic discussion.

34. Virginia Woolf, *Mrs. Dalloway*, 46–47.

35. Luce Irigaray, "This Sex Which Is Not One," 23.

36. Hélène Cixous, "The Laugh of the Medusa," 245–264.

37. Julia Penelope Stanley and Susan J. Wolfe, "Toward a Feminist Aesthetic," 63.

38. Judith Barry and Sandra Flitterman, "Textual Strategies: The Politics of Art-Making," 44.

39. Silvia Bovenschen, "Is There a Feminist Aesthetic," 136.

40. Judith Mayne, "Women and Film: A Discussion of Feminist Aesthetics," *New German Critique* 10 (1977), 83–107 at 96.

41. De Lauretis, "Oedipus Interruptus," 38.

42. *Entre Nous*, directed by Diane Kurys, starring Isabelle Huppert and Miou-Miou, 1983. French title: *Coup de foudre*.

43. *I've Heard the Mermaids Singing*, directed by Patricia Rozema, starring Sheila McCarthy, 1987.

2. "THIS IS NOT FOR YOU": THE SEXUALITY OF MOTHERING

1. Sigmund Freud, "Three Essays on the Theory of Sexuality," 7:198.

2. Jacques Lacan, "The mirror stage as formative of the function of the I as

revealed in psychoanalytic experience," 1–7. The relation of the mirror stage to history is well described by Jane Gallop in *Reading Lacan*.

3. In Freud this "understanding" may well come from his identification with and reading of lesbian sexuality as male homosexuality, a practice Luce Irigaray critiques in *This Sex Which Is Not One*, 65. See also chapter 4 on Freud. Lacan sees female homosexuality as a defiant narrative, different from both male homosexuality and female heterosexuality alike, and that female homosexuals bear "towards femininity" their "supreme interest" (97). "Guiding Remarks for a Congress on Feminine Sexuality," 86–98. Whether his perceptions result from some sympathy, understanding, or insight, they come remarkably close to some lesbian self-formulations. For an analysis of how Julia Kristeva's formulations contest those of Lacan and a slightly different discussion of her use of the lesbian, see Judith Butler, *Gender Trouble*, 79–93.

4. Jane Gallop discusses Kristeva's adoption of the phallic mother at length in her essay, "The Phallic Mother: Fraudian Analysis," in *The Daughter's Seduction*, 113–131.

5. Julia Kristeva, "Motherhood According to Giovanni Bellini," in *Desire in Language*, 237–270.

6. Julia Kristeva, *In the Beginning Was Love*, 238.

7. Julia Kristeva, "Stabat Mater," in *Tales of Love*, 234–263.

8. Jacqueline Rose observes in her "Introduction" to *Feminine Sexuality* that Chodorow displaces "concepts of the unconscious and bisexuality in favour of a notion of gender imprinting. . . . The book sets itself to question sexual *roles*, but only within the limits of an assumed sexual *identity*" (37*n*4). Rose's analysis is another way of accounting for Chodorow's omission of the factor of sexual orientation if in fact that orientation is a product of the unconscious. In Chodorow's account lesbianism cannot exist because it cannot be created.

9. Jacques Lacan, "The Meaning of the Phallus," *Feminine Sexuality*, 81.

10. In "Stabat Mater" Kristeva does seem to laud maternity, even though her analysis of the role of the Virgin is in part a reading of cultural tendencies instead of psychoanalytical truths. In *Soleil Noir: dépression et mélancholie*, she describes the case study of a patient who chooses the illusion of virgin maternity to escape depression and resolve conflicts produced by paternal incest. In this case, the appeal to virgin maternity as a resolution is no longer so clearly positive. *Soleil Noir*, 99–105.

11. While it is true that many novels written by women depict the protagonist as an orphan, the difference between contemporary lesbian novels and other novels lies in the way the lesbian novels make this originary lack irrelevant rather than making the discovery of origins the way to matrimony and maternity. The orphan pattern in contemporary lesbian novels may also represent the daughter's story; fiction by or about lesbian mothers may present a different paradigm of desire.

12. Quoted by Rose in *Feminine Sexuality*, 38.

13. Sigmund Freud, *The Interpretation of Dreams*, 4:146–151.

14. Lacan, "Direction of treatment and principles of its power." *Ecrits: A Selection*, 226–280. See also Cynthia Chase's discussion of this dream in her essay, "Desire and Identification in Lacan and Kristeva," 65–83.

15. Lacan, "Guiding Remarks for a Congress," *Feminine Sexuality*, 96.

16. Teresa de Lauretis, *Alice Doesn't: Feminism, Semiotics, Cinema* (Bloomington: Indiana University Press, 1984).

3. BEGINNING WITH L

1. Judy Chicago's well-known piece *The Dinner Party* celebrates foremothers. Her *Birth Project* also focuses on an archetypal, mythical maternity.

2. Barbara C. Sproul, *Primal Myths: Creating the World*, 157. I am indebted to L. Steven Schmersal, who reminded me of the more cosmological questions of chaos in his University of Delaware Honors Thesis, "Creation: Meditations on Creations, Creators, Creatures, and Chaos," May 1990.

3. This is claimed for Polynesian creation stories by Mircea Eliade in *The Myth of the Eternal Return*, 82.

4. Luce Irigaray, "The One Doesn't Stir Without the Other," 63.

5. Violette Leduc, *La Bâtarde*, 84.

6. Virginia Woolf, *Mrs. Dalloway*, 47.

7. Luce Irigaray, "The 'Mechanics' of Fluids," *This Sex Which Is Not One*, 110–111.

8. Verena Andermatt Conley, *Hélène Cixous: Writing the Feminine*, 131 and 133. Cixous also appeals to this feminine economy in both "The Laugh of the Medusa," 245–264, and "Castration or Decapitation," 36–55.

9. Marcia Holly, "Toward a Feminist Aesthetic," 38–47, appeals almost entirely to a female "real." In their essay "Toward a Feminist Aesthetic," Julia Penelope Stanley and Susan J. Wolfe appeal to a female consciousness that can reshape language in its own image: "The relationship between consciousness and linguistic choice is confronted and articulated as the self expressing itself in and through a language remade, reordered: the feminist aesthetic" (63). Encodement theories clustered around the work of Gertrude Stein, while recognizing Stein's manipulations of reality, depend upon Stein's corporeal image and her lesbian relation to Alice Toklas as a core foundation from which Stein's encodement ensues. See Catherine Stimpson, "The Somagrams of Gertrude Stein," 67–80, and Elizabeth Fifer, "Is Flesh Advisable? The Interior Theater of Gertrude Stein," 472–483.

10. Heide Göttner-Abendroth, "Nine Principles of a Matriarchal Aesthetic," 81–94.

11. Jacques Lacan, "The Mirror Stage As Formative of the Function of the I As Revealed in Psychoanalytic Experience," 4.

12. Jacques Derrida, *Of Grammatology*, 36.

13. In *The Four Fundamental Concepts of Psycho-Analysis*, Jacques Lacan observes that "generally speaking, the relation between the gaze and what one

wishes to see involves a lure. The subject is presented as other than he is, and what one shows him is not what he wishes to see" (104).

14. Mary J. Carruthers, "The Re-Vision of the Muse: Adrienne Rich, Audre Lorde, Judy Grahn, Olga Broumas," 293–322.

15. Annette Kuhn, "Introduction to Hélène Cixous's 'Castration or Decapitation,' " *Signs* 7, no. 1, 36–40 at 39. *Vivre l'orange* quoted in Kuhn. Kuhn identifies the voice from Brazil as Clarice Lispector.

16. See Ann Rosalind Jones, "Writing the Body: Toward an Understanding of *l'Ecriture féminine*," 361–377. Jones rightly contends with Cixous' notion of the body as a prerepresentational space.

17. In *Zami: A New Spelling of My Name*, Audre Lorde responds to the question: "To whom do I owe the woman I have become?" with "To the battalion of arms where I often retreated for shelter and sometimes found it. To the others who helped, pushing me into the merciless sun—I, coming out blackened and whole" (5). Virginia Woolf writes: "Women alone stir my imagination," a line used as the title for Blanche Wiesen Cook's " 'Women Alone Stir My Imagination': Lesbianism and the Cultural Tradition," an investigation of "the literature and attitudes out of which the present lesbian feminist works have emerged, and to examine the continued denials and invalidation of the lesbian experience" (720). This appeal to a feminine community is like what Mary Carruthers dubs a "lesbian *civitas*," a "society predicated upon familiarity and likenesses rather than oppositions" (304).

18. Diane Crowder, "Amazons and Mothers? Monique Wittig, Hélène Cixous and Theories of Women's Writing," 117–144, provides an analysis of the ways these two figures serve as analogies for formulations of women's writing. The split between them that, as Crowder suggests, arises within the history of feminist criticism is an inadvertent but symptomatic return to a heterosexual binary opposition in which the Amazon is phallicized and the mother romanticized. In her introduction to *The New Feminist Criticism: Essays on Women, Literature, Theory*, Elaine Showalter tries to order these two metaphors historically: "By the 1980s, the lesbian aesthetic had differentiated itself from the female aesthetic. As lesbian feminist criticism became more specialized, feminist critics turned their attention to the analysis of mother-daughter relations, and the figure of the mother replaced that of the Amazon, for theorists of the female aesthetic" (7). Wishful thinking, perhaps, and a symptomatic recreation of Kristeva's ordering of lesbian and maternal, but not wholly accurate as a description of the history of feminist criticism.

19. Domna Stanton makes this point in "Difference on Trial: A Critique of the Maternal Metaphor in Cixous, Irigaray, Kristeva," 157–182.

20. Adrienne Rich, "Compulsory Heterosexuality and Lesbian Existence," 631–660. Rich here universalizes lesbian sexuality as a way of defusing the politically derogatory equation made between feminism and lesbians. By making everyone a lesbian, the term loses its sexual meaning.

21. Hélène Cixous, "Rethinking Differences," 74–75.

22. Crowder, "Amazons and Mothers?," 138n38.

23. Though Cixous would probably object to any characterization of a writing said to be feminine as a symbolic structure in Lacanian terms, the writing she proposes bears the same relation to the imaginary as phallocentric writing does. In Lacanian terms Cixous wishes to shift the place of the Law of the Father.

24. Luce Irigaray, "Psychoanalytic Theory: Another Look," *This Sex Which Is Not One*, 65; "This Sex Which Is Not One," *This Sex Which Is Not One*, 23–33.

25. Luce Irigaray, "Commodities Among Themselves," *This Sex Which Is Not One*, 196.

26. Luce Irigaray, "Questions," *This Sex Which Is Not One*, 159.

27. Luce Irigaray, "The Power of Discourse," *This Sex Which Is Not One*, 78.

28. Luce Irigaray, "When Our Lips Speak Together," *This Sex Which Is Not One*, 209.

29. Hélène Wenzel makes this comment about the essay's relation to "When Our Lips Speak Together" in her introduction to Irigaray, "The One Doesn't Stir Without the Other," 58.

30. Ibid., 58.

31. Elizabeth Flynn and Patrocinio Schweickart, eds., *Gender and Reading*, "Introduction," xiii–xiv.

32. Adrienne Rich, *On Lies, Secrets, and Silence: Selected Prose 1966–1978*, 157–183.

33. Marilyn Farwell, in "Toward a Definition of the Lesbian Literary Imagination" (100–118), discusses at length the use of the lesbian metaphor in writing.

34. Adrienne Rich, "When We Dead Awaken: Writing as Re-Vision," *On Lies, Secrets, and Silence*, 35.

35. Judith Fetterley, *The Resisting Reader: A Feminist Approach to American Fiction*.

36. Patrocinio Schweickart, "Reading Ourselves: Toward a Feminist Theory of Reading," 31–57.

37. Jean Kennard, "Ourself Behind Ourself: A Theory for Lesbian Readers," 63–77.

38. Catherine Stimpson, "Mind, Body, and Gertrude Stein," 499. Other essays that explore lesbian encodement include Stimpson's "The Somagrams of Gertrude Stein"; Fifer, "Is Flesh Advisable?"; and Linda Simon, *The Biography of Alice B. Toklas*.

39. Peggy Kamuf, "Writing like a Woman," 298.

40. Elaine Showalter, "Critical Cross-dressing: Male Feminists and the Woman of the Year," 116–136. This is in partial response to Jonathan Culler's "Reading as a Woman" in *On Deconstruction*. In her discussion of "reading as a woman," an idea she attributes to Jonathan Culler, Showalter curiously omits Peggy Kamuf, whom Culler credits with the formulation of the idea. While Culler is careful to credit both Showalter herself and Peggy Kamuf with the analysis of the split woman reader, quoting a substantial chunk from Kamuf's article "Writing like a

Woman," Showalter eclipses both Kamuf and herself in her reproduction of Culler, omitting the influence of feminist thought completely from this part of the discussion and dressing Culler in Kamuf's idea. While the man Culler reproduces the woman Kamuf's reading of a woman reading as a woman, making clear their relation and a consciousness of identity, Showalter reproduces the man Culler in place of the woman, quoting paradoxically around Culler's inclusion of Kamuf's text, producing in her representation of Culler an example of what she fears: that men will become women.

41. Jane Gallop, "The Problem of Definition," 111–132.

42. Jane Gallop makes this point in "The Problem of Definition," and Penelope Engelbrecht in " 'Lifting Belly Is a Language': The Postmodern Lesbian Subject," 85–114, illustrates it.

43. Monique Wittig, "The Straight Mind," 103–111; and Engelbrecht, "Lifting Belly Is a Language."

44. Bonnie Zimmerman, "What Has Never Been: An Overview of Lesbian Feminist Literary Criticism," 205.

45. Dale Bauer, *Feminist Dialogics: A Theory of Failed Community.*

46. Jane Gallop enacts this kind of reading in *The Daughter's Seduction: Feminism and Psychoanalysis, Reading Lacan,* and *Thinking Through the Body.*

4. FREUD READS LESBIANS

1. Sigmund Freud, *Fragment of an Analysis of a Case of Hysteria,* 7:3–122.

2. The phallic metaphor of the "key" is suggested by Freud himself, but is taken up and taken apart by Jane Gallop in "Keys to Dora" included in Charles Bernheimer and Claire Kahane, eds., *In Dora's Case: Freud—Hysteria—Feminism,* 200–220, as well as in Jane Gallop, *The Daughter's Seduction: Feminism and Psychoanalysis,* 132–150. Other essays in the Bernheimer-Kahane anthology that recognize the role of lesbian sexuality in the Dora case are those by Jacqueline Rose, "Dora: Fragment of an Analysis," 128–148; Suzanne Gearhart, "The Scene of Psychoanalysis: The Unanswered Questions of Dora," 105–127; and Neil Hertz, "Dora's Secrets, Freud's Techniques," 221–242.

3. Joseph Breuer and Sigmund Freud, *Studies in Hysteria.*

4. Sigmund Freud, "Three Essays on the Theory of Sexuality," 7:125–246.

5. Sigmund Freud, "My Views on the Part Played by Sexuality in the Aetiology of Neuroses," 7:271–279.

6. Sigmund Freud, "Psychogenesis of a Case of Homosexuality in a Woman," 18:143–170.

7. Sigmund Freud, "Some Neurotic Mechanisms in Jealousy, Paranoia and Homosexuality," 221–232; "Some Psychical Consequences of the Anatomical Distinction between the Sexes," 19:243–258; and "Female Sexuality," 223–243.

8. Sigmund Freud, "A Case of Paranoia Running Counter to the Psychoanalytic Theory of the Disease," 14:263–272.

9. Steven Marcus, "Freud and Dora: Story, History, Case History," 56–91.

10. *The Complete Letters of Sigmund Freud to Wilhelm Fliess, 1887–1904.* Subse-

quent references to these letters will include the date of the letter, then the page of the collection.

11. For example, Freud's letter of September 19, 1901, 449.

12. Letter of October 17, 1899, 380. The rather brief letter reads as follows: "Dear Wilhelm, What would you say if masturbation were to reduce itself to homosexuality, and the latter, that is, male homosexuality (in both sexes) were the primitive form of sexual longing? (The first sexual aim, analogous to the infantile one—a wish that does not extend beyond the inner world) If, moreover, libido and anxiety were male? Cordially, Your Sigm."

13. See, for example, the letters of May 2, 1897, 238, and May 25, 1897, 245.

14. Early in his narrative he had surmised that Dora's former governess, whom Dora liked and who was vicariously a part of a love triangle with Dora's father, had provided Dora with sexual knowledge (36n). This earlier connection, which Freud never quite relinquished, is the heterosexual version of Dora's identifications upon which Freud builds his claim that Dora was attracted to Herr K. Freud earlier observes that Frau K has revealed that Dora's main interest was in sexual matters, her source of knowledge Mantegazza's *Physiology of Love* (26).

15. This reverberates but is not quite the same as Luce Irigaray's analysis of the "hommosexual" quality of dominant culture she argues in "Blind Spot of an Old Dream of Symmetry," in *Speculum of the Other Woman.* Irigaray analyzes some of the effects of Freud's inability to see female relations except within a male homosexual paradigm in *This Sex Which Is Not One.*

16. In "Psycho-analytic Notes on an Autobiographical Account of a Case of Paranoia," known as "the Schreber case," Freud pinpoints the "weak spot in their development" "somewhere between the stages of auto-eroticism, narcissism and homosexuality" (12:62). In "On Narcissism: An Introduction," Freud hypothesizes that homosexuals take themselves as love objects (14:88).

17. Sigmund Freud, *New Introductory Lectures on Psychoanalysis,* lecture 33, 22:112–135.

18. Sigmund Freud, "The Dissolution of the Oedipus Complex," 19:173–179, and "A Child Is Being Beaten," 17:175–204.

19. The fixation of the lesbian in adolescence was pointed out to me by Jane Gallop in her essay "The Attraction of the Matrimonial Metaphor," in *Around 1981: Academic Feminist Literary Criticism,* forthcoming from Routledge. I had been too caught in Freud's attraction to infantile etiologies.

20. This was the case in Ohio circa 1980.

21. *South Atlantic Quarterly* 88, 1 (Winter 1989).

22. Many feminist anthologies published in the 1980s regularly include and set off special chapters on "lesbian" criticism while most of the rest of the included essays tend to ignore sexual orientation. See chapter 5 of this book.

23. Kate Millet. *Sexual Politics.* In her subchapter "Freud and the Influence of Psychoanalytic Thought," she centers her explanation of Freud's thinking about women around penis envy, a choice that determines her inevitable dissatisfaction. Simone de Beauvoir in *The Second Sex* also, but more briefly, dismisses

Freud (34–35). I am still trying to track down the elusive "Myth of the Vaginal Orgasm," which circulated through my adolescence in photocopied form.

5. ALL ANALOGIES ARE FAULTY: THE FEAR OF INTIMACY IN FEMINIST CRITICISM

This essay was generated during and owes much to Jane Gallop's 1988 NEH Summer Seminar, Feminist Criticism: Issues in Literary Theory, at the Center for Twentieth Century Studies, University of Wisconsin–Milwaukee. The original version, "All Analogies Are Faulty," was presented as part of the panel Difference and Differences: Gender, Race, Class, and Sexuality in Mass Culture at the 1988 MLA convention in New Orleans.

1. In *Technologies of Gender*, Teresa de Lauretis credits such early eighties anthologies as Cherrie Moraga and Gloria Anzaldua's *This Bridge Called My Back* and Gloria Hull, Patricia Bell Scott, and Barbara Smith's *All the Women Are White, All the Blacks Are Men, but Some of Us Are Brave* with making different perspectives available to feminists. De Lauretis says: "The shift in feminist consciousness that was initially prompted by works such as these is best characterized by the awareness and the effort to work through feminism's complicity with ideology, both ideology in general (including classism or bourgeois liberalism, racism, colonialism, imperialism, and, I would also add with some qualifications, humanism) and the ideology of gender in particular—that is to say, heterosexism" (10–11). National Conventions of NWSA, notably those held in 1981 and 1983, were forums where questions about the white, middle-class assumptions of academic feminists were raised and critiqued. For a summary of the 1981 NWSA conference, see Mary Papke, Eileen Manion, and Julia Visor, "Women Respond to Racism," 180–187.

2. I leave until the end any discussion of Shirley Nelson Garner, Claire Kahane, and Madelon Sprengnether, eds., *The (M)Other Tongue: Essays in Feminist Psychoanalytic Interpretation*, another anthology of feminist literary criticism, because of the special problems presented by psychoanalytic methodology. The formula of black and lesbian as synechdochal of diversity also seems to be very much an introjection of the white feminist critical community. It is not as if black and lesbian live a separate but somehow amalgamated existence. Marjorie Pryse and Hortense Spillers, eds., *Conjuring: Black Women, Fiction, and Literary Tradition*, a collection devoted to essays on the writing of black women, barely even refers to lesbian sexuality. In a brief discussion of Ann Allen Shockley's *Loving Her*, a novel about the lesbian relation between a black and a white woman, Elizabeth Schultz sees its attention to questions of sexism almost as an alternative to considerations of racism: "Although neither Allison Mills's *Francisco* (1974) nor Ann Allen Shockley's *Loving Her* (1974) protests racism or explores the racial dimension of the interracial friendship, each of these novels reflects the destructive potential of sexism to a friendship" (81). Bound up in issues of class *(Francisco)* or lesbian sexuality, differences seem to alternate rather than combine. The analogy seems to be no different; differences seriatim rather than together.

3. Annette Kolodny, "Dancing Through the Minefield: Some Observations on the Theory, Practice and Politics of a Feminist Literary Criticism," 1–25. This essay with some revision is reprinted in Showalter's *The New Feminist Criticism*. After publication of the first version of this essay, Elly Bulkin, Rena Grasso Patterson, and Judith Kegan Gardiner criticized the essay's blindness to issues of race, class, and sexual orientation despite (and partly on the basis of) an explanatory note provided by Kolodny: "This essay intentionally deals with white feminist critics only, because it was originally conceived as the first of a two-essay dialogue with myself. The second essay, "Sharp-shooting from the Outskirts of the Minefield: The Radical Critique by American Black and Third World Feminist Literary Critics," was to argue that black and Third World American feminist literary critics stand as a group apart from the whites, united by their more probing analysis of the institutions which give rise to current literary tastes and their angrier indictment of current critical practice and theory" (22).

4. Jane Gallop, "The Problem of Definition," 111–132.

5. Judith Kegan Gardiner, Elly Bulkin, Rena Grasso Patterson, and Annette Kolodny, "An Interchange on Feminist Criticism on 'Dancing Through the Minefield,' " 629–675.

6. Jane Marcus, "Still Practice, A/Wrested Alphabet," in Shari Benstock, ed., *Feminist Issues in Literary Scholarship*, of which ten essays were originally published in *Tulsa Studies in Women's Literature* 3 1/2 (1984–85).

7. June Howard, "Review Essay: Feminist Differings: Recent Surveys of Feminist Literary Theory and Criticism," 167–189. In this review Howard considers the anthologies discussed here as well as Marjorie Pryse and Hortense Spillers' *Conjuring: Black Women, Fiction, and Literary Tradition*.

8. Jacqueline Rose, *Sexuality and the Field of Difference*, 11–12.

9. Jane Gallop offers an analysis of the penultimate positioning of these black and lesbian chapters in *Making a Difference* in "The Attraction of the Matrimonial Metaphor," in a chapter of her book *Around 1981: Academic Feminist Literary Theory*, forthcoming from Routledge.

10. Toril Moi, *Sexual/Textual Politics*, 86 (emphasis Moi's).

11. See Elizabeth Meese's analysis of Benstock's volume of *Tulsa Studies* in *(Ex)tensions: Re-Figuring Feminist Criticism*, 4–23.

12. This point was originally made by Jane Gallop in the 1988 NEH summer seminar during discussion of Benstock's volume.

13. In *About Chinese Women*, Julia Kristeva clearly relegates lesbians to the realm of the apolitical (15).

14. Peter Shaw, "Feminist Literary Criticism: A Report from the Academy," 495–513.

15. Bella Brodski and Celeste Schenck, *Life/Lines: Theorizing Women's Autobiography*.

16. Marleen Barr and Richard Feldstein, eds., *Discontented Discourses: Feminism, Textual Intervention, Psychoanalysis*, and Richard Feldstein and Judith Roof, eds., *Feminism and Psychoanalysis*. Both of these anthologies contain essays gen-

erated around 1986; only in the latter collection in Mary Poovey's essay, "The Anathematized Race: The Governess and *Jane Eyre*," and Carol Neely's "Constructing Female Sexuality in the Renaissance: Stratford, London, Windsor, Vienna" is class a major component to the arguments and only in Madelon Sprengnether's essay, "(M)Other Eve: Some Revisions of the Fall in Fiction by Contemporary Women Writers," is there any discussion of work by a black woman author.

17. Audre Lorde, "The Master's Tools Will Never Dismantle the Master's House," 98–101.

18. Gloria Anzaldua, *Borderlands: La Frontera: The New Mestiza*, preface, page unnumbered.

6. POLYMORPHOUS DIVERSITY

1. Ironically, the same week Court made this statement, *Sports Illustrated for Children* carried a humorous picture story on how to beat Martina Navratilova featuring photographs of Navratilova cavorting with children, recreating this ambivalence again. Court's comments formed the basis for tabloid stories about predatory lesbian tennis professionals (complete with a photograph of Martina), filtering the configuration out to its most extreme rendering for grocery store consumption.

2. In *Lesbian Images*, Jane Rule traces the emergence of the medical model as well as other cultural stereotypes of lesbians.

3. Ibid., 32.

4. Sander Gilman, *Difference and Pathology: Stereotypes of Sexuality, Race, and Madness*, 215.

5. Luce Irigaray, "Commodities Among Themselves," *This Sex Which is Not One*, 196.

6. This is Monique Wittig's logic in "The Straight Mind," 103–111.

7. Peter Shaw, "Feminist Literary Criticism: A Report from the Academy," 495–513; Walter Jackson Bate, "The Crisis in English Studies." Bate uses the title of an MLA paper, "Lesbian Feminist Poetry in Texas," as one example of how he sees the profession going wrong.

8. Cherrie Moraga, *Giving Up the Ghost*, 29.

9. Teresa de Lauretis, "Sexual Indifference and Lesbian Representation," 174.

10. Sigmund Freud, "Psychogenesis of a Case of Homosexuality in a Woman," 18:143–170.

11. Wittig, "The Straight Mind," 110.

12. Monique Wittig, "One Is Not Born a Woman," 47–54. See also Judith Butler's excellent analysis of the ideology of gender, *Gender Trouble: Feminism and the Subversion of Identity*.

13. D. H. Lawrence, *Lady Chatterley's Lover*, 262–263. For more analysis of literary representations of lesbian sexuality as masculine, see Judith Roof, " 'The Match in the Crocus': Representations of Lesbian Sexuality," 100–116.

14. For a feminist Bakhtinian analysis of carnival, see Mary Russo, "Female Grotesques: Carnival and Theory," 213–229.

15. In "Sexual Indifference" de Lauretis points to Esther Newton's observations that the womanly woman is "most troublesome" for Havelock Ellis (175).

16. Quoted in de Lauretis, "Sexual Indifference," 168.

17. Teresa de Lauretis, "Feminist Studies/Critical Studies: Issues, Terms, and Contexts," 9.

18. Audre Lorde, *Zami: A New Spelling of My Name.*

19. Other texts important in making this lesbian diversity visible are Cherrie Moraga and Gloria Anzaldua, eds., *This Bridge Called My Back;* Gloria Anzaldua, *Borderlands: La Frontera: The New Mestiza;* and Norma Alarcon, Ana Castillo, and Cherrie Moraga, eds., *Third Woman: The Sexuality of Latinas.*

20. "Celebrate Diversity—Our Way," 13.

21. Marks' and Case's arguments are summarized by de Lauretis in "Sexual Indifference."

22. This is particularly true of Gallop's collection of essays, *Thinking Through the Body*.

23. Olga Broumas, "Artemis," *Beginning with O*, 23–24.

Bibliography

Alarcon, Norma, Ana Castillo, and Cherri Moraga, eds. *Third Woman: The Sexuality of Latinas*. Berkeley: Third Woman Press, 1989.

Anzaldua, Gloria. *Borderlands: La Frontera: The New Mestiza*. San Francisco: Spinsters/aunt lute, 1987.

Barr, Marleen and Richard Feldstein, eds. *Discontented Discourses: Feminism, Textual Intervention, Psychoanalysis*. Urbana: University of Illinois Press, 1989.

Barry, Judith and Sandra Flitterman. "Textual Strategies: The Politics of Art-Making." *Screen* 21, 2 (1980), 35–48.

Barthes, Roland. *The Pleasure of the Text*, trans. Richard Miller. New York: Hill and Wang, 1975.

Bate, Walter Jackson. "The Crisis in English Studies." *Harvard Magazine* (Sept.-Oct. 1982).

Baudry, Jean-Louis. "The Ideological Effects of the Basic Cinematographic Apparatus," trans. Jean Andrews and Bertrand Augst. In Theresa Hak Kyung Cha, ed., *Apparatus*, 25–37. New York: Tanam Press, 1980.

Bauer, Dale. *Feminist Dialogics: A Theory of Failed Community*. Albany: State University of New York Press, 1988.

Bernheimer, Charles and Claire Kahane, eds. *In Dora's Case: Freud—Hysteria—Feminism*. New York: Columbia University Press, 1985.

Bovenschen, Silvia. "Is There a Feminist Aesthetic?" *New German Critique* 10 (1977), 111–137.

Breuer, Joseph and Sigmund Freud. *Studies in Hysteria*. In *The Standard Edition of the Complete Psychological Works*. James Strachey, trans. and ed. London: Hogarth, 1955, vol. 2 (1893–1895).

Brodski, Bella and Celeste Schenck, eds. *Life/Lines: Theorizing Women's Autobiography*. Ithaca, N.Y.: Cornell University Press, 1988.

Broumas, Olga. *Beginning with O*. New Haven: Yale University Press, 1977.

Brown, Rita Mae. *Rubyfruit Jungle*. New York: Bantam, 1977.

Butler, Judith. *Gender Trouble: Feminism and the Subversion of Identity*. New York: Routledge, 1990.

Carruthers, Mary J. "The Re-Vision of the Muse: Adrienne Rich, Audre Lorde, Judy Grahn, Olga Broumas." *Hudson Review* 26 (1983), 293–322.

"Celebrate Diversity—Our Way." *On Our Backs* 6, 2 (1989), 13.

Chase, Cynthia. "Desire and Identification in Lacan and Kristeva." In Richard Feldstein and Judith Roof, eds., *Feminism and Psychoanalysis*, 65–83. Ithaca, N.Y.: Cornell University Press, 1989.

Chodorow, Nancy. *The Reproduction of Mothering: Psychoanalysis and the Sociology of Gender*. Berkeley: University of California Press, 1978.

Cixous, Hélène. "Castration or Decapitation," trans. Annette Kuhn. *Signs* 7, 1 (1981), 36–55.

——. "The Laugh of the Medusa," trans. Keith Cohen and Paula Cohen. In Elaine Marks and Isabelle de Courtivron, eds., *New French Feminisms*, 245–264. Amherst: University of Massachusetts Press, 1980.

——. "Rethinking Differences." In George Stambolian and Elaine Marks, eds., *Homosexualities and French Literature*, 70–86. Ithaca, N.Y.: Cornell University Press, 1979.

Cleland, John. *Memoirs of a Woman of Pleasure (Fanny Hill)*. New York: Oxford University Press, 1985.

Colette. *Ces Plaisirs . . .* Paris: J. Ferenczi, 1932.

——. *The Pure and the Impure*, trans. Edith Dally and with an introduction by Joseph Collins. New York: Farrar and Rinehart, 1933.

Conley, Verena Andermatt. *Hélène Cixous: Writing the Feminine*. Lincoln: University of Nebraska Press, 1984.

Cook, Blanche Wiesen. " 'Women Alone Stir My Imagination': Lesbianism and the Cultural Tradition." *Signs* 4 (1979), 718–739.

Crowder, Diane. "Amazons and Mothers? Monique Wittig, Hélène Cixous, and Theories of Women's Writing." *Contemporary Literature* 24 (1983), 117–144.

Culler, Jonathan. *On Deconstruction*. Ithaca, N.Y.: Cornell University Press, 1982.

de Beauvoir, Simone. *The Second Sex*, trans. and ed. H. M. Parshley. New York: Bantam, 1952.

de Lauretis, Teresa. *Alice Doesn't: Feminism, Semiotics, Cinema*. Bloomington: Indiana University Press, 1984.

—— "Feminist Studies/Critical Studies: Issues, Terms, and Contexts." In Teresa de Lauretis, ed., *Feminist Studies/Critical Studies*, 1–19. Bloomington: Indiana University Press, 1986.

—— "Oedipus Interruptus." *Wide Angle* 7 (1985), 34–40.

—— "Sexual Indifference and Lesbian Representation." *Theatre Journal* 40, 2 (1988), 155–177.

—— *Technologies of Gender: Essays on Theory, Film, and Fiction.* Bloomington: Indiana University Press, 1987.

Derrida, Jacques. *Of Grammatology*, trans. Gayatri Chakravorty Spivak. Baltimore: Johns Hopkins University Press, 1976.

Diderot, Denis. *Memoirs of a Nun*, trans. and with an introduction by Francis Birrell. New York: Brentano's, 1928.

—— *Oeuvres romanesques*, ed. H. Bénac. Paris: Garnier, 1962.

Doane, Mary Ann. *The Desire to Desire: The Woman's Film of the 1940s.* Bloomington: Indiana University Press, 1987.

—— "Film and Masquerade: Theorising the Female Spectator." *Screen* 23 (Sept./ Oct. 1982), 74–88.

Dworkin, Andrea. *Pornography: Men Possessing Women.* New York: Perigree, 1981.

Eliade, Mircea. *The Myth of the Eternal Return*, trans. Willard Trask. New York, Pantheon, 1954.

Engelbrecht, Penelope. " 'Lifting Belly Is a Language': The Postmodern Lesbian Subject." *Feminist Studies* 16, 1 (1990), 85–114.

Farwell, Marilyn. "Toward a Definition of the Lesbian Literary Imagination." *Signs* 14, 1 (1988), 100–118.

Feldstein, Richard, and Judith Roof, eds. *Feminism and Psychoanalysis* Ithaca, N.Y.: Cornell University Press, 1989.

Fetterley, Judith. *The Resisting Reader: A Feminist Approach to American Fiction.* Bloomington: Indiana University Press, 1978.

Fifer, Elizabeth. "Is Flesh Advisable? The Interior Theater of Gertrude Stein." *Signs* 4 (1979), 472–483.

Fischer, Lucy. *Shot/Countershot: Film Tradition and Women's Cinema.* Princeton: Princeton University Press, 1989.

Flynn, Elizabeth and Patrocinio Schweickart, eds. *Gender and Reading.* Baltimore: Johns Hopkins University Press, 1986.

Foster, Jeannette. *Sex Variant Women in Literature.* Tallahassee: Naiad, 1985.

Freud, Sigmund. *Standard Edition of the Complete Psychological Works.* James Strachey, ed. and tr. London: Hogarth Press, 1953–1974; New York: Macmillan.

—— 1900. *The Interpretation of Dreams.* In *Standard Edition*, vols. 4–5.

—— 1901. The Psychopathology of Everyday Life. In *Standard Edition*, vol. 6.

—— 1905. "Fragment of an Analysis of a Case of Hysteria." In *Standard Edition* 7:3–122. 125–245.

—— 1905. *Jokes and Their Relation to the Unconscious.* In *Standard Edition*, vol. 8.

—— 1905. "My Views on the Part Played by Sexuality in the Aetiology of Neuroses." In *Standard Edition* 7:271–279.

—— 1905. "Three Essays on the Theory of Sexuality." In *Standard Edition* 7:125–246.

—— 1911–13. "Psychoanalytic Notes on an Autobiographical Account of Paranoia." In *Standard Edition* 12:1–82.

Freud, Sigmund. 1914–16. "A Case of Paranoia Running Counter to the Psycho-analytic Theory of the Disease." In *Standard Edition* 14:263–272.

—— 1914–16. "On Narcissism: An Introduction." In *Standard Edition* 14:67–102.

—— 1917–1919. "A Child Is Being Beaten." In *Standard Edition* 17:175–204.

—— 1920–22. "Psychogenesis of a Case of Homosexuality in a Woman." In *Standard Edition* 18:143–170.

—— 1922. "Some Neurotic Mechanisms in Jealousy, Paranoia, and Homosexuality." In *Standard Edition* 18:221–232.

—— 1923–24. "Some Psychical Consequences of the Anatomical Distinction Between the Sexes." In *Standard Edition* 19:243–258.

—— 1924. "The Dissolution of the Oedipus Complex." In *Standard Edition* 19:173–179.

—— 1927–31. "Female Sexuality." In *Standard Edition* 21:223–243.

—— 1927. "On Fetishism." In *Standard Edition* 21:152–157.

—— 1933. *New Introductory Lectures on Psychoanalysis*, Lecture 33. In *Standard Edition* 22:112–135.

Freud, Sigmund. *The Complete Letters of Sigmund Freud to Wilhelm Fliess, 1887–1904*. Jeffrey Masson, tr. and ed. Cambridge, Mass.: Harvard University Press, 1985.

Gallop, Jane. *The Daughter's Seduction: Feminism and Psychoanalysis*. Ithaca, N.Y.: Cornell University Press, 1982.

—— "The Problem of Definition." *Genre* 20 (Summer 1987), 111–132.

—— *Reading Lacan*. Ithaca, N.Y.: Cornell University Press, 1985.

—— *Thinking Through the Body*. New York: Columbia University Press, 1988.

Gardiner, Judith Kegan, Elly Bulkin, Rena Grasso Patterson, and Annette Kolodny. "An Interchange on Feminist Criticism on 'Dancing Through the Minefield.' " *Feminist Studies* 8 (Fall 1982), 629–675.

Garner, Shirley Nelson, Claire Kahane, and Madelon Sprengnether, eds. *The (M)Other Tongue: Essays in Feminist Psychoanalytic Interpretation*. Ithaca, N.Y.: Cornell University Press, 1985.

Gearhart, Suzanne. "The Scene of Psychoanalysis: The Unanswered Questions of Dora." In Charles Bernheimer and Claire Kahane, eds., *In Dora's Case: Freud-Hysteria-Feminism*, 105–127. New York: Columbia University Press, 1985.

Gilman, Sander. *Difference and Pathology: Stereotypes of Sexuality, Race, and Madness*. Ithaca, N.Y.: Cornell University Press, 1985.

Göttner-Abendroth, Heide. "Nine Principles of a Matriarchal Aesthetic." In Gisela Ecker, ed., *Feminist Aesthetics*, 81–94, trans. Harriet Anderson. Boston: Beacon Press, 1985.

Greene, Gayle and Coppélia Kahn, eds. *Making a Difference: Feminist Literary Criticism*. New York: Methuen, 1985.

Heath, Stephen. "Difference." *Screen* 19 (Autumn 1978), 51–112.

Hertz, Neil. "Dora's Secrets, Freud's Techniques." In Charles Bernheimer and Claire Kahane, eds., *In Dora's Case: Freud-Hysteria-Feminism*, 221–242. New York: Columbia University Press, 1985.

Holly, Marcia. "Toward a Feminist Aesthetic." In Josephine Donovan, ed., *Feminist Literary Criticism*, 38–47. Lexington: University Press of Kentucky, 1975.

Howard, June. "Review Essay: Feminist Differings: Recent Surveys of Feminist Literary Theory and Criticism." *Feminist Studies* 14, 1 (Spring 1988), 167–189.

Hull, Gloria, Patricia Bell Scott, and Barbara Smith, eds. *All the Women Are White, All the Blacks Are Men, but Some of Us Are Brave*. New York: Feminist Press, 1982.

Irigaray, Luce. "The One Doesn't Stir Without the Other," trans. Hélène Wenzel. *Signs* 7, no. 1 (1981), 58–67.

—— *Speculum of the Other Woman*, trans. Gillian C. Gill. Ithaca, N.Y.: Cornell University Press, 1985.

—— *This Sex Which Is Not One*, trans. Catherine Porter. Ithaca, N.Y.: Cornell University Press, 1985.

Jardine, Alice. *Gynesis: Configurations of Woman and Modernity*. Ithaca, N.Y.: Cornell University Press, 1985.

Jones, Ann Rosalind. "Writing the Body: Toward an Understanding of l'Ecriture féminine." In Elaine Showalter, ed., *The New Feminist Criticism: Essays on Women, Literature, Theory*, 361–377. New York: Pantheon, 1985.

Kamuf, Peggy. "Writing like a Woman." In S. McConnell-Ginet et al., *Women and Language in Literature and Society*, 284–299. New York: Praeger, 1980.

Kaplan, E. Ann. *Women and Film: Both Sides of the Camera*. New York: Methuen, 1983.

Kennard, Jean. "Ourself Behind Ourself: A Theory for Lesbian Readers." In Elizabeth Flynn and Patrocinio Schweickart, eds., *Gender and Reading*, 63–77. Baltimore: Johns Hopkins University Press, 1986.

Kolodny, Annette. "Dancing Through the Minefield: Some Observations on the Theory, Practice and Politics of a Feminist Literary Criticism." *Feminist Studies* 6 (1980), 1–25.

Kristeva, Julia. *About Chinese Women*, trans. Anita Barrows. New York: Urizen, 1977.

—— *Desire in Language*, ed. Leon Roudiez, trans. Thomas Gora, Alice Jardine, and Leon Roudiez. New York: Columbia University Press, 1980.

—— *In the Beginning Was Love: Psychoanalysis and Faith*, trans. Arthur Goldhammer. New York: Columbia University Press, 1987.

—— *Revolution in Poetic Language*, trans. Margaret Waller. New York: Columbia University Press, 1984.

—— *Soleil Noir: Dépression et mélancholie*. Paris: Gallimard, 1987.

—— *Tales of Love*, trans. Leon Roudiez. New York: Columbia University Press, 1987.

Kuhn, Annette. *The Power of the Image: Essays on Representation and Sexuality*. London: Routledge and Kegan Paul, 1985.

Lacan, Jacques. *Feminine Sexuality: Jacques Lacan and the École Freudienne*. Juliet Mitchell and Jacqueline Rose, eds.; Jacqueline Rose, trans. New York: Norton, 1985.

Lacan, Jacques. *The Four Fundamental Concepts of Psycho-Analysis*, trans. Alan Sheridan. New York: Norton, 1981.

—— "The Mirror Stage As Formative of the Function of the I As Revealed in Psychoanalytic Experience." In *Ecrits: a selection*, trans. Alan Sheridan, 1–7. New York: Norton, 1977.

Lawrence, D. H. *Lady Chatterley's Lover*. New York: Grove Press, 1959.

Leduc, Violette. *La Bâtarde*, trans. Derek Coltman. New York: Farrar, Strauss and Giroux, 1965.

Lorde, Audre. "The Master's Tools Will Never Dismantle the Master's House." In Cherrie Moraga and Gloria Anzaldua, eds., *This Bridge Called My Back: Writings by Radical Women of Color*, 98–101. Watertown, Mass.: Persephone Press, 1981.

—— *Zami: A New Spelling of My Name*. Trumansburg, N.Y.: Crossing Press, 1982.

Marcus, Jane. "Still Practice, A/Wrested Alphabet." In Shari Benstock, ed., *Feminist Issues in Literary Scholarship*, pp. 79–97. Bloomington: Indiana University Press, 1987.

Marcus, Steven. "Freud and Dora: Story, History, Cast History." In Charles Bernheimer and Claire Kahane, eds., *In Dora's Case: Freud-Hysteria-Feminism*, 56–91. New York: Columbia University Press, 1985.

Mayne, Judith. "The Woman at the Keyhole: Women's Cinema and Feminist Criticism." In Mary Ann Doane, Patricia Mellencamp, and Linda Williams, eds., *Re-Vision: Essays in Feminist Film Criticism*, 49–66. Los Angeles: American Film Institute, 1984.

Meese, Elizabeth. *(Ex)tensions: Re-Figuring Feminist Criticism*. Urbana: University of Illinois Press, 1990.

Metz, Christian. *The Imaginary Signifier: Psychoanalysis and the Cinema*, trans. Celia Britton, Annwyl Williams, Ben Brewster, and Alfred Guzzetti. Bloomington: Indiana University Press, 1982.

Millet, Kate. *Sexual Politics*. New York: Ballantine, 1969, 1970.

Moi, Toril. *Sexual/Textual Politics*. London: Methuen, 1985.

Moraga, Cherrie. *Giving Up the Ghost*. Los Angeles: West End Press, 1986.

Moraga, Cherrie and Gloria Anzaldua, eds. *This Bridge Called My Back: Writings by Radical Women of Color*. Watertown, Mass.: Persephone Press, 1981.

Mulvey, Laura. "Afterthoughts on 'Visual Pleasure and Narrative Cinema' Inspired by *Duel in the Sun* (King Vidor, 1946." *Framework*, nos. 15, 16, 17 (1981), 12–15.

—— "Narrative Cinema and Visual Pleasure." *Screen* 16 (1975), 6–18.

Neely, Carol. "Constructing Female Sexuality in the Renaissance: Stratford, London, Windsor, Vienna." In Richard Feldstein and Judith Roof, eds., *Feminism and Psychoanalysis*, pp. 209–229. Ithaca, N.Y.: Cornell University Press, 1989.

Newton, Judith, and Deborah Rosenfelt, eds. *Feminist Criticism and Social Change: Sex, Class and Race in Literature and Culture*. New York: Methuen, 1985.

Nin, Anaïs. *The Delta of Venus: Erotica*. New York: Bantam, 1979.

—— *The Diary of Anaïs Nin: 1931–1934* (vol. 1). New York: Swallow Press and Harcourt, Brace and World, 1966.

—— *Henry and June: From the Unexpurgated Diary of Anaïs Nin*. New York: Harcourt, Brace, Jovanovich, 1986.

Nin, Anaïs and Henry Miller. *A Literate Passion: Letters of Anaïs Nin and Henry Miller, 1932–1953*, ed. Gunther Stuhlmann. New York: Harcourt, Brace, Jovanovich, 1987.

Papke, Mary, Eileen Manion, and Julia Visor. "Women Respond to Racism." *Telos* 50 (1981–82), 180–187.

Poovey, Mary. "The Anathematized Race: The Governess and *Jane Eyre.*" In Richard Feldstein and Judith Roof, eds., *Feminism and Psychoanalysis*, pp. 230–254. Ithaca, N.Y.: Cornell University Press, 1989.

Pryse, Marjorie and Hortense Spillers, eds. *Conjuring: Black Women, Fiction, and Literary Tradition*. Bloomington: Indiana University Press, 1985.

Rich, Adrienne. "Compulsory Heterosexuality and Lesbian Existence." *Signs* 5 (1980), 631–660.

—— *On Lies, Secrets, and Silence: Selected Prose 1966–1978*. New York: Norton, 1979.

Roof, Judith. " 'The Match in the Crocus': Representations of Lesbian Sexuality." In Marleen Barr and Richard Feldstein, eds., *Discontented Discourses: Feminism/Textual Intervention/Psychoanalysis*, 100–116. Urbana: University of Illinois Press, 1989.

Rose, Jacqueline. "Dora: Fragment of an Analysis." In Charles Bernheimer and Claire Kahane, eds., *In Dora's Case: Freud—Hysteria—Feminism*, 128–148. New York: Columbia University Press, 1985.

—— *Sexuality in the Field of Difference*. London: Verso, 1986.

Rule, Jane. *Lesbian Images*. Trumansburg, N.Y.: Crossing Press, 1975.

—— *This Is Not for You*. Tallahassee: Naiad, 1988.

Russo, Mary. "Female Grotesques: Carnival and Theory." In Teresa de Lauretis, ed., *Feminist Studies/Critical Studies*, 213–229. Bloomington: Indiana University Press, 1986.

Schweickart, Patrocinio. "Reading Ourselves: Toward a Feminist Theory of Reading." In Elizabeth Flynn and Patrocinio Schweickart, eds., *Gender and Reading*, 31–57. Baltimore: Johns Hopkins University Press, 1986.

Sedgwick, Eve. "Across Gender, Across Sexuality: Willa Cather and Others." *South Atlantic Quarterly* 88, 1 (Winter 1989).

Shaw, Peter. "Feminist Literary Criticism: A Report from the Academy." *American Scholar* (Autumn 1988), 495–513.

Showalter, Elaine, ed. *The New Feminist Criticism: Essays on Women, Literature, Theory*. New York: Pantheon, 1985.

—— "Critical Cross-dressing; Male Feminists and the Woman of the Year." In Alice Jardine and Paul Smith, eds. *Men in Feminism*, 116–136. New York: Methuen, 1987.

Silverman, Kaja. "Lost Objects and Mistaken Subjects." *Wide Angle* 7 (1985), 14–29.

Simon, Linda. *The Biography of Alice B. Toklas*. New York: Avon, 1978.

Sprengnether, Madelon. "(M)Other Eve: Some Revisions of the Fall in Fiction by Contemporary Women Writers." In Richard Feldstein and Judith Roof, eds., *Feminism and Psychoanalysis*, pp. 298–322. Ithaca, N.Y.: Cornell University Press, 1989.

Sproul, Barbara C. *Primal Myths: Creating the World*. New York: Harper and Row, 1979.

Stanley, Julia Penelope and Susan Wolfe. "Toward a Feminist Aesthetic." *Chrysalis: A Magazine of Women's Culture* 6, 57–71.

Stanton, Domna. "Difference on Trial: A Critique of the Maternal Metaphor in Cixous, Irigaray, Kristeva." In Nancy Miller, ed., *The Poetics of Gender*, 157–182. New York: Columbia University Press, 1986.

Stimpson, Catharine. "Mind, Body, and Gertrude Stein." *Critical Inquiry* 3, 3 (Spring 1977), 489–506.

—— "The Somagrams of Gertrude Stein." *Poetics Today* 6 (1985), 67–80.

Suleiman, Susan Rubin, ed. *The Female Body in Western Culture: Contemporary Perspectives*. Cambridge, Mass.: Harvard University Press, 1986.

Wittig, Monique. "One Is Not Born a Woman." *Feminist Issues* 1, 1 (1980), 47–54.

—— "The Straight Mind." *Feminist Issues* 1, 1 (1980), 103–111.

"Women and Film: A Discussion of Feminist Aesthetics." *New German Critique* 10 (1977), 83–107.

Woolf, Virginia. *Mrs. Dalloway*. New York: Harcourt, Brace, Jovanovich, 1925.

Zimmerman, Bonnie. "What Has Never Been: An Overview of Lesbian Feminist Literary Criticism." In Elaine Showalter, ed., *The New Feminist Criticism: Essays on Women, Literature, Theory*, 200–224. New York: Pantheon, 1985.

Index